A Step-by-Step Guide to the Joy of Winetasting

Winetaster's Secrets

Andrew Sharp

With a New Foreword by David Lawrason

Warwick Publishing

Toronto

We acknowledge the financial support of the Government of Canada through the Book Publishing Industry Development Program for our publishing activities.

ISBN: 1-894622-47-2

Published by Warwick Publishing Inc.
161 Frederick Street, Suite 200
Toronto, Ontario M5A 4P3 Canada
www.warwickgp.com

Distributed in Canada by
Canadian Book Network
c/o Georgetown Terminal Warehouses
34 Armstrong Avenue
Georgetown, Ontario L7G 4R9
www.canadianbooknetwork.com

Distributed in the United States by
CDS
193 Edwards Drive
Jackson TN 38301
www.cdsbooks.com

Design: Clint Rogerson

Printed and Bound in Canada

A Step-by-Step Guide to the Joy of Winetasting

Winetaster's Secrets

Andrew Sharp

With a New Foreword by David Lawrason

Table of Contents

Acknowledgements

THE sentiments expressed in the first edition of *Winetaster's Secrets* (1981) have only been reinforced by additional years of tasting experience since then. "No book is a singular effort." That statement is even more true with this new, completely re-written volume. Although there have been no "giant steps forward" in our understanding of how we sense and interpret the marvelous complexities of wine, small doors have been opened and we have peered more deeply into the whys and hows of taste and smell, and the marvelous and mysterious ways the human brain interprets a wealth of sensory input for our benefit and pleasure. My unreserved gratitude is extended to those researchers who have continued their efforts in this field. My task—a delightful one, admittedly—has been to interpret and translate some of this information for winelovers.

In addition, I would like to acknowledge the following list of people: Dayle Sharp, Jim Lapsley, John Buechsenstein, Javier Rodriguez, Markus Riedlin, Monika Potsos, Angelika Schmidt, Dorian Weiner, Trevor and Maria Davidson, David and Monika Gray, and Rob and Sarah Voth. My creditors continue to thank each and every purchaser of a copy of *Winetaster's Secrets*.

Foreword

MOST wine books oxidize as quickly as most wines. This edition of Andrew Sharp's legacy to tasters everywhere is a tribute to the durability and importance of its subject matter. Tasting never goes out of date precisely because it is a science, a physiological function. Few wine writers have understood this as deeply as Andrew Sharp, whose mind was always inquiring and comparing wines for the benefit of all those who might take more than passing and subjective interest.

Andrew was the founder of the Toronto-based Intervin Wine Competition, the only one in Canada to put hopeful judges through a rigorous blind taste test, and the only double-blind competition where not even origin or varietal were known.

"I want to know about its quality as a wine," he used to remind his panelists before each tasting. "That is what we must interpret on behalf of consumers."

But for all his studious and serious intent, Sharp had a presence and style, in his teachings and writings, that was friendly and logical. This is why I was able to summon the nerve, back in 1982, to phone him out of the blue and ask what it took to be successful as a wine writer.

"Taste, taste and keep tasting," he said.

So I did, and once armed with the science of *Winetaster's Secrets*, I have never doubted my frame of reference or my own abilities. It remains, simply, the most important consumer-oriented work on the subject that I have come across. And it will outlive me.

David Lawrason
Editor-in-Chief
Wine Access

Foreword to First Edition

Secret: ... a thing kept from general knowledge.

—The Living Webster Encyclopedic Dictionary

READERS anticipating revelations of heretofore unknown grape varieties, arcane fermentation practices, or illicit compounds designed to enhance organoleptic abilities will be disappointed in this book, since Andrew Sharp uses the word "secret" in the traditional sense of something not known to the general public, rather than in today's usage of something deliberately hidden from view. If truth were told, a book of winemaking trade secrets would be both boring and short. As quality-oriented winemaking has become international in scope, so has the diffusion of oenological science. What remains "secret" are formulae for flavored wines, a category that continues to decline in popularity.

Yet a paradox does exist: as oenological science has spread internationally, it has also become more specialized, and thus less accessible to the general reader. The knowledge is not "hidden" in the common sense of the word, but unless one is a veteran peruser of scientific and trade journals it is easy to fall behind the latest work in flavor chemistry, sensory science or viticulture. Sharp has thus performed a service to all wine lovers in bringing out this second edition. Not only has he culled through a decade's worth of scientific articles on wine along with the informed opinions of other writers, he has integrated this information with his two decades of experience as a communicator about wine and his nine years directing an international wine competition, InterVin.

As a teacher about wine, Sharp knows well the common problems beginners have with understanding wine types. And as a director of

InterVin, he knows first hand the problems (both logical and philosophical) associated with judging wine quality. The result is a book that can be read easily with profit by the novice wine imbiber, the passionate collector, or the technical producer. The first group will learn the most, having the most to learn, but all will come away with new insights.

Ultimately, learning about wine mirrors other facets of education. One becomes knowledgeable by becoming conscious of differences, of likes and dislikes. Any system that encourages the reader to become aware of how his or her senses operate, describes how to assess and remember differences, and provides examples of how to test and stretch sensory memory, will be successful. But this volume delivers more than that. Like fine wine it combines pleasure with aesthetics. Although it may be downed in one gulp, we suggest it is best taken in small sips and savored. Enjoy!

James Lapsley, PhD
Outreach Specialist
Department of Viticulture and Enology
University of California, Davis, California

John Buechsenstein
Winemaker
Hidden Cellars
Ukiah, California
co-author, "The Aroma Wheel"

Preface

IT is still an unfortunate fact, but the average consumer rarely perceives the differences in wine quality. One goal of this book is to alter that fact, at least to some degree. We must start, of course, by helping to generate more consumer interest in learning how to do that. By gaining some insight into what goes through a winemaker's mind, for example, it will help us all better understand and appreciate what is in his bottle. So, some technical information will have to be considered.

Winetaster's Secrets is not intended to be an original piece of research, or to add to the growing body of scientific investigation into our perceptions as they relate to the analysis of wine. Rather, it is very much an attempt to better communicate such findings to the consumer, and to inspire a passion for wine and its pleasures.

Another goal of this book is to help you develop an objective sense of taste as it pertains to wine; to assist you in a fundamental way to learn how you can evaluate and judge wine quality accurately, much the way winemakers and professional tasters do—in other words, to focus on the keys winetasters use to unlock the secrets of any wine, using a systematic approach to tasting.

The benefit? A better understanding and greater enjoyment of all wine. The bonus? Money—the money you'll save by learning to become a *wine* drinker instead of a *label* drinker.

I must temper this by adding it is not my goal, with this book, to swell the ranks of professional winetasters, those who are qualified to sit with a panel of experts and critically analyze such things as Claret and Burgundy vintages. Such a skill, an art really, comes from years of experience and training in an environment no author could re-create with just the written word. But being able to judge between the good, the bad, and the undrinkable is well within the grasp of every winelover—with just a little help from a friend.

However, much of the literature available to guide budding oenophiles (winelovers) too often comes across as either somewhat elitist and dogmatic (the "pronouncement from on high to the unwashed masses" approach) or anarchistic (the "do your own thing," totally promiscuous approach). The old "it's all a matter of individual taste" philosophy finds a kindred spirit with the taste anarchist.

Winetaster's Secrets charts what I fervently hope is a very balanced, down-to-earth course. If this little work can add to both your knowledge and enjoyment of all well-made, honest wines, it will have accomplished its purpose.

To establish and maintain the degree of objectivity and consistency I'm advocating, there is need for a dependable pattern or guide. This guide should prompt or induce you to evaluate each wine in a systematic and consistently objective manner. In other words, a consistent evaluation system is needed. There are almost as many wine evaluation systems in use today as there are winetasters. It is not an objective of this book to select or promote one system as superior to another. However, our human senses do impose upon us (if we choose to heed them) a natural sequence in the sensory evaluation of wine. A good system should follow this pattern and take into consideration only the objective elements of sensory perception.

If we then consistently apply these objective, genuinely qualitative judgments, the true, inherent merits of each wine you taste should easily become apparent. As well as identifying the stature of the wine, you will also be able to relate this to market prices and determine for yourself whether the wine you're tasting is a bargain or fair value for money, or you've been had by another slick commercial, misguided friend, or artistic wine label.

Surprisingly, all this may have little to do with you liking the wine. There are a number of wines I enjoy immensely; however, I do not delude myself into thinking that that makes them anything more than what some of them are—simple, ordinary wines. It just so happens they have a nature, a personality I enjoy. But when evaluating them professionally, I must be unbiased, rating them for what they really are.

An important part of the objective of this book is

1. to encourage you to expand the use of your natural senses, increasing your enjoyment of all wine,
2. to help you develop the ability to evaluate the quality of wines consistently and accurately, for yourself, and
3. to help you appreciate the differences in qualitative and non-qualitative wine characteristics.

While my primary focus is on table wines—red, white, and rosé—I will briefly consider factors involving sparkling, fortified, and dessert wines. I will also detail tasting techniques that can be applied to assessing brandies and ice wines; the effects of age on the taster and the wine; and wine competitions and scoring systems.

Winetaster's Secrets does not pretend to be a winetasting party guide. It does not elaborate on the traditional hints about table settings, the number and arrangement of glasses, the bread vs. cracker vs. cheese debate, how to be the ideal host or hostess, wine and food matches, and so on. The focus is specifically on helping you to learn **how** to judge wine quality, **why** wines differ, and **what** causes them to smell and taste as they do.

An Introduction to the Pleasures of Tasting Wine

SOMETIMES the question can be more important than the answer. The understanding and appreciation of wine is riddled with questions. Though debated for generations, many wine issues remain unresolved. Some of these questions confuse, even inhibit consumers from a pursuit of winetasting as a part of their everyday life. So, they remain convinced of that sad old cliché, "It's all a matter of personal taste." It's only appropriate, therefore, that we address some of these thorny issues at the very outset of this book. *Winetaster's Secrets* may not provide all the answers, but it is my hope you will better understand the questions.

🐝 🐝 🐝

What Is "Taste"?

Taste is a funny thing! Not *ha ha* funny but *peculiar* funny. Even the definition of the word is a bit confusing. It's both a verb and a noun. It means to "eat or to drink; to have or to get experience; a manner or style."

You can describe your appreciation for fine literature, an operetta and a hamburger with the same word—taste. That's the confusing latitude the English language permits at times. So, we're forced to address this word from several different aspects if we're ever to understand how it applies to wine and our ability to determine wine quality. Tasting wine is a quest for quality.

Much of the confusion appears when you try to describe the taste of something to someone else. In this situation taste is too often expressed as a very individual, subjective judgment—"I like it" or "I don't like it," in its most basic assessment.

In a manner, this introduces a major stumbling block to your being able to judge wine quality accurately—your personal taste, your likes and dislikes, in other words. They have very little to do with assessing the inherent, intrinsic quality or stature of a wine. Oh, I know you've been told so often that the best wine is the one you like, and you're probably asking yourself, "Am I not supposed to drink the wines I personally like?"

Certainly you are! That's only natural.

But your personal likes and dislikes are not the objective standards by which wine can be accurately judged. Some people simply don't like wine at all. Are their tastes sufficient reason to discount all wines as quality beverages?

Hardly!

However, even as one who enjoys wine, your individual preferences may not coincide with the wines the so-called experts judge as being fine or great. In fact, they may rate your choices quite inferior by comparison. What then? Should you switch brands? Should the judgments of the experts dictate your wine selections instead of your own taste?

Never!

How foolish, and at times pretentious, to allow your own taste to be dominated by someone else's, even that of an expert. That's when taste becomes taste in a very artificial way.

"So what's the point?" you ask. "First you tell me my personal likes and dislikes are not the standards by which true wine quality can be judged, then you tell me to keep drinking the wines I like."

Confusing? Not really. The point is simply this: your taste, as the word describes your individual likes and dislikes, is not static. It invariably changes, and is therefore something less than a dependable judge of the true, innate quality of wine. This is often the difference between a professional and a novice winetaster, even a good amateur. The professional is able to set aside his personal preferences and judge the wine on its inherent merits, or lack of them.

You see, your taste is largely, if not completely, a learned experience, an acquired characteristic. So it's obvious that a little experience and experimentation can alter your likes and dislikes considerably.

Your present taste for wine, or anything for that matter, simply indicates your individual sense of appreciation (not *level* of appreciation) at this particular moment. Consequently, if your wine knowledge and experience grow together, so will your ability to discern objective wine quality. To ever increasing degrees, you will become more sensitive to the qualities that distinguish genuinely fine and great wines from those more ordinary in nature.

🐞 🐞 🐞

What Does "Tasting" Wine Mean?

Tasting wine is a delightful and rewarding search for quality. But winetasting is not a consumer opinion poll. More, much more than personal preference needs to be expressed. In the end, it is really a means of discovering and assessing genuine wine quality, which may identify for you *value*.

Tasting wine has been defined as both an art and a science. As a science it is truly a part of a discipline called "sensory analysis," where the human senses are both the instrument and the judge. It is a deliberate organoleptic examination, a human measurement and interpretation of stimulations sensed by the mouth, nose, and eyes.

Some scientists, oenologists, and technicians draw a distinction between "tasting" wine and "sensory assessment." To them, sensory assessment involves four distinct steps, starting with the assessment; then a technical description of those perceptions; a comparison to known standards or samples; and finally, a reasoned judgment.

Though technical sensory analysis is more of a discipline than an art it is not all that far removed from simple, amateur or commercial winetasting. Though certainly more demanding and focused, technical tasting and ordinary tasting can both be taught; they can be learned; they can be mastered; they can bring us a great deal of pleasure.

While their goals may differ, both technician and amateur seek a better understanding of what is in the glass before them. They consciously and deliberately submit the wine to their human senses to identify its merits and faults. While their vocabularies may not always harmonize, they seek to describe their sensations to others—one to define and analyze, the other simply to express and share the pleasures of their experience.

Winetasting is, for some, a rewarding part of normal living, not an exception. It is an expression of deep interest in what they choose to put into their bodies. It requires neither a deliberate agenda nor a rigorous, analytical approach. Our blessed human senses accomplish much of this without ever being asked. We simply need to listen, to pay closer attention. To some extent tasting is a memory exercise, the act of retaining our perceptions so that we can bring back to mind those moments of pleasure and satisfaction.

The simple act of drinking to satisfy our thirst can be pleasurable in itself. What differentiates drinking from tasting is the heightened use of our intelligence and perception.

🐜 🐜 🐜

Why Should I Bother Learning To Taste Wine?

The simplest of all answers to this question is that it is one of the most pleasurable forms of education imaginable.

There exists with wine, as perhaps with no other beverage, a genuine hierarchy of quality. This is not just something that exists only in the "eye of the beholder," but in many ways is a measurable reality. Learning how to distinguish that innate quality is really a remarkable way of training our human senses. To master that skill brings us an immense and deserved sense of accomplishment.

And with this accumulated reservoir of knowledge and insight, our pleasure grows, as does our appreciation for moderation. Rarely do we abuse the things we truly love. Abusing such pleasures, when they are yoked with understanding, is the exception. Dedicated winetasters rarely cross the line of alcohol abuse.

Unfortunately for some, the deliberate act of "analyzing" anything suggests a suppression of pleasure. With wine the opposite is true. Innumerable pleasures will escape our notice if we ignore the training of our senses of smell and taste. Instead of suppressing or regimenting our enjoyment this increased understanding magnifies it.

Those marvelous smells and tastes of wine do even more. They literally stimulate the production of saliva and the digestive juices secreted by our stomach. In turn, our anticipation and enjoyment of food is immensely enhanced. It sounds a trifle clinical perhaps, but the stimulation extends to the bowel, too, assisting in the assimilation of what we have already enjoyed consuming so much. We receive both physical and emotional benefits when we include a glass of wine with our meals.

In even more practical terms, learning the art and joy of tasting wine can also be involved with the professional side of life. Some examples:

• Winemakers and cellar staff need to be accomplished winetasters to do their jobs well.

- Official government agencies have several reasons to employ trained winetasters.

- Quality control and research laboratories cannot depend solely on sophisticated, technical equipment—in many cases there is nothing as sensitive as the human instrument and a well-trained tasting panel.

- From restaurateurs to importers to retailers, from buyers to sellers, in-depth winetasting skills are basic requirements.

- Wine competitions and their awards are gaining consumer favor—a seasoned, consistent tasting ability is a pre-requisite for any wine judge.

- Then there is you—after all, you probably purchase wines for yourself and to serve to others; whether it's for family use or for some special business or social occasion, you should be able to step outside your personal tastes and competently judge wines that may not specifically appeal to you, but certainly will to your guests.

And think of what is involved in developing this skill. You get to—you *must*—taste the wines. Despite the lofty intentions of this book, no author can precisely relate to you all the subtle differences among wines. You must experience the essence, the nature of each wine for yourself. Then, with a bit of guidance, discipline, and objectivity—what these few pages hope to assist you with—you will begin to appreciate these differences far more easily and consistently than ever before. No matter how literate or ingenious the author, the written word can only go so far, providing a sort of concentrated version of the real thing. The re-constituting agent is the personal experience you must add by tasting the wines.

But this is often the opposite of a rather widespread and disconcerting habit. Too often novice winedrinkers pick a favorite wine and stick to it like a brand of beer or whiskey. This may please immensely the fortunate producer, but it does little for your wine education. Winetasting is one form of education you not only benefit from ultimately, but where you also enjoy the learning process every bit as much.

By limiting yourself to a favorite wine, or even several, you sell yourself considerably short when it comes to experiencing your share of the infinite pleasures of wine. There are considerably more than 500,000 wine labels floating around the world market today. Besides, your favorite, if it is a better wine, will probably vary in quality from vintage to vintage, whether you change brands or not.

Now, this doesn't mean you won't discover a number of labels you'll come to depend on for everyday use. Just don't stop there! Keep on experimenting. Your appreciation of wine quality will never grow without such experience.

※ ※ ※

What Is a Winetaster?

Only two ounces of the red liquid is poured. The man lifts his glass to eye level and studies it closely. As if some inaudible message had been received, the glass is replaced on the starched, white linen tablecloth and a few notes are hastily scratched on the paper in front of him.

Again, the glass is raised, but this time he swirls the liquid round and round. Even before the it has settled down, his nose is thrust well into the glass and his body swells as he inhales deeply.

More notes are hurriedly added to the paper. He stops; returns his nose to the glass; sets it down once more, adding more cryptic scribbles to his growing chronicle.

At long last the glass reaches his lips. A small sip is taken, followed by an odd gurgling sound. A pause . . . and as if something had offended him he dispels the liquid into a nearby bucket.

Sitting back in his chair now, a pensive, quizzical look crosses his face. Leaning forward, more notes are penned. And he passes on to the next glass.

A professional winetaster is at work.

And he does his job well—very well, indeed. In fact, he's so proficient his tolerance for error when evaluating wines on a one-hundred-point scale is less than three points on the average.

The secrets of that wine, its nature, revealed themselves quite easily to his trained palate. In a matter of minutes our taster has accurately determined the true quality of the wine. He knows where it ranks, its stature, in the wonderful world of wine.

But the art of tasting wine is a relatively modern concept, certainly in professional terms. From the moment someone bought or sold the first cup of wine an informed opinion was sought. Judgments then were usually uncomplicated—the wine was simply judged good or bad.

As generations passed, tasting skills grew. Yet, the basics have changed little from the Roman days: *colore—odore—sapore*.

The word "taster" (*degustateur*) was first defined in France in 1793 as "one whose profession is to taste wine." A word we know and so often abuse today—"gourmet"—was a synonym of the word "taster," even preceding it in common usage, as did the ancient French expression *piqueurs des vins* (winetasters). The French verb "to taste" (*deguster*) didn't even make a formal appearance until 1813, according to Emile Peynaud, renowned French taster, scientist, and author.

Does this mean then that "winetaster" is a title reserved for the level of professional accomplishment? Can we, as novices, amateurs, simple lovers of wine, ever be as skilled in assessing the wines we drink? Or are the secrets, those so-called mysterious talents, of the winetaster so abstruse we must all be content with being barely more than spectators in this respect, forever passing from wine to wine, never knowing whether one is really better than another?

Can we ever learn how to judge wine quality with any degree of consistency and accuracy? One man, writing to a wine columnist, expressed his frustration rather eloquently:

> Ten years and ten wine books later I still don't know. Oh, I can pinpoint on a map all the classic wine regions and discuss first-hand a number of little wine villages I've visited in France and Italy. I can translate all the "winesse" on the labels of French, German and Italian wines and I've memorized several vintage charts and their ratings . . . but I still can't tell you, except in the most fundamental terms, whether one wine is really superior to another.

This winelover's plight is hardly unique or surprising, for there is precious little wine information that details precisely the keys to tasting wine—in simple language, *how to*.

Oh yes, all those impressive "coffee table" wine books describe in eloquent and pictorial language the quaint history and customs of the famed wine lands, which wine to serve with certain foods, and the authors' personal rating of innumerable wines.

Yet, with the rarest of exceptions the *how* and *why* of winetasting is glossed over or presented in such technical terms you would think the author had reached a sensitive, restricted area clearly marked "For Professionals Only."

Winetaster's Secrets focuses on this very facet of wine. Step by step, this book reveals how it's done, how the experts—and now you—can assess and understand wine quality. It does so in a manner that hopefully neither oversimplifies nor complicates the subject.

❋ ❋ ❋

Is Winetasting an Objective or Subjective Determination?

This question touches a raw nerve in the wine trade. It is a festering wound among writers, amateurs, and professionals alike. It obviously has not been resolved and is unlikely to be so in the near future.

It is my personal view that the debate involves a deadly lacing of semantics that often clouds the issue, making progress in resolving the debate excruciatingly slow.

It is somewhat like witnessing an argument between friends, only to grasp—as an outsider—that they are really talking about two different things. They have a misunderstanding of what is at issue, not genuinely different viewpoints of the same subject.

The issue of objective vs. subjective is further complicated by the very definitions of the words. And it is the variations in definitions that are frequently at the heart of the debate. To complicate it even more, consumer usage of these words extends beyond the dictionary meanings. Notice the latitude involved in the following dictionary definitions of:

SUBJECTIVE
1. "belonging to the thinking subject; personal; individual"
2. "without foundation in reality; illusionary; imaginary"

There is enough variation here alone to fuel a lively debate. A definitive understanding is further frustrated by the definition of the word "subjectivism."

SUBJECTIVISM: "the theory that all knowledge is subjective and that objective knowledge is impossible."

Let's look at that other key word, objective, and how it's defined:

OBJECTIVE
1. "outside of the human subject."

This seems to suggest that it is therefore quantifiable, measurable, and more than just opinion.

2. "intent upon or dealing with things external to the mind rather than thoughts or feelings."

This second definition appears to imply (as does #2—subjective) that human minds are not capable of unbiased assessments, simply imaginative guesses. When the second definition is applied for both words, it is little wonder that this debate continues to plague our understanding of the art of tasting wine.

Such definitions fuel views such as the one expressed by Quittanson, who said, "Quality, like truth is above all subjective." His view is expressed, in variations of this theme, by many in the wine arena. Persons who believe this will be unlikely to perceive genuine wine quality because in essence, like truth, they don't believe it exists.

Increasingly, however, there is some movement towards the center. Due largely to the expanding level of wine technology, we have begun to realize that much of what is perceived by our human senses is also measurable by laboratory instruments. More are now willing to accept the concept that winetasting can be an objective assessment even though we employ subjective, human senses. Such views are certainly compatible with the first definition for both words.

To clarify the picture even further I would suggest the insertion of another word into this touchy equation—"affective." Webster defines affective as, "pertaining to emotion, not to thought." Entering this word into our equation may indeed settle a significant portion of this debate and the misunderstandings that are associated with it.

Saying that something is too sweet, for example, may arguably be a subjective statement. But to insist that all sweetness is bad is definitely an "affective" viewpoint. Professional winetasters cannot afford to be affective. Their challenge is not to tell you if a given wine pleases them, but to examine, describe, and conclude. Their conclusions are again, arguably "subjective," but should never be "affective."

The debate will continue, no doubt. So, depending upon your definition of these two words, winetasting is most reasonably the skillful blend of objectivity and subjectivity. The "affective" response is only pertinent when you think somebody might actually be interested in what you like or don't.

★ ★ ★

How Do You Define Quality in Terms of Wine?

To some, wine quality is defined in the marketplace. It is a measure of consumer satisfaction. Unfortunately, it is still trendy in some circles to view quality as something completely personal—in essence, undefinable, or at least only to the individual.

According to one wine writer, "It is the totally subjective pleasure provided by drinking the wine which conditions judgment."

Another states flatly, "Quality is always relative."

"Quality is a concept which simply indicates the consumer's preference regarding a product, preferences created by fashion or advertising," adds another authority.

"Quality itself is a theoretical notion which signifies nothing in practical terms. It depends on numerous factors among which the consumer's environment plays a preponderant role," is one more viewpoint.

But is it really that vague? That theoretical? That personal? You may have already guessed—we are now confronted with another major wine debate. Perhaps not a totally separate question, for it is closely allied with the subjective/objective issue. Indeed, if wine judgment is completely subjective, wine quality is indeed a matter of personal taste. If it is objective, or even a blend of both, something more real than one's likes or dislikes is involved. "Like and dislike" judgments imply that wine is either good or bad. Few matters are that simple.

But concepts and ideas change. And this is more than "the flavor of the month" kind of change, too. The notion that wine has an innate, inherent quality has been held by many for some time. In the past decade it has been slowly advancing to center stage, firmly backed by technological advances. It is in sync with our ability to achieve these standards of quality, a quality growing numbers of consumers now demand.

International standards of quality are beginning to dominate the marketplace. A common goal of winemakers worldwide is to improve their products. If nothing but those so-called subjective concepts exist, how would they know what to improve, or even that it could be improved? Quality control has become an important factor to every serious producer of wine. Yet, how could such controls exist if there were no standards by which to measure quality?

With the advancement in winemaking skills many of wine's traditional flaws can be all but eliminated. Underneath those flaws is found the innate, inherent quality of the wine. And today it is the blossoming quality of the consumer that stimulates the spread of quality wine.

Such quality does not come automatically, not even with exquisite grapes and a wonderful "terroir" (see Glossary). The wine will only be as good as the person who nurses it to its full potential.

Poor wines are no longer excusable, even under a subjective, "it's good if you like it" banner. A regional wine may have once been acceptable, even though it was traditionally oxidized and unbalanced, because that's the way it's always been. With more clearly defined quality standards, and real-life wine examples to prove the point, such wines will have to improve or wither on the proverbial vine.

However, can quality be defined in such succinct, even scientific terms? Most researchers will agree—we are a long way from being able to define the quality of a wine in analytical terms. There is no scientific measurement scale for quality. At least, not yet.

Before wine quality can be achieved a set of pre-existing conditions must be met:

- the appropriate climate and soil (terroir)
- noble grape varieties
- a high level of technical competence in viticulture (grape growing) and viniculture (winemaking)
- a discerning consumer who will pay for the quality

Accepting the reality of "objective quality" is an important step in comprehending what constitutes quality, but definitions don't come easily. Wine authorities have long acknowledged this difficulty:

"The quality of wine is easier to experience than to demonstrate."
—*Poupon*

"Quality in wines is easier to recognize than to define."
—*Amerine*

"Quality is something perceived more than defined."
—*Pisani*

"Few people can verbalize their opinion of quality."
—*Young*

"The quality of wine is difficult to define in an entirely unequivocal way."
—*Paranotto*

I will forego any attempt to suggest a succinct, definitive definition of wine quality. The dictionary defines quality as "a level of excellence; superiority." The question remains—how do you determine if a wine is superior to its contemporaries or achieves this excellence?

In keeping with Dr. Ann C. Noble's definition, "Quality is a composite response to the sensory properties of wine," the following factors must exist in a wine if it is ever to aspire to superior quality:

- purity—free of measurable faults (a minimal quality threshold)

- visual appeal—color and clarity—it doesn't have to be "squeaky clean" but any suggestion of haze or off-color, faulty odors or tastes, removes it from the "superior" classification

- a richness of aromatics, primary (fruit), secondary (from the fermentation), and tertiary (the complexity of age)

- good length—expressed in flavor persistence

- a clean finish

- a distinctive personality

- a harmony and balance among all of its components.

There are those who would add "pleasure" as a necessary requisite of quality. After all, if a wine doesn't give you pleasure why would you drink it? That's a fair question. Yet, I have omitted pleasure from my list of qualitative factors because it is purely a matter of like or dislike. It's too affective. A competent winetaster will recognize quality even when he doesn't like a particular taste or smell. Such unbiased assessments are made in everyday life. Does the produce manager of a grocery store have to like broccoli to be able to buy quality bunches for his customers who do? Must a sommelier like Sauvignon Blanc to recommend it to his patrons?

A vital step in determining the quality of any wine is the realization that not all elements in wine are truly qualitative—some are purely personality factors. Objective qualities are real, not contrived. They are the factors that allow you to fairly compare one wine with another. They stamp each wine with a fundamental character or stature that does not depend on the rather fickle intricacies of anyone's personal likes or dislikes.

To further illustrate let me use the very old, but very graphic example of the "apple and orange" comparison. For those who are still convinced it's all a matter of personal taste, this helps:

Imagine sitting in front of you on a table a perfect, luscious, juicy navel orange and beside it a sparkling, garnet-red apple. Which is better, the apple or the orange? Is that a fair question? Most will respond, "No, it's not a fair question. You can't compare apples with oranges, they're different." However, before you make your final decision consider this scenario:

In front of you again is that perfect, juicy, navel orange. But this time the apple is not quite so appealing: it's still partially green with several obvious blemishes and bruises. When you bite into it you find it pulpy and lacking the crispness it should have. Now, I ask that same question—which is better, the apple or the orange? It's obvious the orange is superior, for specific reasons—the apple possessing certain faults. Reversing the situation, using a poor, dried-out orange compared to a perfect apple gives you the same example.

So now, think of the things that are common to the apple and orange that account for their quality. Both should be free of blemishes; both should have good color (albeit different colors); both should have a good fruit texture, pleasing levels of juiciness, a nice acid/sugar balance, and so on.

So, you *can* compare apples and oranges—when they are less than perfect—but only when you compare the truly qualitative factors, not the elements, the essences that differentiate an apple from an orange. When both are perfect, indeed it is a matter of individual preference which you like best or which is better to you or gives you the greatest pleasure.

The same is true for wine. Less than perfect (I haven't seen too many perfect wines around lately) and you can compare them, evaluating one as superior to the other for specific, qualitative reasons. Of course, you may still prefer a second-rate orange to the world's greatest apple, but objectively you should realize the poor orange is of lesser quality than that perfect apple.

We can rightfully conclude then that wines have both qualitative factors that can be evaluated and compared, and factors that are non-qualitative but simply identify a style or personality and cannot be compared or assessed as being superior or inferior, just different.

Britain's highly respected Institute of Masters of Wine (a wine industry educational organization) has begun to shift its tasting exercises more towards assessment than the traditional exercise of identifying wines. Personality factors can very often identify a wine, but rarely do they address its level of quality. Is a wine with an aroma of cherries better than one distinguished by a raspberry smell? That's personality—not quality!

✻ ✻ ✻

The Composition of Wine

Wine is one of the most complex biological liquids. Unlike most other beverages, even water, it is not subject to food spoilages or food poisoning, nor will it carry or support any disease organisms that can infect humans.

In our attempts to better understand the ways we can taste wine, thus benefiting from the experience and adding to our pleasure, it will immensely assist us as winelovers to have at least a general understanding of a wine's makeup, its composition.

The figures in the table below are broadly representative of this makeup. A great many wines will vary considerably. The list of volatile amines in wine alone would be more than 20. This is a very simplified list of major wine components in percentages.

You may notice that "yeast" is missing from our chart. Although it is absolutely vital to the very creation of wine, it is not an "ingredient" as generally thought. In a finished, properly fermented wine there are no remaining yeasts.

Major Wine Components

Component	Dry Table Wines		Sweet Wines	
	White	Red	White	Red
Water	83.5%	83.5%	76.5%	76%
Alcohol	11.0	11.0	11.5	11.7
Other Volatiles	0.04	0.04	0.05	0.05
Extracts	2.3	2.6	2.8	3.0
Sugars	0.58	0.01	7.0	7.0
Pectin & Related	0.3	0.3	0.32	0.32
Glycerol & Related	1.1	1.1	0.9	0.9
Acids	0.7	0.6	0.5	0.5
Ash	0.2	0.2	0.2	0.2
Phenols	0.01	0.28	0.01	0.1
Amino Acids & Related	0.25	0.25	0.2	0.2
Fats, Terpenoids	0.01	0.02	0.01	0.02
Misc. vitamins, etc.	0.01	0.01	0.01	0.01
Total	100%	100%	100%	100%

Chapter 2

Tools of the Trade

BEFORE we get to the actual "how to" assessments of wine quality and the human sensory tools we employ to make those evaluations, we need to have some understanding of two major aspects of our human sensory nature:

How our senses work

and

How our brain perceives and interprets stimulations.

Such an understanding helps us avoid making errors of perception, arriving at incorrect conclusions, and most important, being victimized by the power of suggestion, both from others and from ourselves.

How Our Senses Work

We need to appreciate that when we enter the world of human sensory perception, we enter an imperfectly understood world. While much has been accomplished, our understanding of it is far from complete. A number of opposing theories seem to hold weight, causing lay writers to "suggest" rather than to be overtly didactic about their views.

Some scientists suggest that our visual and hearing senses are ever on the alert, whereas smell and taste "kick in" only when they are alerted to do so. Somehow, I can't grasp why they would ever shut down completely. Could it be more a matter of our paying attention to those senses only when we have sufficient reason to do so? When confronted with a powerfully obnoxious smell our nose is usually the first sensory tool to perceive it. Essentially, there is no other sense that instructs it when to start functioning. But when the smell becomes strong enough, it certainly commands our conscious attention. While our sense of smell was aware of it much earlier, our mind was, perhaps, occupied with something else.

In technical terms, tasting wine is a neurophysiological function. When they accumulate in sufficient numbers, specific types of molecules (and fractions of molecules) have the ability to stimulate the sensory nerve cells in our nose and mouth.

These stimulations travel along nerve fibers to the brain. The processing and decoding of these stimulations takes place in a specialized zone of the brain—the olfactory cortex. We accomplish this extraordinarily complex function with unbelievable speed—a tiny fraction of a second. When you consider the amount of data to be evaluated it's even more staggering.

The foregoing is obviously a grossly simplified version of what is truly an awesome process. Further details are considered in later chapters.

☘ ☘ ☘

Our Human Information Sources (Tools of the Trade)
EYES
NOSE
MOUTH
COMMON CHEMICAL SENSE
(see page 59 for details about this severely under-rated human sense)

Four key words should enter our tasting vocabulary at this point. They will enhance our understanding of how our human senses operate and how we can taste wine consistently and objectively:

Stimulus: any physical or chemical agent that generates a response in a sense receptor;

Neurons: nerve cells whose endings in the eyes, nose, mouth, skin, and mucus membranes sense the stimulations, sending them to the brain and spinal cord;

Sensation: the phenomenon resulting from the stimulation of sensory receptors;

Perception: our conscious acknowledgement of a sensation when our brain interprets it.

☀ ☀ ☀

The Brain

In computer terms, we must now consider our CPU (central processing unit). In human terms, we're talking about the unequalled and awesome human brain. No matter what experience or natural level of sensitivity we may possess, nothing will register in a cognitive fashion unless our brain first interprets it. To get the most out of our visual, smell, and taste senses we need to comprehend something of how the brain works, how it analyzes and integrates data simultaneously.

This tireless, ever-active organ not only keeps us alive literally but brings to life every sensation we experience. It is the source of all our thoughts, our feelings, and our hopes. Sadly, we know very little about it. After thousands of years of human speculation, highlighted by a few, recent decades of intensive scientific research, the functions of our brain remain essentially a mystery.

Why so little progress? Neurologist Richard M. Restak phrased it well when he said, "Since the brain is different and immeasurably more complicated than anything else in the known universe, we may have to change some of our most ardently held ideas before we're able to fathom the brain's mysterious structure."

Barely two percent of the average body weight, this grayish-colored matter is constantly nourished with oxygen, food (mainly glucose), amino acids, and hormones by an ever-attentive body orchestrated, of course, by the brain itself. This nourishment supports in excess of 100 billion nerve cells—neurons—and many more billions of supporting cells (glia).

The fissured cerebral cortex of the human brain (surface layer) is less than a quarter of an inch thick. If flattened out, the cortex would measure about 2.5 square feet, with some 10,000 miles of connecting fibers per cubic inch—yes, per cubic inch.

Coupled with the other parts of the inner brain, the power of the cerebral cortex is truly incredible! Every second, 100 billion bits of information assault the brain from the body's various senses. Yet it handles this load with ease. According to science writer Morton Hunt, "our active memories hold several billion times more information than a large contemporary research computer."

But how can we consciously cope with such a tidal wave of sensory input? In reality, only a few hundred stimulations at most enter the conscious mind at a time. How can the brain do this? Two factors are in play:

Firstly, in the brain stem there is a network of nerves about the size of your little finger. This "reticular formation" acts as a kind of traffic control center, monitoring millions of messages, sifting, sorting, and selecting priorities for attention by the cerebral cortex.

Secondly, further focus of our attention seems to come by waves that sweep the brain at a rate of about eight to twelve times per second. These waves cause periods of high sensitivity during which the brain takes note of the stronger impulses and acts upon them—in other words, a means of self-scanning with a focus selector to highlight only the essentials.

Computer science uses the term "hard wired" to refer to built-in characteristics based on fixed circuitry. This is in contrast to functions that can be entered into a computer by a programmer. Applied to the human brain, one authority expressed it this way: "Hard wiring refers to our innate abilities or, at least, predispositions." Sight, smell, touch, and taste abilities are "hard wired" human programs. This pre-programming of some of our neural equipment processes what our sensory circuits feed us. Then, with our "conditioned" brain, plus the sensory input, we perceive, we form concepts, and interpret what we see, smell, and taste.

It doesn't stop here, either. It is suspected that such stimulation can move on through our limbic system pathways to effect the release of hormones, further influencing human emotion, our conscious and unconscious behavior.

As awesome as the sheer number of neurons is, the interconnection of 100 billion or so nerve cells and their ability to process data is even more incredible. With each neuron possessing potentially thousands of connections with other neurons, estimates suggest a possibility of as many as a quadrillion interconnections (see Figure 1).

Neurons do not actually touch one another, they communicate electrochemically. The tiny space separating neurons (about one millionth of an inch) is called a "synapse." Estimates put the number of synapses at 100 trillion. Within the neuron itself signals are electrical. The tiny gap is bridged by a chemical messenger called a "neurotransmitter," about 30 of which have been isolated and identified. In his book *The Brain*, Richard Thompson explains: "Learning and memory could not develop in a nervous system that had only electrical synapses."

Figure 1

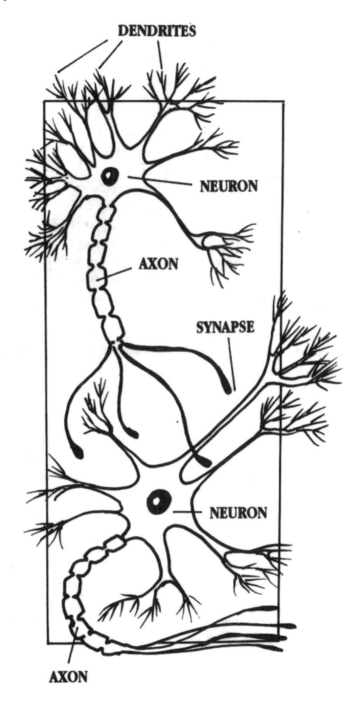

These chemical messengers are received at one end of the neuron by a delicate maze of tiny filaments called "dendrites." The signals are then transmitted (fired) at the other end of the neuron by a nerve fiber called an "axon." Each impulse apparently has the same strength; the intensity of the signal depends upon the frequency of the impulses, which may be as high as 1,000 per second.

Not only do these connections exist between neurons, but there are also microcircuits that directly connect the dendrites themselves. According to one neurologist, "these microcircuits add a totally new dimension to our already mind-boggling conception of how the brain works." And all this is barely the tip of the proverbial iceberg.

It has been stated that the human brain, functioning correctly, could take any load of learning and memory we could impose upon it, and a billion times more than that. Science is still not certain just what physiological changes actually take place in the brain as we input our experiences (learn). But we do know continued use strengthens those connections (synapses), reinforcing what we learn.

Thus, our brain is somewhat like a muscle, at least in one respect. It is strengthened by use, weakened by disuse. As the cliché suggests, "If we don't use it, we'll lose it." Supported by considerable research, we now know for certain that unused, our mental powers will fade.

So, two elements control our visual, smelling, and tasting abilities: our genetic programming, and how we impose stimulations upon our sensory tools. Whether or not genetic factors account for different impressions of the same wine in different people is a matter for much more research by taste scientists, as they continue to explore the psycho-physics of taste.

As it is with the most important of all our sensory tools—our brain—chances are you'll have the four major sensory tools in more or less functional condition. These vital keys or tools of the wine trade are, of course, four of the basic human senses—sight, smell, touch, and taste. When liberally mixed with that sixth sense, common sense, much of the mystery and mystique surrounding wine quality quickly evaporates.

Unlike some rather imaginative writers, we'll overlook our fifth sense, that of hearing, as part of our wine judging equipment. The suggestion that the sound of fine wine cascading into an elegant glass is one of the true pleasures of wine stretches even my liberal imagination. Although such sounds have admittedly been known to command my instant attention, I don't think even the best wine judge could differentiate between the splash of stale coffee and that of fine wine. And as far as the scintillating fizz of a sparkling wine? Well, what about the "champagne of ginger ales" and its fizz?

In a negative sense, however, music and extraneous sounds, such as crowd noises, can produce predictable variations in your wine judging. Even well meaning, off-handed comments about the wine can affect the objectivity of other tasters. Without trying to create a sanctimonious silence, at least a few minutes of *Quiet Please!* is in order when tasting in a more serious vein.

Now to the tools.

☀ ☀ ☀

Sight

To start at the bottom and work upwards is not an unreasonable sequence to follow. And so we shall. Sight is at the bottom of your senses in that it is the least perceptive of the four senses you'll employ in assessing wine quality. But it is probably the sense you'd least like to lose.

Despite all this, the human eye is a marvelous device. In a *New York Times* report it was candidly admitted, "After two decades of research, they have yet to teach machines the seemingly simple act of being able to recognize everyday objects and to distinguish one from the other. Instead, they have developed a profound new respect for the sophistication of human sight . . . The human retina is the envy of computer scientists. Its 100 million rods and cones, and its layers of neurons perform at least 10 billion calculations per second."

And every second 10 trillion particles of light pass through the pupils of your eyes and are received by 130 million rod and cone cells in the layers of the retina. Stimulated by the light, the nerve cells begin transmitting signals to various parts of the brain (see Figure 2).

The paper-thin retina is truly one of the most marvelous tissues in the body. Its 125 million rods are sensitive to small amounts of light, making night vision possible. The five million–plus cones respond better to brighter light, making possible detailed color vision. Some cones are more sensitive to red light, others to green, and others to blue. Their combined response enables you to see the full spectrum of color. When all three types of cones are excited equally, what you see is pure white.

Applied to wine the value of our sight is most often underestimated, but it is the necessary beginning to all of our evaluations. Frequently, the problem is that your eyes see only what you *want*

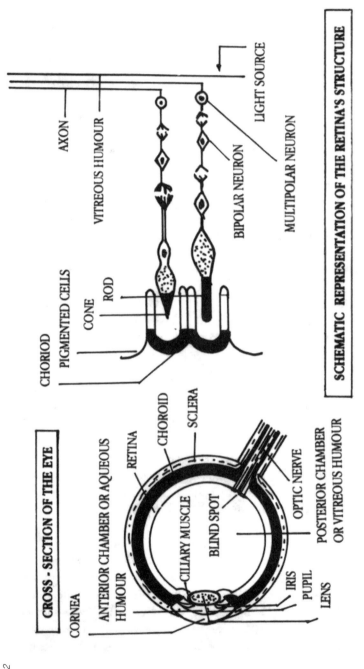

CROSS - SECTION OF THE EYE

CORNEA
ANTERIOR CHAMBER OR AQUEOUS HUMOUR
RETINA
CHOROID
SCLERA
CILIARY MUSCLE
BLIND SPOT
OPTIC NERVE
POSTERIOR CHAMBER OR VITREOUS HUMOUR
IRIS
PUPIL
LENS

AXON
VITREOUS HUMOUR
CHORIOD
PIGMENTED CELLS
CONE
ROD
BIPOLAR NEURON
MULTIPOLAR NEURON
LIGHT SOURCE

SCHEMATIC REPRESENTATION OF THE RETINA'S STRUCTURE

Figure 2

them to see. Though each human eye has those 130 million light-receiving neurons, it's the brain that appraises or evaluates the picture transmitted to it. Often, the brain details greater or lesser reality than what is actually there to see.

Appearance and color are the two major factors to be determined visually. However, that's considerably easier to say than to do. Our visual sensitivity is limited to a rather narrow band, between 390 and 820 nanometers. A nanometer is a unit of wavelength—1 nm = one millionth of a millimeter (there's about 25 mm in one inch).

Color

To see color, three elements are necessary:

1. a light source

2. something that is illuminated by it,

3. the eye/brain combination to perceive it.

The color of wine is created because it absorbs light rays in different ways as they pass through it. This is called the "absorption spectrum" and wine color can be accurately measured by a device called a spectrophotometer. It measures both depth and hue.

As an example, in determining the depth of color and its tint, a red wine would be measured using a thin film of liquid. Readings would be made at wavelengths of 420 nm (the yellow band) and at 520 nm (in the purple band).

The ratio of the yellow to red will give you the hue, while the sum of the two optical densities (the absorbed light at these two wavelengths) give you the color depth. The color depth of a white wine is measured at a wave length of 440 nm (in the yellow band) using a centimeter of the wine.

The absorption of light is the basis of color. Red wine appears red because it absorbs the other colors, allowing only red light to reach your eye. Some white wines look yellow because they absorb the blues and violets.

The table on the next page lists some of the absorbed colors leading us to see or perceive the remaining color. There is no clearcut line at which the tint automatically switches to the next color. Anyone who has witnessed a rainbow realizes that the colors blend into each other. Interestingly, purple, a color favored by so many people, is really a mixture of red and blue, colors at opposite ends of the spectrum. Though it is our brain that determines or interprets the colors we see, we still have no idea why individuals prefer certain colors more than others.

Wave Length	Absorbed Color	Perceived Color
Below 380 nm	X-Rays	Invisible
380–440	Violet	Yellow-Green
435–480	Blue	Yellow
480–490	Green-Blue	Orange
490–500	Blue-Green	Red
500–560	Green	Purple
560–590	Yellow-Green	Violet
580–595	Yellow	Blue
595–605	Orange	Green-Blue
605–750	Red	Blue-Green
Above 800 nm =	Infra-Red/Radio Waves = Invisible	

Lighting

Our ability to accurately identify the colors of wine—so to some degree determine its quality—depends very much on the quality of the light we use. This is perhaps one of the major shortcomings in the wine evaluation process, even to some degree among professionals—a failure to secure proper lighting.

Not only do various light sources alter what we perceive as color but not even "natural lighting" can be considered a panacea. While natural lighting, especially indirect north-facing light, is an artist's friend, winetasters have to take into account the tremendous variations in natural lighting, all of which can affect their color perception. For example, morning light is different from noon or late afternoon light. Overcast skies and sunny days can create profound differences in the color you perceive in the same glass of wine. Even geography gets involved. Light in the northern hemisphere is said to be softer than that "down under."

However, not many serious winetastings take place outdoors, so man-made lighting becomes an important factor. The unfortunate reality is, there is no commercially available light source that can simulate optimum natural lighting. Filtered tungsten lamps may be the closest relative.

The most common source of light in tasting venues such as large banquet halls, meeting facilities, hotels, even laboratories, is usually the poorest—fluorescent lighting. The high energy spikes emitted by fluorescents, in contrast to the smooth curve of natural light, can mislead our color perception significantly. The graphs below demonstrate the variations.

Figure 3: Light type can affect perception of wine color

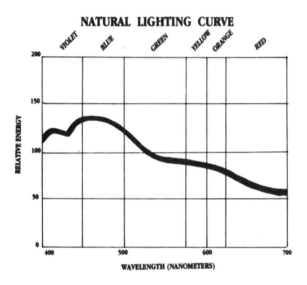

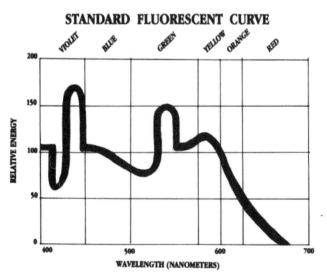

Lighting intensity is expressed as temperature Kelvin. Some common lighting sources and their approximate Kelvin measurement are listed here:

Candlelight	1500 K
Incandescent lighting	3000 K
Ordinary Fluorescent	5000 K
Full spectrum Fluorescent	7500 K

As is apparent, candlelight, though highly appreciated for its role in generating a warm and inviting ambiance (for something other than tasting) is not very practical for wine purposes. Aside from that, candles add heat to a room, use up the oxygen, and frequently have a smell. So, wait until the tasting is over, then light the candles if you must.

To suggest that sight is the sense most easily led astray would not be out of place. Just consider what can happen to your assessment of wine colors as influenced by different sources of prevailing light a phenomenon called "metamerism." As the light source changes, our brain perceives different colors. This must be factored into our color assessments of wine.

Using common fluorescent tubes as your major source of light can cause white wines to appear more brilliant or clear than they really are. The tendency under this light will be to consistently judge a white wine as being more yellow, while reds seem to be less red than in reality. Incandescent lighting (your everyday 60-watt bulbs and so on) has much the same effect, but not quite so pronounced.

While strong, indirect, natural lighting is optimum, the most practical and economical source of reasonably accurate light I've found is clear (unfrosted) incandescent bulbs. Some full-spectrum fluorescents allow fairly good assessments as well.

But not even natural lighting is problem-free. There are factors with natural lighting that must be taken into consideration in using it to judge wine coloring. On cloudy days whites show more yellow, while reds appear more intense. And against a brilliant blue sky, red wines display an unnatural brownish tinge.

With so many lighting pitfalls you may wonder if the wine expression "blind tasting" shouldn't really mean tasting blindfolded. Don't worry though; that's not likely to become a trend. Some wine experts even mistake a red for a white under such visually deprived circumstances.

Background Color

Background colors can at times also be a nuisance. While indispensable to the interior decorating trade these color influences can play havoc when you're trying to correctly assess wine colors. This type of distraction can come from walls, large pieces of furniture, lamp shades, carpeting, draperies and any number of colorful objects in close proximity to your wine glass. Keep in mind, a wine glass reflects images on its 360-degree circumference. So if you're wearing a bright yellow tie or a vivid green blouse, guess what color will reflect in your glass.

I'm not suggesting that starched, white lab coats are a necessity, but soft pastels—better yet, soft whites—will eliminate any color reflection problems from your clothing.

The color of nearby walls can also influence your judgments. Try to avoid any bright colors. French experiments have demonstrated that wall colors can cause some wines to appear to taste sweeter, others more acidic.

Red lighting or a strong red reflection tends to make wine appear more brilliant, clear. A yellow influence causes white wines to shift noticeably towards a deeper shade of yellow; reds also become darker. Under a green influence little color effect is noticeable on white wines, but reds take on darker hues. Blue has the least aberrant influence and relatively accurate assessments can be made under this shade of lighting, with only a slight browning of red colors.

Green can make wines taste somewhat more acidic; blue emphasizes bitterness; a red influence tends to make all wine a little more pleasant than they may truly be.

It becomes obvious, then, your objective should be to assess wine colors under conditions that are as consistent as possible. Optimum may be out of reach, but eliminating as many of the potential problems as possible will generate a more desirable and effective tasting environment. In laboratory settings, serious wine competitions, and in teaching institutions it is not uncommon for each taster to work in a specially designed booth, isolated from fellow tasters. Although this rather clinical setting has a number of practical advantages, some wine judges balk at this kind of setting, most often because they have become used to interactive tastings and have little experience judging in isolation.

Such a tasting booth certainly lacks practicality for the home. However, a very simple white cardboard backdrop can be easily assembled. It can provide you with the consistent, white background you need at a negligible cost. You may want to keep it at home, though—taking it to winetastings may create for you a reputation which may not be all that desirable. "Wine nut" is not a snack item.

We could go on and on cataloging the various influences that can affect our visual judgments. But I think you get the picture by now. Sight gives us clues to the character of the wine, a sneak preview if you will. Our anticipation of the wine can be led off in various directions, good and bad, by how well and accurately we take advantage of our visual talents. So, sight is a key factor for which each wine judge, professional or amateur, must make considerable allowance. There is need to make these visual evaluations under as consistent conditions as possible, recognizing and factoring in what various environmental influences can do.

※ ※ ※

Smell

Phew!!

Most of us have had more than one occasion to personally express that qualitative opinion. It may have been a totally individual sentiment or one shared by most persons when confronted by a particular smell. Some smells are like that—universally disagreeable. Whichever the case, propriety prevents me from elaborating on the more graphic examples of this type of odor.

In just a few pages you will quickly realize that this is the lengthiest single section in this book. It is so for good reasons. Most of what we sense about wine involves our ability to smell.

But what is it that actually happens to cause this curious function of smell? It can repulse you totally or start you smacking your lips in anxious anticipation of a taste delight.

Both smell and taste are chemical senses. They respond to chemical molecules. Our smell (olfactory) sensitivity extends to so many chemicals (10,000 different odors) it far exceeds the abilities of the most sophisticated, modern laboratory equipment.

With this incredible sensitivity our sense of smell also acts as a defense mechanism, reacting to potentially harmful stimulations that all other sensory organs would miss until some physical damage may have occurred.

Earlier I suggested the nose was significantly superior to all other senses. How much superior? Some experts claim this most extraordinarily efficient human device is ten thousand times more sensitive to odors than your tongue is to tastes. Now that's superior! Perhaps you can begin to appreciate the role this little proboscis plays, or should play, in improving your wine judging abilities. I still claim Jimmy Durante could have been one of the world's greatest wine judges.

Despite our awareness of the awesome power of the nose and the amount of research carried out in this field, our knowledge of how smelling (olfaction) actually works remains in its infancy. The stimulations sensed by our nose have not been rigidly defined in quite the same way that we can measure sound or light. And it is not so much a question of what we "know" about smell, but what the knowledge we have accumulated leads us to "suspect."

Not only should we recognize the importance of the nose in the wine judging process, but we should also realize that the nose and our sense of smell usually represents a considerable gap in the sensory education of most persons.

Much time and effort is spent in training other inferior human senses. Think of the training we give to our ears for music and the spoken word. Our visual sense is cultivated and taught to appreciate various forms of art, design, and color combinations. But how many of us have ever attended a smelling class, in any institution of learning? It's all but an ignored discipline. Most take it for granted. "We can all smell, can't we?" Most of us can, yes! But do we really know what it is we're smelling and how to differentiate between one smell and another similar to it?

Think of the fragrant smell of freshly mown grass, leaves burning in the fall, a chicken roasting in the oven, a baby fresh from a bath. They're unforgettable scents. As powerful and sensitive as the nose is, with a little exercise and concentration it can become a facet of your senses to be appreciated far more than it is now.

When it comes to wine, its aromatics (200 known odorous compounds) can be so rich and complex, so stimulating and satisfying that at times they can actually waylay our drinking the wine.

Never to be overlooked in the olfactory equation is the personal factor. Our state of health is intimately linked to our smell sensitivity. Certain diseases—even beyond the obvious colds and flus—can seriously alter our smelling efficiency. A vitamin A deficiency can reduce our smell sensitivity (hyposnia), while adrenal insufficiency can actually enhance it.

Assuming that our health is not a factor, we would still be on shaky ground to assume that the playing field is completely level. Human response to odor stimulation varies considerably, even to the point that some are completely "blind" to certain smells (specific anosmia). Fortunately, only $1/10$ of one per cent of the human family is totally anosmic. But we all have genuine blind spots, and very probably, there are a number of other odors we handle poorly as well.

Even then, the smells we can perceive invariably reflect individual acuity. This factor helps us appreciate, to some degree, why we have such individualistic fragrance preferences and why when you clearly detect a "raspberry" aroma in a wine's bouquet someone else might look at you as if you'd suddenly taken leave of your olfactory senses. "I smell strawberries," they state in no uncertain terms. And probably you're both telling the truth. The difference in perception of odor intensity, from individual to individual, can vary by a factor of as much as 100,000. I am constantly amazed at how humans achieve any sensory agreement.

Physiology of Smell

We are about to enter a more technically detailed description of how we smell. For some, this may go far beyond what you care to know. But this knowledge is much more than just so much excess mental baggage, for it will unquestionably enhance the appreciation and pleasure you receive from wine.

From our nasal openings we will take you on an incredibly fascinating journey through a mysterious and awe-inspiring maze, reaching our destination in the innermost recesses of the mind. You unconsciously make this journey innumerable times every moment of your life.

Our travels will follow a fundamental pathway that is essentially the same for all human senses. First, we must consider the very nature of the stimulus and how it reaches our receptor cells. Next, we will gain some insight into the interaction between the stimulus and the receptors. Then, we follow the reactive nerve impulses and how they are sorted and coded by the central nervous system in a way that gives to us perception, in this case, a distinctive smell.

For anything to have a smell it must be in a volatile (gaseous) state. Its molecules must readily dissolve in a mucus covering in the olfactory region in the nasal passage. It must be strong enough to activate the nerve endings. Some very aromatic substances are easily detected in the air but have little smell within a liquid solution. The reason? Low volatility. However, our sense of smell recognizes and classifies these volatile molecules only if they reach an intriguing little yellowish-brown patch (olfactory epithelium) located in the upper third of the nasal cavity, near the back (see Figure 4).

Figure 4: The olfactory system

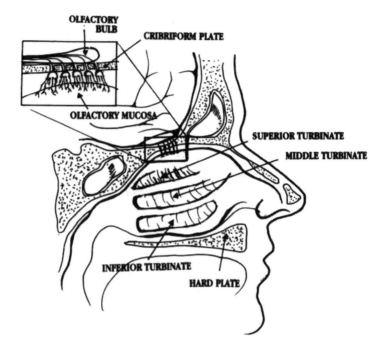

It is here that the odor-laden molecules are trapped and dissolved in the mucous covering the small patch. It is in this patch that the staggering performance of the nose begins.

The odorous vapors enter the nasal cavity to begin their fantastic journey. The lining of the nasal passages (respiratory mucosa) filters and warms the gases as they move through the first and second conchae in a bit of a turbulent motion. They seek the "high road," the top of the nasal cavity (superior concha), where the olfactory epithelium and its sensors are waiting.

But how do we start the process in our attempt to "nose" a wine? *Breathe in!* might appear as the obvious first step. But how? According to smell researchers, normal breathing breathing allows only about 20 per cent of any available odor to actually enter the nasal passages, where as little as two per cent actually gets past the mucus-covered lining of the passages to make contact with the receptors in the olfactory patch. This helps us appreciate how easy it is to totally miss a prominent smell, let alone some subtle aromatic nuance.

Fortunately though, we can intensify these odors by inhaling more deeply at specific intervals. Not only does this intentional, deliberate action "vacuum" in more of the aromatic molecules, but sniffing vigorously intensifies their impact on the moist layer on top of our smelling patch. With greater impact more molecules remain to engulf the nerve endings (receptors, sensors).

So, a couple of short, deep sniffs are necessary. But a word of caution. Whether we are tasting one or 101 wines it is of great value to develop a breathing or an inhaling pattern. If your technique varies, so will your results. Some wines have very "shy," or backward noses, and when tasters encounter them they often take some extraordinary steps to "get at the nose." But that will usually yield misleading results. If wines are to be assessed on an even footing, special antics like extra inhalations, even shaking the glass, should be avoided. The identical pattern of inhaling will make for more accurate comparisons. This applies most importantly to your assessment of the wine's aromatic intensity.

But we're only halfway there in our breathing techniques. Because there's another very important factor to keep in mind, the dual manner in which we smell—in a sense, frontwards and backwards. When we inhale, air passes over the olfactory region and we smell something, hopefully. However, when we take something into the mouth, the odor of this substance again passes the olfactory region when we exhale—odors coming up the back way, so to speak (oronasal or retronasal smelling).

After you have swallowed some of the wine you can close your mouth and breathe out in a kind of nasal snort or huff. Remember to put a little muscle into it. More molecules will impact with greater force onto that moist olfactory patch.

Retronasal smelling is often a superior way to smell. This is due primarily to the fact that when in your mouth the wine is closer to your smelling region. As well, the wine warms up in the mouth, and the warmer the wine the more volatiles released, and the more volatiles released the more prominent the odor, and the more prominent the odor the easier it is to identify. By and large, a great deal of what is thought to be taste is really just in-mouth odors. Simply pinch your nose shut and see how little you really do taste without your nose, or recall your last cold when your nasal passages were congested. It's almost as if your sense of taste disappeared.

Some wine and taste authorities prefer to describe that first method, inhaling, as smelling. Not much to argue about there. But the second, exhaling odors from the mouth through the nose, they define as "savoring." A few get quite insistent about differentiating between the two. At the risk of incurring their learned disapproval I choose to disagree with them. Smelling is smelling, whichever direction the airflow. To savor something suggests an intensity of examination, not a direction of airflow. I take this recalcitrant stance not out of personal bravado, but because both Master Webster and Master Oxford seem to agree with my definition of savor, or should I say I agree with theirs. So as you happen upon the word smell in this book it defines odors from both inhaling and exhaling.

Olfactory Epithelium—Smelling Patch

Our nasal journey finally brings us to a human device with staggering sensitivity—technically, the Olfactory Mucosa. As shown in Figure 4, this yellow-brown patch (about two to four cm^2) is situated a little ways from the main air passage (respiratory stream), and is accessible only through a narrow cleft (superior concha or concha of santorini).

As odorous molecules dissolve in its mucous layer they come into contact with olfactory hairs (cilia), which are really just extensions of the receptor nerve cell itself. Humans have 10 to 20 million of these receptor nerve cells (neurons), each with six to twelve fine cilia at the end. These flask-shaped receptor cells are situated between supporting cells, the source of the mucous secretions. They continually bathe the cilia in this precious fluid (see Figure 5).

Some researchers suggest these supporting cells and their hair-like endings (microvillae) play an as yet unknown role in the smell function. The variable thickness of the mucus layer certainly influences the length of time and the number of molecules that reach the receptor cell hairs, so obviously has some influence on odor identification.

This gives us some understanding of how wine odors reach this delicate smelling zone, which is constantly renewing its olfactory neurons every 30 days or so. But from here on we are largely traveling in the world of theory and conjecture. Theories abound, but the fact is we really don't know the exact mechanism of stimulation, the precise relationship between chemical structure and smell. The theories are often confounded by the reality that there are odor molecules of very different structure that have the same smell. Other chemicals change odor profoundly by a minute variation in the quantity or concentration, making odor identification by chemical analysis alone incredibly difficult. Or some chemical molecules have no smell at all, even though they are in the gaseous state. Carbon dioxide and carbon monoxide are well-known examples of odorless gases.

Figure 5

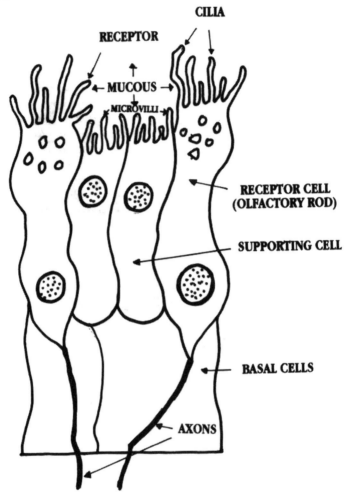

Rather than having only a flat olfactory surface, the extended nerve cell cilia greatly increase the receptor area, and one theory has it that there are "lock and key"–like receptor areas on each cilium. Different odor molecules, the theory states, lock onto the compatible receptor site, triggering a specific smell identity (see Figure 6).

Though it is not known for sure if there even are specific receptor sites for specific odors, another theory postulates there are in fact many different receptor sites on each cilium. Some experiments have shown that a cilium can respond to more than 20 different odor stimulations.

Figure 6: The "lock and key" theory of odor identification

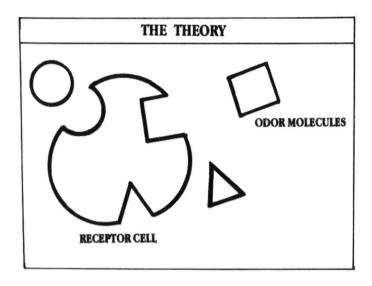

Further attempts to explain how the odors are identified have included groupings of receptor sites; recognition of the pattern of activity (across fiber-firing); differences in retention time in the mucous layer; differences in regional absorption of the odor molecules; and spatial/frequential impulses. Some have theorized that since we have identified 30 specific odor blindnesses in humans (specific anosmia), that may indicate the number of different types of odor reception. Various combinations of these 30 specific receptor types could identify thousands of odorous compounds.

None of the current theories will ever be provable until we know a great deal more about the chemical and physical properties of the receptor sites and the odor-causing molecules. As you will appreciate, the process of human odor identification is an extremely complex one, requiring the integration of messages from millions of receptor sites. Our job would be easier if these receptors were consistent in their sensitivity and distribution across the olfactory patch. They aren't!

What we do know is that the brain interprets electrical impulses. And we know that an electrical charge (neuro-transmission) originates from the receptors along its axons to the olfactory bulbs. Our "olfactory brain" then interprets the electrical impulses. The nature of those impulses is governed by molecular size, the arrangement across the mucous sheet, the molecular charge, even the way in which a molecule's atoms are arranged.

Obviously, we need to provide a few more details about these two terms—"axon" and "olfactory bulbs." Looking back at Figure 5 you will see the axons extending from the base of the receptor cell. Axons are fine unmyelinated fibers (like a thin wire without its plastic coating), about 0.2 microns in diameter. They carry the electrical messages from the receptor cells. Quickly they bundle together in groups of 20 to 100 fibers called a fascicle. The fascicles further group together in the filia olfactoria (see Figure 7). These bundles pass through the porous cribiform plate at the base of the brain and skull.

At this juncture, some 2,000 bundles of olfactory nerves enter the two olfactory bulbs. These reddish-gray bulbs are situated behind the nose, at the base of the skull, under the frontal lobe. Unlike any other region of the brain, the olfactory bulbs—thick bands of whitish brain matter (olfactory tract)—extend backwards to enter the brain in two places.

Inside the olfactory bulbs the axons of the receptor cells form synapses with what are called mitral and tufted cells (see Figure 7). These cells in turn form the second link (lateral and medial stria) in the olfactory pathway, leading to the olfactory cortex of the brain. This central cortex then acts something like a master control panel, distributing the olfactory messages to various sectors of the brain.

Some suggest it even goes further, that some of the olfactory signals also reach the limbic system (and others) so are thought to be able to influence a number of human behavior patterns. Included are learning functions and sexual behavior. It also involves memory.

Thankfully our memory banks seem to be well attached to our sense of smell. It's not often that we will have smelled something and then fail to recognize it when it presents itself again. And that's one talent you will want to cultivate. A good memory for smells is invaluable. It helps you identify the basic character of the wine, to be recalled and compared with other wines you'll drink in the years to come. Some experienced tasters have such well-tuned memories in this respect that they are able to recall easily wines they tasted even decades ago.

Without developing such a memory you lose much of your capacity to make quality comparisons. Most often it's by comparison to a known, accepted set of standards that allows you to evaluate the stature of the wine in your glass.

Figure 7: Smells seem to be transmitted to the brain via olfactory bulbs

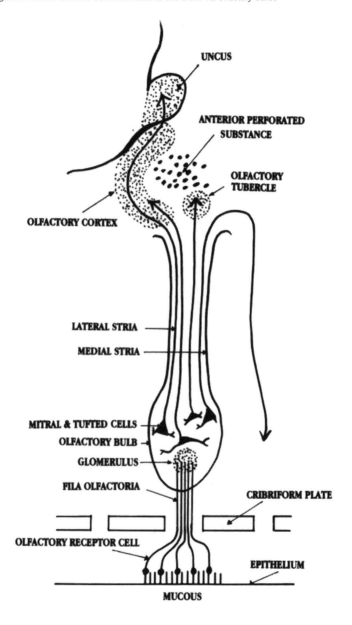

Adaption

As neophyte winetasters begin to broaden their experience they soon realize there exists a rather disconcerting consequence of "nosing" the same wine over a length of time. Without being aware of it, these tasters have come face to face with a phenomenon called "adaption." The smell literally fades into oblivion.

This sensory response has other names; some descriptive, some misleading. To some tasters it is also called "olfactory familiarization." Others label it "olfactory fatigue." To me, "fatigue" is a rather unfortunate choice of words. Though used in technical circles it conveys to the layman a considerably less than clear idea of what is taking place. "Fatigue" suggests weariness and exhaustion due to overwork. That is not what has taken place. What is occurring is that the nose has become used to or even "jaded" with that aroma. So it proceeds to push that one smell into the background, allowing you to smell other odors.

So if you were to continue immediately sniffing the same wine, you would soon lose the ability to smell that wine at all. By spacing out your sniffs (15 to 45 seconds) you avoid the nose's ability to adjust or adapt to that wine's aroma and bouquet. Many a novice taster has wondered why his initial impression of a wine seemed so much better than later assessments. Now you know at least one cause—smelling without long enough intervals between sniffs.

While this incredible smelling device can adapt to smells by ignoring them, blocking them out completely, this is generally to our benefit. If this were not true and, for example, first thing in the morning you were to apply a perfume or cologne, one with good staying power, that's about all you would smell for the day. It would simply overpower most other smells by being so close to you.

Many wine books are full of warnings about not sniffing any wine more than a few times or the "adaption" factor will take over. Some even suggest you should only pay attention to that first, initial sniff or sip. What may be overlooked is that adaption can take place in as little as 30 to 45 seconds, and that it very much depends upon the wine being nosed.

Also, adaption can be rather selective, so that while yes, you are adapting to one odor, you will be increasing your sensitivity to others. In terms of wine, if you didn't "adapt" all you would ever smell is the strongest component of the aroma or bouquet. But because you adapt to that smell, less aggressive, more subtle aromatics are allowed to move forward. Some have even confused this with a wine's bouquet "growing" or, "becoming more complex in the glass," as they say. What can happen is an adaption to the major odor element, which now reveals the more subtle complexities behind it.

If you were to follow the traditional tasting wisdom, ceasing the nasal investigation after only a sniff or two, you would probably miss a wealth of vinous treasures hiding behind the principal aromatic.

In more general fashion this principle of adaption can also affect your overall sensory impression of a wine. As you continue drinking the same wine over a period of, let's say, an evening, you may notice how the wine may never quite live up to your earlier impression. It does really, but you've begun to adapt to that wine, taking its qualities a little for granted. The moral of this story—test first, then drink. Don't try to evaluate wines after you've been drinking them for a period of time.

Some very experienced winetasters suggest (with a certain degree of merit) that the only way to really evaluate a wine is by drinking the better part of the bottle, over a period of several hours. Granted, you may indeed achieve a certain intimacy with that wine, but the practicality of this suggestion leaves a little to be desired, should there be a number of wines to taste.

This section on smell has done much, I hope, to convince you of the power of the human nose. Indeed, it is our most sensitive and pleasurable investigational tool, especially in our search for quality wine. Use it wisely but learn to use it well!

However, just as we're about to pat ourselves on the back and remind each other of how sensitive we really are, remember the dog. His olfactory region is six times larger than ours, and some say forty times as effective. A cat's is larger still. Fortunately, they tend not to like wine.

Olfactory research continues. Much more is needed. Profound questions relating to how we decipher the direction of smells, even if we perceive odors "in-mouth" the same as those from outside, remain unanswered, as do so many others.

🐝 🐝 🐝

Touch

Having passed by the eyes and nose we've now reached the mouth and first, our consideration of your sense of touch. The primary instrument you'll employ is, of course, your tongue, since it's still considered a little crude and somewhat impractical to stick your fingers into the glass to feel the texture of the wine that way.

Two basic factors about wine are identified and evaluated by your sense of touch: the body or texture and the astringency (tannin content) of the wine. Playing an enormous role in how we sense or react to touch is temperature and pain. We should also understand something very common to us all—our common chemical sense.

Without a fundamental understanding of how and why our sense of touch functions we will fail to grasp how it can affect our assessment of a number of wine elements. This will allow our perceptions of certain wines to be severely distorted.

Touch is a reaction to physical properties. When we experience such common vinous elements as bubbles, a creamy texture, a full-bodied character, thinness in a wine, heat (as in spicy), roughness or smoothness, a chilled wine, and so on, these are tactile or touch responses. This is often referred to as "mouth-feel."

Our skin and the lining of our mouth contain a variety of nerve endings with different sensitivities to different physical properties. Nearest the surface are the protective, free nerve endings, which register pain, cold sensitivity, and touch. Deeper we find pressure receptors, followed by heat sensitivity a bit deeper yet.

This sensitivity not only varies from individual to individual but in different parts of the body. Every safecracker knows that the back of the hand is not as sensitive as the tips of our fingers. Inside the mouth it is the tip and center of the tongue that demonstrates the greater sensitivity in this manner. The insides of our cheeks, the roof of our mouth, the lips, and so on, are all capable of tactile (touch) sensations, but are in need of the tongue to accurately accomplish the more delicate evaluations. So, our "in-mouth" touch assessment of a wine involves:

1. pressure—from a light, to a firm, or heavy touch;

2. temperature;

3. common chemical sense; and

4. pain, or irritations such as spicy, burning, itching.

When winetasters, writers, merchants, and makers of wine seek to describe the physical properties of a wine the word "texture" has become one of the main descriptors. But researchers have really not agreed upon a precise definition of "texture." And the debate has no resolution in sight. However, when we combine the above factors we get as close to understanding it as I think we can, at this point.

Pressure

A variety of wine components generate different pressures or weight in our mouth. A light tap on the shoulder compared to a vigorous but friendly slap on the back, is differentiated by our pressure sensors, and perhaps the rattling of our dentures.

Major sources of structure or texture include tannins from both the grapes and wooden barrels, sugar, alcohol, glycerol, and flavor extracts.

Temperature

We feel the sensations of heat and cold because of an important segment of our tactile receptors, the thermal variety. Nerve fibers in our mouth, lips, and tongue react to even minute variations of temperature.

Our lips and the tip of our tongue demonstrate the greatest temperature sensitivity, offering a frontline warning system against potentially harmful temperatures before they can do much damage in the oral cavity.

When a flight of wines is tasted, equivalent temperature is extremely important. When you have two glasses of the same wine, but served at different temperatures, you are, in effect, judging two different wines, unless you postpone any evaluations until both wines have achieved an equal temperature in-mouth. (For specific effects see pages 114–16.)

Common Chemical Sense

Humans possess an ability to react to chemicals applied to the skin. Quite reasonably, the greatest sensitivity to chemical irritants is centered on the exposed mucous membranes of the eyes, nose, mouth, upper respiratory tract, and the anogenital openings. This ability is called our "common chemical sense." It can also warn us against harmful chemical irritants.

Spicy food is one of many such irritants. They are not tastes, but truly chemical irritants, and they are sensed by this common chemical sense (served by the fifth cranial nerve-trigeminal). When such irritations become strong enough, they literally cause pain—in essence, a warning to "cool it." Even when some irritants fall below your personal threshold they can play almost a silent but still influential role in our sensory perceptions.

Pain/Irritation

In wine, few such irritants exist, at least when the wine is healthy.

When alcohol levels rise above 12 percent we are approaching normal but very mild pain thresholds. Unless its impact is softened by other wine components, each degree of additional alcohol increases the perceptible pain sensation. Again, because each of us has a different and personal pain threshold, that sensitivity to pain will vary considerably.

A natural by-product of grape fermentation is sulfur dioxide, but it is also a fairly common wine additive. It acts as a wine preservative, an anti-browning substance, and an anti-bacterial agent.

If free sulfur dioxide (SO_2) is present at levels above 150 ppm (parts per million), for some it may become evident in a physical way as well as in its odor form. It can do so by causing, in those individuals sensitive enough, to feel a burning or prickle in the nose—for some even a sneeze. Technically, it's the trigeminal nerve endings (fifth nerve) in the mouth and nose that react in such an abrupt manner. This is not a frequent event, but common enough to bring it to your attention. Even far below this level, we may not smell the SO_2, but we may be able to "feel it," as it can leave a dry coating in the mouth as part of the finish of the wine.

Some experts feel that a sense closely related to touch, called "kinesthesia," comes into play as well. This involves the senses that our muscles possess. Some suggest that such examples as the prickly sensation from both natural and artificial carbonation and a burning or hot feeling from the alcohol are partly kinesthetic. Even highly acidic wines, like Portugal's Vinhos Verdes, can stimulate our tactile sensors in this muscular manner.

Whatever the source—pressure, pain, temperature, common chemical sense, even kinesthesia—these tactile data end up in the brain's "central information clearing house," the thalamus. The data then stimulate various parts of the cortex (surface area of the brain) to perceive that particular sensation. In the case of our general sense of touch, because it involves so much of our body, it is handled by a wide band across the brain.

❊ ❊ ❊

Taste

In its everyday usage this word covers a great many sensations. We often use the word "flavor" as a synonym or substitute term for taste. But flavor has a very specific definition in the winetaster's vocabulary. Flavor combines what we taste (true taste) with our smell impressions, our tactile sensations, and that common chemical sense we all possess.

Together they generate a powerful perception, flavor. Thankfully the nose and tongue work well in tandem. "True taste" alone is just not enough, as too many substances stimulate our taste receptors in exactly the same way. Without the nose's ability to further evaluate the nuances of odor we would be unable to distinguish between tastes like a peach and a mango, or an apple and a pear.

However, our focus for the moment is on "true taste," the mechanism that applies to the function of the tongue, almost exclusively. Although we appear to know more about this sense than we do about smell, we still have more questions about taste than answers. There is as yet no comprehensive, widely accepted explanation of how the sense of taste really functions.

In fact, of all our senses one of the poorest, one of the least exacting is taste. It's downright primal in comparison to our sense of smell. For all intents and purposes our taste sensitivity depends solely on 3,000 papillae on our tongue. It sounds like 3,000 would be more than enough to do an admirable job. Yet, you sense only four basic stimulations—saltiness, sweetness, acidity (sourness), and bitterness.

For any substance to be "sapid" (have a taste) it must be soluble in our saliva. The movement of our tongue ensures that not only is it constantly lubricated and moistened by this complex fluid, but it has the effect of distributing the sapid elements to all of our taste receptors.

Saliva is a fascinating liquid, one that requires much more research if we are ever to understand it completely. It can exercise a remarkable influence on winetasting. The pH (acid activity) of saliva is very close to being neutral, so it can certainly influence how well we sense acids, for example. Coupled with a basic ability to dilute the volume of wine you take into your mouth, we need to realize that saliva can chemically alter a wine. For instance, the protein in saliva can fix (stabilize) the tannins in the wine. In a visual sense you may have seen this already, as the purple, stringy matter when we use a spittoon or a bucket.

This reality should make any winetaster take note of how long he keeps the wine in his mouth. The longer there, the more saliva and dilution occurs, along with a neutralization of acids and a fixing of the tannins. This does not make for good assessments. It reminds us of the value of imposing a rather strict and consistent pattern of tasting. Otherwise, our perception of different wines can vary by how long we keep them in our mouth.

Movement of the wine across the tongue to evenly distribute the taste elements and the various locations of our taste buds partially explains why you see wine judges and those so-called connoisseurs doing all that "sloshing and gurgling" during a tasting. Some colorfully term this "chewing" the wine, but I like "sloshing and gurgling" better. Besides, the only things I can chew are things I can bite. And any wine you can bite has a shade too much body for me.

The Tongue

In clinical terms, the tongue is a small muscular organ covered with a mucous membrane, and is attached to the floor of our mouth. As a sensory tool, it is divided into two parts—the oral (front two-thirds) and pharyngeal (rear one-third). A shallow **V**-shaped line of circumvallate papillae on the surface of the tongue marks the junction of these two parts. But remember, a large part of the tongue is completely insensitive to taste. And, of course, our tongue, though a relatively small instrument, can also get us into a lot of trouble when we abuse its other major function (see Figure 8).

Figure 8: The tongue has a sensory geography. If put to proper use it can become far more valuable to the winetaster than is normally expected.

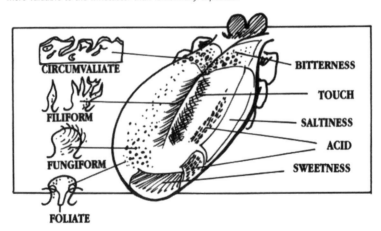

Those 3,000 papillae (Latin: nipple) come in four varieties. Some appear as little bumps on your tongue. Without them you would be minus your ability to taste, in the true sense of the word.

Each papilla contains several hundred "taste buds" and each taste bud has about a dozen taste receptors or cells whose sensory hairs (microvilli) extend outward through a taste pore to make contact with the sapid liquids. Human taste buds measure about 60–80 microns in length and 40 microns in width. The taste cells are the chemoreceptors.

Our tongue, though, is not the exclusive host of papillae. Less sensitive and much fewer in number, you can also find papillae on the surfaces of the oral cavity, such as the roof of the mouth, lips, gums, cheeks, pharynx, larynx, tonsils, and the epiglottis (the thin plate that covers the glottis opening during the act of swallowing, preventing food or liquid from entering the larynx).

The taste buds themselves seem to have a rather short lifespan. Their turnover is said to be about 3,000 to 5,000 every day. Within four to seven days you will have a completely new set of taste buds. However, this means that at any given time your taste buds will exist in fully mature form, in a smaller developing stage, as well as a degenerative form. This may provide us with at least one reason why the sensitivity of our taste mechanism is so much inferior to our smell sense.

The papillae on the surface of the tongue certainly represent the most powerful area of taste sensitivity. These papillae come in four basic versions: filiform, fungiform, foliate, and circumvallate.

> *Filiform* papillae are thread-like and perform only tactile (touch) functions, having no taste receptors (non-gustatory). They are located across the front surface of the tongue, but seem to have more tactile sensitivity down the center of the tongue.
>
> *Fungiform* papillae look like tiny button mushrooms and appear to the naked eye as those tiny red spots (because of their rich blood supply). Their taste buds respond primarily to sweet and salty stimulations. You find the largest concentration at the front (oral) sector of the tongue.
>
> *Foliate* papillae also support taste buds; they are more prominently situated on the sides and upper edges of the tongue, from just in front of that separating circumvallate line, towards the tip. The taste receptors in these papillae are more sensitive to acidic stimulations.
>
> *Circumvallate* papillae are to be found primarily on the rear surface of the tongue (on the pharyngeal section). They are sunken structures with a trough to collect the sapid liquids. Lining the trough are tiers of taste buds. Their sensitivity is essentially exclusive to bitter and sour (acid) stimulations. Going back to the earlier mention of our tongue's movement, it's this movement which forces the fluids into and out of these troughs (see Figure 9).

Figure 9: Unlike olfactory cells, taste cells are not neurons

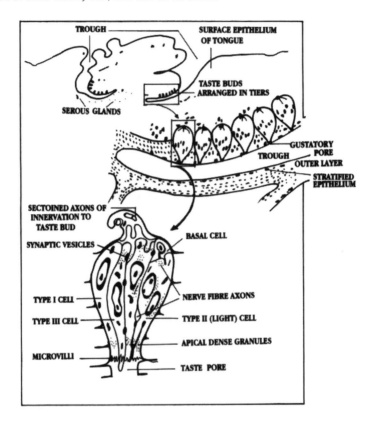

I must quickly correct any impression the foregoing descriptions might suggest that each papilla has an exclusive response to only one of the four basic taste stimulations, or that individual tastes can be perceived only on one area of the tongue. Some taste buds do that, but others can respond to two, even three of the primary tastes.

This multiple-response ability has led some to conclude that the traditional "taste geography," so long applied to the tongue, is no longer valid. Such conclusions would be equally misleading. The tongue does have its own sensory geography. The most effective sour (acid) sensors are located on the upper edges of the tongue; bitterness is sensed more accurately by taste buds on the rear surface of the tongue; sweetness sensors found on the tip of the tongue work best for that stimulation. Saltiness is best detected on the sides of your clapper.

However, this does not assert a taste specificity for each taste bud. While individual taste buds can respond to more than one type of stimulation, it has been discovered that there is a definite response pattern across a population of papillae. While one region may demonstrate a certain proclivity for one stimulation, that taste sensitivity is even stronger when we expand the sensory area. So, while a sensation of sweetness, for example, is strongest as we move it around in our mouth, the tip of the tongue remains the most sensitive sweetness zone. Perhaps that is why we savor a candy by rolling it around at the front of our mouth.

You may have noticed in our sensory travels over the tongue there appears to be a rather large blank spot in the center two-thirds. You are quite correct—it is insensitive to all tastes.

It's also worth remembering that when a liquid that contains all four of the primary taste stimulations—as is true with some wines—each taste is not perceived simultaneously. They tend to evolve or develop their sensations at different rates. Sweetness is sensed almost immediately, in two seconds or less. The acidic (sour) impression is also quite rapid but hangs around for a longer period of time. Bitterness takes some time to develop, but the intensity increases over a longer period and it usually gives us a lengthy reminder of its existence.

This difference in development time also suggests the reality of a sensory geography on the tongue, and supports the different nature of the papillae structures.

Receptor Mechanisms

When a stimulation reaches the hair-like microvilli in the taste pore, it obviously reacts with some form of receptor. The process of this attachment and the way in which electrical impulses are generated along the gustatory nerves is not known.

Theories do exist, including the "lock and key" approach and the idea that the stimulating molecule and the receptor form a protein-substrate complex. But the fact remains, we are only guessing. And I'm not all that certain I would understand it if someone *could* explain it.

Tasting Nerve Pathways

My earlier comments accusing taste sensitivity of being rather primitive was not a bias against the tongue. Part of the reason for that comparatively poor performance (compared to the nose) may have a lot to do with the fact that the taste receptor cells are not neurons and have no axons. The tremendous sensitivity of our eyes and nose depends on these direct neural receptors.

Our tongue's receptors act only as receivers, use neural taste fibers to connect up with a true neuron to send its messages to the brain. They do this by transmitting their impulses along three cranial nerves (seven, nine and ten). The front two-thirds of the tongue use the seventh cranial nerve (chorda tympani) while the rear one-third follows the ninth nerve (glossopharyngeal). Those taste buds in other parts of our mouth (pharynx, epiglottis, etc.) connect to the tenth cranial nerve (the vagus).

This may seem a bit clinical for a winetaster. Why should we care if different groups of taste sensors use different nerves to transmit their messages to the brain? We should! Knowing this will help us to see why we need to swallow at least some of the wine, even when we are tasting many wines. The rear third of the tongue and its "bitter" sensitivity is served by a different nerve than sweet, acid, and salty stimulations at the front. If we don't swallow we will fail to communicate this vital gustatory element to our brain.

The taste impulses travel to the medulla (the marrow at the top of the spinal cord), to the pons (a communication bridge), then the thalamus, and ultimately to the cortex. From these impulses we perceive the tastes of wine, adding it to the complex of sensory signals used to assess the very nature of the wine. Our challenge is to evaluate these perceptions.

Our taste buds, like the rest of our body, are influenced by and react to outside stimuli. Stress, pressure, and illness can decimate our taste sensitivity. As we age we consistently lose some of that acuity.

"Adaption" can also affect our taste judgments, as explained in the olfactory section. With our adaption to acid tastes we need to be even more careful. Once we "adapt" to one acid, and lose our sensitivity to it, we adapt to all of the acids in wine. This reminds us of the need to keep the wine in our mouth moving. This will help us to avoid developing a "zone" adaption.

Our taste sensitivity can also be affected by psychological influences. So, allowances must be made for your frame of mind and physical well being at the time of tasting. And it seems our taste, and most of our sensory devices, are really keenest when we are hungry. I don't think this is just cause to starve your winetasting guests, but do your tasting first followed by whatever edibles you have in mind.

🐜 🐜 🐜

Summary

My selection of these points and their order of presentation has not been arbitrary. We've been following the very natural sequence imposed by our own senses. In fact, each time you partake of a glass of wine you follow this sequence without even having to think about it.

When a wine is presented to you, your first impression is what you see; it's visual. Unless you're blindfolded or in a very dark room, you can't help but see the wine first.

Following this, even if you were to immediately bring the glass to your mouth to take a sip, it's difficult to avoid smelling it before that first drop touches your lips. So, whether it was your intention or not, you've remained true to the pattern so far—visual to olfactory (nose).

Once that first drop does reach your mouth, again, though your intention may have been to simply drink it, your sense of touch comes automatically into play as first, physical contact is made with the wine. Only then does it finally reach your taste buds and a final taste impression registers.

Unconsciously, you have been following the very pattern professional winetasters pursue: *visual—olfactory* (nose)—*tactile* (touch)—*taste*. It's the natural way.

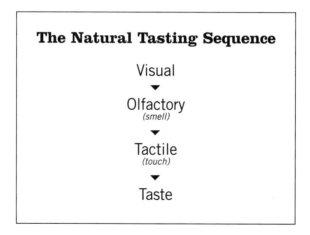

Now that some of the factors that can influence the use of your sensory tools have been detailed, the time has arrived to put them to work. Precisely how you will use these tools is the subject of the next few chapters. Use them wisely and accurately and they will reward you with an insight into wine that will significantly increase both your knowledge and pleasure.

CHAPTER 3

A Sight To See

AS already mentioned, it's quite difficult to avoid first making visual judgments about wine. We see a glass of this glorious nectar and immediately our sense of sight has made an assessment, of sorts.

The task at hand, though, is now to focus that ability and evaluate two specific visual aspects of wine—general appearance and color. This may at first sound rather simple, but there is truly more here than meets the eye, if you'll pardon the pun.

To the professional winetaster, appearance and color play an important role in any quality assessment. These two considerations are invariably included in the evaluation process used by wine competitions. Some disagreement remains as to how vital they are to the overall evaluation.

Some suggest these two assessments should account for as much as 40 percent of the total numerical result. While this view underscores the traditional under-evaluation given to these elements, 40 percent is, to me, pushing it. If a numerical evaluation system gives less than 20 percent to these two factors we have perhaps regressed too far in the other direction. From 20 to 25 percent of a wine's total merit could reasonably be credited to these two elements.

We also need to remember that it is our brain that ultimately gives value to what we perceive. Our visual acuity has a great deal of built-in prejudice. To be competent wine judges, professional or amateur, we need to give this visual sense a little exercise. It will require concentration coupled with some unbiased training.

Since "appearance" and "color" should be considered separately, we'll start with . . .

※ ※ ※

Appearance

Our prime concern under the heading of Appearance is for the clarity (limpidity) of the wine, as well as for the condition of the surface (meniscus) or "disc" of the wine. A limpid, crystalline appearance can be the very first indication of a truly fine or great wine. An ordinary, a severely blended, or a straight out poor wine will frequently demonstrate a dull, lack-luster appearance.

But a note of caution: Modern wine production methods must be given special consideration here. With the advent of improved filtering and polishing processes, wines of very insignificant stature can be produced easily and economically, with a marvelous appearance. Of course, that may be their sole redeeming merit, but they still look great. So we must be aware of this possibility and not be misled by such a good first impression.

We also need to keep in mind that the filtration of a wine—if carried out properly—does not mean that it has been stripped of its flavor and character. In reality, proper filtration removes a great deal of the impurities that could cause severe problems for the wine later on, in bottle.

On the other side of the coin, the growing popularity of unfiltered wines is a reality that must enter into the evaluation equation. Though refusing to filter a wine can be a risky proposition, we should not allow our assessment of clarity to over-ride all other judgments. Sediment is not incompatible with the demand for clarity. In fact, it can be somewhat comforting to see some sediment in fine red wines, even some of it clinging to the sides of the bottle. It can be an indication of proper handling without over-processing.

Before you ever pick up the glass to make this first "appearance" evaluation, it might be wise to review the earlier section on "Sight" (page 39). Removing the "visual impediments" discussed in that section can be the first step to making accurate appearance assessments. If more than one wine is to be judged, be sure that the "fill" in each glass of the "flight" (a series of wines) is equal. This kind of variation can and has led astray many a taster. If someone else is pouring the samples, *insist* on equal pours.

Clarity

If you've ever seen grapes shortly after they've been crushed you might marvel at how wine ever gets to be so clear in the bottle. Even new wine has "shreds of skin and and pulp from the crushed grapes, the results of flocculation and crystallization, and above all, the microorganisms that have transformed the must into wine. Each liter of wine contains billions of yeast cells, bacteria," according to Emile Peynaud. He says wine "is born troubled."

This helps us appreciate the reality that if a wine is going to develop into a healthy, truly fine wine, it will need near perfect clarity—permanently. Only when a wine is stable can it continue to improve its quality with age. And if you are ever to obtain that limpidity (clarity), fining and filtration are a virtual necessity.

As long as a wine remains in an unstable condition it is wide open to a variety of influences that can seriously alter that wine's clarity, which in turn, can affect its aroma, structure, and color. Some wines are so fragile simple exposure to air can turn them cloudy.

The technical wine definition of clarity is "the absence of haze/particles in liquid suspension." It might better be defined as an acceptable absence of visible particles. The simple fact is, no wine is perfectly clear, having no suspended particles.

The unaided human eye is not a bad judge of clarity. It can do the job reasonably well. We must take into account, of course, human variation. We don't all see perfectly. Some particles can be a hundred, even a thousand times smaller than the human eye can reasonably detect. These "colloidal" particles are normally too small to precipitate as a sediment so remain invisibly in suspension, unless flocculation (the formation of tuft-like particles—see page 75) occurs.

Though the human eye fails to detect particles this small, there are ways to precisely measure any degree of clarity. A "nephelometer" is able to give us a numerical assessment of clarity by measuring the penetration and dispersion of light rays as they pass through wine. A "particle counter" can also be used. It is capable of counting solid particles dispersed in a liquid according to size, from a micron (1,000th of a millimeter) upwards.

To describe wine clarity we use such words as "brilliant" for a perfect crystal-clear appearance; "bright" for something slightly less; and "clear" for an acceptable degree of clarity. On the negative side, "dull" would indicate a minor fault; "hazy" a serious problem; and "cloudy" could be totally unacceptable. Be careful here, especially when you're judging wines that may have been chilled—whites more probably. A very fine mist can coat the glass (condensation) and create a faint cloudy impression.

Surface ("Disc")

Start your visual examination by first considering the upper surface (meniscus or "disc") of the wine. First, view it almost at eye level, or laterally, and then look straight down on it. It should be bright, shiny, and reflective, almost mirror-like.

If not, if it's flat, dull or has a matte finish, assess it as a negative factor. At best, it will indicate simply an ordinary wine, at worst some potentially serious faults with that bottle. All is not well with this wine. Occasionally you will stumble across a wine with an iridescence, a film of sorts, floating on its surface. This may be indicative of a number of very grave wine ailments such as the growth of microorganisms or enzymatic problems. Such factors could lead to the wine being oxidized if its source is yeast, or to vinegariness if the problem stems from bacteria.

Poor handling of the wine could also cause this surface iridescence, from machinery oil getting into the wine during processing, or on rare occasions it could result from an excessive iron content.

There are a number of other technical surface faults like *mycoderma vini* and *aceti*, which are whitish and grayish films. We'll stop at this point, before this turns into a rather feeble attempt at being a scientific paper on the subject. Besides, you probably know more about this factor than you want to by now.

That's also why we want to make it clear that your job is not necessarily to identify which of these faults prevails or its original cause. They will all be judged as negatives and will be recorded appropriately in your numerical evaluation.

Pressing on with our visual inspection, we can approach the actual aspect of wine clarity. Using a white background or a backlight of some sort, you now look through the wine for suspended particles. Again a note of caution is sounded, as not all factors that may cause a wine to be temporarily hazy or cloudy are ultimately negative. And be aware that a red wine with great depth of color, though not transparent, may well be quite clear.

With the growing consumer demand for what amounts to a clinical clarity for all wines, it's becoming increasingly difficult to convince some people of the validity of the previous two statements. But there are legitimate reasons why a wine may temporarily display a haziness. Too often this alone puts off the inexperienced wine drinker who, without further investigation, proceeds to pass over such a wine, when it may indeed have been a genuine delight.

This temporary haziness, in fact, may be a fine, well-aged wine (more often a red) quite naturally "throwing" a sediment, as the expression is used in the wine world. In the early stages of leaving this natural deposit (primarily of color matter and tannins) the suspended particles can be quite noticeable. However, it clears as the sediment drops to the bottom of the bottle or clings tenaciously to the sides.

The degree of deposit will depend greatly on the depth of the wine's original color. As deposits continue, the color alters, reds becoming more brown and whites taking on gold or amber shades. Fine white wines that age well only throw a sediment after many years of proper ageing.

Once this process has fairly well run its course and the bottle has rested or remained in one position for a period of time, the wine should become quite clear. But on serving or transporting the wine the sediment may become disturbed, thus you could be momentarily confronted with a hazy wine that was clear only moments ago.

Beware! Any premature or hasty judgments can cascade into other errors. Being convinced that a visual fault exists can often lead to convincing yourself that faults in the nose and taste also exist. All that may be perceived is an unfamiliar smell or taste, but with one fault in mind that negative perception may point an accusing finger at a totally innocent sensation.

An experienced wine judge will take all this into consideration, watching carefully for the handling of the wine and its age. So, a fine, aged wine roughly handled, with its natural sediment disturbed, despite its displaying a haziness should not be prematurely judged as having a fault. Decanting may be necessary.

Decanting (removing the wine from the bottle to another container) can present you with some rather awkward moments. The sediment may cling tightly to the side of the bottle making it fairly easy to decant. However, the deposits can also be very light and easily disturbed. Often your only option is to pour it through some fine gauze, and even then very carefully. But with wines of this nature it will be well worth the extra care and attention.

If decanting is deemed necessary, do remember to remove all the neck foil so that you have a better view of the sediment as it approaches the neck of the bottle. A light source behind the bottle neck (candle or flashlight) will allow you to see its approach and cease your pouring in time to avoid any sediment reaching the decanter.

Don't be afraid to sacrifice an ounce or two. It's better to have 725 ml of clear wine than 750 ml of cloudy wine. The residue, with a few milliliters of the wine, makes an excellent addition to some sauces or as a deglazing liquid for the skillet.

Decanting wine has become a major issue in itself. You can find this topic discussed in more detail on page 159.

This whole matter indicates the value of one major principle you would do well to keep in mind for all your wine judging: The more you know about the wine, the more accurate will be your evaluations. Blind tastings can be a challenge, a test of your growing wine sensitivity. But remember, evaluating a wine is not a contest; it's a genuine attempt to establish the quality of that individual bottle of wine. The purpose? to help you purchase wisely, while learning from the experience.

It was a pleasure to read similar comments, so well expressed, in two other wine books. Alexis Bespaloff in his *Wine: A Complete Introduction* released in 1980, conveyed the thought succinctly:

> It's often assumed, by the way, that wine experts are people who can taste wines whose labels have been covered up and then name the vineyard and vintage. Although some members of the wine trade amuse themselves by putting their colleagues through such blind tastings, the real skill of a wine buyer is demonstrated in exactly the opposite manner. He stands in a particular cellar, tasting a specific wine, and has even noted the barrel from which it was drawn. He must now determine how good it is, how good it will be six months or six years later, and what it is worth. It is precisely this ability to concentrate on the wine at hand—in order to judge its value, not guess its origin—that is the primary attribute of his expertise.

And in the *Signet Book of American Wine*, third edition, Peter Quimme asserted boldly, "Assessing wines blind is common in winetasting; identifying them blind is a stunt. To identify wines is not the point of tasting, appreciation or even connoisseurship. The point is evaluation."

Amen!

This all may sound quite reasonable in this context, but you may not appreciate that these comments and views, in a number of wine circles, verge on sheer heresy.

For many decades now the objective of a good number of influential wine aficionados has been to develop the ability to identify a wine's place of origin. And this was supposed to be a comment on quality. If it ever was, it certainly is no longer true today.

Many of those classic wine regions have, shall we say, altered over the years, with many new wine regions in various corners of the globe challenging the traditional classics with wines that occasionally surpass them. After all, identifying which wine it is says little about how good it is. Most often the very factors that distinguish one wine from another, as a personality let's say, are non-qualitative factors to begin with.

At the risk of sounding repetitious—the objective of winetasting is to evaluate quality. Only then can you judge whether or not your wine money has been well spent.

If you'll please excuse this slight detour, it's time to return to the point of *clarity*. Before we create the erroneous impression that haziness or cloudiness is only rarely a negative factor, let's look at the darker side of the picture for a few moments.

Keep in mind that truly fine or great wines are often characterized by an added luster and clarity. The haze or cloudiness in wine doesn't just present us with a visual impairment. The cause of that problem can often distort or mask some of the wine's other fine qualities.

So haziness, or worse, cloudiness, is most often a warning sign of a serious problem. It could be an undesirable yeast growth, or what is called a protein imbalance. An excess of iron can also cause a milkiness. If the cloudiness is accompanied by a crystalline deposit, a harmful excess of potassium bitartrate (tartaric acid) or calcium tartrate may exist.

We should not forget this one point, however: Tartrate crystals in a clear wine are nothing to be concerned about. They may appear as tiny flakes or crystals at the bottom of the bottle or be adhering to the bottom of the cork. They offer no impairment to the wine and should not reflect negatively in your scoring. White wines seem to be most affected this way. But if it's accompanied by cloudiness, we do have a genuine fault on our hands.

Flocculation is another fault you may run into. It's a technical term used to describe the clustering of tuft-like particles, usually caused by an undesirable yeast growth. But again, your function is not to play scientific detective and sort out the various causes of these faults, but simply rate their positive and negative effects on the wine. Although this is probably more technical than the average wine drinker will want to pursue this matter, there is a practical side to all this. Knowing which is a genuine fault and which isn't may prevent an evaluation error, even better, it will save many a bottle from the sad destiny of being poured down the kitchen sink unnecessarily.

Because of those earlier discussed technical advances in the filtration and polishing of liquids, poor and great wines too often seem to stand as equals in this one respect. Over the years wine clarity, as a measure of wine quality, has declined somewhat in its significance to wine assessments. Yet we can't simply ignore it. It remains one of the keys in assessing wine quality and potential problems. Perhaps then, its weight, its overall significance to the wine judging process, should be adjusted downward, remaining an important factor to be noted, but with less significance than it once held.

Some Causes of Haze or Cloudiness

- exposure to air in unstabilized wine

- cold and heat instability

- prolonged exposure to light

- absence of sterility

- traces of copper and iron (metal salts)

- unstable tannins and colors

- bacterial or microbiological infections

- yeast proteins

✻ ✻ ✻

Color

Before discussing what color is, where it comes from, and what it indicates in a wine, we need to appreciate its power. It can have a profound effect upon both judge and consumer.

Appreciation of any color is a very subjective and individual matter. Colors we find attractive—and there's no known reason to explain our preferences—can soften the critical edge of our evaluations. If we strongly dislike a particular shade our assessment can humble the toughest Broadway critic. Color can also influence the way we react to certain smells and tastes.

These very facts alert us to be wary of being influenced by personal color preferences. Unless you're careful your personal color likes and dislikes could seriously color your judgment. The remedy: (a) keep foremost in mind the color standards we're going to discuss and what they indicate for wine quality; (b) ignore your pet shades.

While color can without question lead us down some rather wayward paths, by itself it can provide a surprisingly accurate indication of a wine's body, its maturity, and its health.

There's one other reality we need to come to grips with early on in our color discussions. It would take an encyclopedia to list all the possible color variations. Some experts suggest the human eye can distinguish 300,000 different color judgments—if they were placed side by side. In our day-to-day life we encounter a small fraction of this potential. This inborn ability is rarely taxed. With printed material it is difficult to provide visuals to assist the process. Few printers would be capable of reproducing all the exact shades and their various nuances. So, from the outset we must realize this limitation.

Each wine has its individual color and a range of colors it will span during its lifetime. For the most part, age is what causes the wine to travel its full color range—at varying rates, quite naturally. Grape variety, soil conditions, weather, cellar practices, and a number of additional elements combine to produce wine colors that are unique to that particular wine. Only experience will teach you to recognize and remember the subtle differences.

It wasn't my intention to start us off on a negative foot with this point. For indeed, there is a great deal we can learn from that broad range or spectrum of wine colors, the ones we can easily recognize. Evaluation of broad color groupings can go a long way to help us determine the quality and maturity of each wine that crosses our path. Before discussing individual colors and what they mean, it's beneficial to understand where wine colors originate and why they differ.

For all intents and purposes, wine colors originate from only two sources—the skins of the grapes and the effects of oxidation. If you were to strip the skins from white or red grapes, the juice obtained from the flesh or pulp is basically the same color—a little like fresh lemon juice (a rare few varieties do have a tinge of reddish or pink color).

For white wines that's almost it. On occasion the juice will be allowed a short period of time in contact with the skins for flavor extraction. But it is then left up to the winemaker, the effects of ageing, and oxidation. The maturity of the fruit at the time of harvesting plays an important part, too.

For red wines the process is much more involved and complex. Red wine colors originate with pigments in the grape skins. These pigments, common in nature, generate the color in fruits and flowers. They are called "anthocyanins" and are members of the phenolic family, related to the tannins found in the skins, pips, and stalks.

The other source of wine color is attributed to the effect of oxygen. Fruits, including grapes, contain more than one compound that can encourage a "browning" in contact with air. A certain type of phenolic (catechin) likes to turn brown. And an enzyme naturally found in grapes (tyrosinase) likes to accelerate that process. There are other causes, but no doubt you have seen the browning after a bite or slice has been taken from an apple. Uncontrolled exposure to oxygen causes the same effect with grape juice or wine. The degree and control of that exposure exercises a profound influence on the color of white and red wine.

Influences on Wine Color

1. **Climate:** cool climate versus warm climate can cause considerable differences in skin thickness and the number of pigments available for color.

2. **Soil/Subsoil:** soil composition and structure can influence the maturity and mineral content of a wine, thusly its color.

3. **Fruit maturity:** color pigments increase in the grape skin with fruit maturity.

4. **Grape Variety:** varietal differences in grapes provide a full range of pigment concentration—they can also vary widely in their degree of maturity at harvest.

5. **Fermentation:** the modern winemaker has a tremendous latitude available in winemaking—the tools are many; styles can vary enormously; color extraction can be altered and corrected in a variety of ways.

6. **Ageing:** as wine ages, regardless of the color, it passes through a wide range of tints. This is not necessarily a measure of literal years, but an evolution exclusive to that wine; reds actually lighten in depth, whites darken.

7. **Wood:** the very slow, controlled oxygenation in wooden barrels has a definite impact on the color of any wine. Some color can even be extracted from the wood.

Just to add to your considerations, you should be aware that wine-makers can do much to, shall we say, supplement a wine that has poor color, primarily reds. By simply blending their wine with wine made from certain other grapes they can significantly improve the look of their own product. Those certain grapes (teinturiers) are varieties whose singular merit may be their deep, dark color. Again, it may even be a variety that has a juice that has some red coloring. The most famous of these varieties are Alicante Bouschet and Rubired.

This blending will most often improve only the visual aspect of the wine, not its many other necessary qualities. But wine judges must be aware of this possibility. Once they have considered the other aspects of the wine and discover that the visual factors are grossly exaggerated by comparison, they will then understand what may have taken place. It simply reaffirms the old adage, "Looks can be deceiving."

Before making individual color evaluations we would be wise to recall from the "Visual" section in chapter 2 that color is perceived through the different ways wine absorbs light rays that pass through it. As well, keep in mind the influences both lighting and background can have on color judgments. Since you're utilizing the weakest of your senses, your eyes, do take some care in choosing your setting.

Depth

But just what are we looking for as far as color is concerned? Two major factors: tint or hue, and the depth or density of the color (some authorities refer to this as "luminance," others suggest it is a separate factor). Let's deal with the latter attribute first, depth of color. It is also referred to as "saturation" or "intensity."

Two wines may have a tint or hue quite similar, but vary considerably in their depth of color. A very simple experiment can be done with a red wine. Using two identical wine glasses, half fill one glass with a selected red wine. Before doing the same for the second glass, dilute some of the wine in another glass at about a three wine to one water ratio. Now half fill the second glass with the diluted wine. The volume of fluid is obviously the same. Now, look down from the top of the glass, through the wine. Make sure you use a white background. You'll immediately notice the pure wine has a deeper color. It is actually more opaque, more difficult to see through.

Another illustration: lightly stroking a piece of paper with a crayon, then pressing down hard, several times, over the same spot produces marks of the same color or tint, but one mark has obviously much more density to it. It's darker. It is also physically more dense, with more crayon material on the paper, causing the added color. Our sample wines are not different in this respect. The darker shade of the pure red wine is caused by literally more color pigments in that volume of liquid. This same principle applies to wines in their natural state.

Those color pigments found in each grape variety (in the skin) also demonstrate different degrees of resistance to extraction. Most of these pigments are not generally that soluble in water. They are in alcohol, however. So if the wine is allowed to ferment on the skins the alcohol extracts the pigments to greater depths of color, varying according to the grape variety.

What do these various color depths indicate? Several possibilities, in general terms. In a positive vein, good color depth may denote good tannin content from fully ripened grapes, thusly a wine that should age well, benefiting from its years. Also, it may mean that the wine has been allowed a reasonable length of time in contact with its skins, giving it added fruit, bouquet, as well as those added years.

White wines are becoming almost an exception to this as more and more producers are fermenting the white juice without skin contact—the skins having been removed beforehand.

Depending on what the rest of your evaluations reveal, good color density could also signify grapes grown in a very sunny climate. Usually those grapes with heavy, sun-thickened skins produce wines of very ordinary overall stature, but will possess great depth of color. These grapes can be the types we spoke of earlier, tinting wines, used for blending with other wines for color adjustment.

A pale color, though occasionally a characteristic of certain grape varieties, could also indicate a fast, poor vinification process. Or, it may indicate too high a yield per acre, causing low extract in the harvested grapes. An inferior vintage, having had fewer sun hours during the growing season, will also fail to produce the required pigments in the skins. As expected, a weak, low-density color results.

There are more factors involved, but again, we must keep in mind our task is not so much to identify the precise reason for the deficiency, but to determine its degree and evaluate it accordingly.

"Window dressing" is a phrase used by some wine authorities to designate a wine that has excellent visual qualities, both appearance and color, but fails to follow through in most other respects. We must be cautious we are not led too far astray by a wine's glorious *robe*, as wine colors are called in France.

While sound color is definitely a major ingredient contributing to the overall quality of a wine, there are wines that have rather poor depth of color, yet are quite acceptable or may even excel in all other aspects. Be careful not to quickly create in your mind a negative feeling for such a wine because of this singular deficiency. But do remember this depth of color will most often be related to increased fruit, body, and structure, leading to other qualities that will characterize a superior wine.

Sulfur Dioxide
I would be remiss if I did not at this point give some consideration to the wine industry's almost universal use of sulfur and its effect on wine color, especially its intensity.

Winemakers have a love/hate relationship with sulfur. Although small amounts of it are a natural by-product of fermentation, it is the most common wine additive. The love/hate part revolves around the positives vs. negatives associated with its use. As mentioned earlier, SO_2 is anti-bacterial, anti-browning, and an anti-oxidation agent. It does a lot for wine. But it also has an effect on color—good and bad.

When the winemaker adds SO_2 to the fresh crushed grapes before fermentation, it does aid in some degree to the greater extraction of color pigments from the grape skins. That's good. In fact, many modern wines would be somewhat lighter in color depth today if it weren't for SO_2.

But our benefactor now turns on its host, once it has been transformed into wine. When SO_2 attaches itself to the pigment molecule (temporarily) it "bleaches" out the color. The process is much more complicated than this simple statement reflects. However, when oxygen, which enters the wine in its busy early life of racking, filtering, pumping, and so on, finally oxidizes the SO_2, the color reappears. But in the process some of that color depth is lost. In some white wines the bleaching effect can leave it colorless. It becomes a balancing act between the winemaker's skill and the effects of SO_2. What this means is, at times color depth in a wine may be quite light when we first see it, but could very well return later on. If SO_2 has been used injudiciously you will very probably notice its pungent, burnt-match smell.

Winemakers today are looking for ways to restrict their use of SO_2, and in fact, industry-wide have chopped it by as much as 50 percent. Some of their staunchest allies are wines with higher acidity. The increased acidity (and lower pH) is responsible for more vibrant colors and healthier wines.

At last, to that other color key, hue or tint, the actual color differences themselves and what they mean.

Tint

Each wine has its own unique color and each color its own tale to tell. The limitless variations in hue originate from a number of sources. Grape variety, maturity, time on the vine, length of fermentation on the skins, climate conditions for that particular vintage, soil makeup, general cellar practices, and so on, are all elements that affect the final color (tint) of the wine. However, these limitless variations can be grouped into several broad color ranges that can give us a fascinating insight into the nature and stature of that wine.

Red Wine

Red, as a wine color, originates from the pigments in the grape skin (anthocyanin pigments) that are extracted primarily during fermentation. With it comes a close relative, tannins, but there are some differences. Both pigments and tannins come from the skins, but tannins also come from the pips and stalks. Because the color pigment molecules are smaller, they are extracted faster than the larger tannin polymers. With about five days of maceration you've gotten most of the pigments that are available. If you leave the skins in contact with the juice any longer almost all you'll get is more tannins. (See page 123 for a description of "extended" maceration.)

It is these "free" pigments that give to the young wine most of its color. Lilac, mauve, and purple tints dominate young reds. But every winelover knows that the color of red wine can change dramatically with age, evolving from its youthful purple glow to a brick or tile red at maturity. Why?

As the wine ages it oxidizes at various speeds, dependent upon numerous factors. With time the pigments also "polymerize." They become part of much larger molecule chains (including some tannins) which are then less coarse on the palate. When they become too large to be soluble in the wine they begin to precipitate as sediment.

As these purplish pigments begin to diminish in number they gradually lose their dominant influence on the overall color. The remaining tannins, some that do not fall out, now begin to emerge with their own colors—yellowish, then orange, and on to browns. As some tannins age further they also polymerize and join the precipitation parade with any remaining pigments. As the colors in the tannins begin to take over, the wine color ranges from a bright red to increasingly brownish tinges. This color progression is the most accurate way to assess a wine's maturity, though not its age; the rate at which wines mature does not always coincide with the calendar.

For this evolution of color to be of any benefit it must occur with a wine that will respond positively to age. Otherwise the wine, like all wines, simply gets older, not better. Age is a common achievement for every wine—improvement is not.

Now, to some specifics!

Purple is indeed the color of youth and immaturity. It implies a wine freshly fermented—a wine still wearing diapers, so to speak. Most red wines, as a type of wine, will at least start their life with something of this shade, progressing towards other fascinating hues as they mature. The precise time needed to make these vital transformations from youth to adolescence to maturity is governed by grape variety, depth of original color, and a number of handling practices in the winery. Yet, like some people who never grow up, a few, usually lesser quality wines may never leave this infantile purple or violet stage. They may have neither the breed nor the time, as they will be consumed, some before they ever reach the bottle, others long before their second birthday.

In addition to these wines, which are consumed so young, there are a number of native North American varieties and their hybrids that have such strong pigments in this color range that their purple blush never really disappears all together. It remains an identifiable characteristic throughout their various stages of ageing.

Ruby is the next step. Assuming that the wine is a fine wine or certainly a better "vin ordinaire," it will continue to make progress, at least to this point. This is the shade immediately following the loss of that newly vinted purple tone. It is often a dark color. Perhaps the wine has reached two or more years of age, having finished any wood ageing, and is now resting quietly in bottle.

For those better vins ordinaires that fall into this category they may well be on the retailers' shelves, having reached their personal pinnacle. Many have been produced with this lifespan in mind and are often referred to as "commercial-grade" wines. For truly fine wines a further stage or two lies ahead.

Red, true red, a color of adolescence for fine wines, marks the traditional period between youth and full maturity. Some wines, however, will demonstrate shades more like garnet at this stage. The best of the vin ordinaires and some of the more humble fine wines should be drunk at this stage, as further ageing will do them little good (two to four years of age).

Red/Brown, brick red or tile red is definitely a sign of maturity in well-handled wines. The brownish tinge is first noticed at the edge, where the wine touches the glass. I use the term "well-handled" because this shade can also result from too much exposure to air (oxidation). A quick sniff, however, should tell you immediately whether the wine is over-oxidized or not.

There are also those rather impatient producers who will try to circumvent the time needed to reach these mature stages by employing some short-cuts. Usually they heat the wines for a period of time trying to create a semblance of maturity. But such wines will frequently exhibit a cooked, madeirized (Madeira-like) taste easily identifiable and really not worth the effort in the end. Many truly fine wines will reach their peak at this stage, further ageing doing them few favors (five to ten years).

Mahogany represents a shade few wines ever achieve—in good shape. This is primarily true because few have the inherent stamina to attain this plateau and still be worth drinking. The vast majority of wines (80 percent or more) are ordinary at best, and once to the red stage decline quickly into senility. Some extremely fine and truly great wines of noble character and classic variety will reach the softer, more subtle red/brown tint of mahogany, with strength to spare. It most often represents 10 to 15 years, or more, in bottle. Such vigorous wines may remain essentially in this superior condition for another 10, 20, or more years before a serious decline in quality becomes evident. But keep in mind, we're talking about the elite of the wine world. Less, far less than five percent of any vintage will ever aspire to such lofty heights. And in some years no vineyard will sire a wine that attains this plateau of excellence.

Amber/Brown shades cause polite professional disagreement among wine authorities. For some tasters, this means three strikes and out. The wine is over the hill in their view, hardly worth drinking. There's no doubt it represents a wine of advanced age, but for other experts this elderly robe and its associated qualities are still to be admired and savored.

I'm not about to even attempt to help you resolve this point. You'll just have to experience this stage for yourself and formulate your own conclusions.

Inferior wines may, however, acquire a similar appearance within a very few years. But smelling and tasting them should quickly inform you that their funeral took place, or should have, quite some time ago.

White Wine

You have a slight advantage judging white wines. The human eye is more capable of sensing tint differences in the yellow/green region of the color spectrum.

Of course, when we speak of white wines we do so euphemistically, as no wine, or grape for that matter, is truly white in color. We're actually talking about a range of colors from a watery yellow/green to a rich gold/brown, even pale pink. Sweet white table wines and those dry whites made from fully matured grapes, generally speaking, display deeper shades of yellow right from the beginning. With bottle age golden hues begin to appear, developing definite brownish tinges in advanced age.

White wines with reductive ageing (no air contact) often have tints that tend more towards that "golden" hue, while tawny, brown hues may be evidence of air contact.

The term "white" has been used for so long and is so deeply entrenched in our languages at this point, it's like some relatives—it's here to stay for the foreseeable future.

Frequently in wine writing you will come across the word "straw" to denote a certain white wine tint. But this has always confused me. Having spent some time "on the land" I've seen straw with a definite greenish tinge, to that which was a bright yellow/gold. For me the term straw does not consistently bring to mind one particular shade. If those who are used to using this descriptive term will forgive me, I'll avoid using this word during our discussions, as I think you should.

Oenologists have several theories that account for white wine colors—phenolic compounds, flavones (yellow), chlorophyll (green). When the color deepens it is said that this occurs because the phenolic molecules join together, having gold, amber, and brown hues in this form. But our knowledge is imprecise. There is no certainty when it comes to the source of white wine colors. In some cases the total lack of skin contact provides an even greater mystery as to why such wines have any color at all.

Pale yellow/green is a shade particularly common to wines grown in cooler climates, where the grapes may not have ripened fully. The greenish tinge will be especially noticeable in young, dry wines (said to be residual chlorophyll). Chardonnay and Riesling grape varieties will occasionally demonstrate this quality. White wines from warmer climates rarely exhibit these greenish tinges.

A few years in bottle, however, should transform any touches of green to pale yellows. If not, it may arouse some legitimate suspicions that excess amounts of added sulfur are retarding the normal ageing process, thus the natural color progression. One purpose of adding sulfur in the first place is to inhibit the browning of the fruit. But some producers go a little overboard, trying to keep their wines young-looking forever. In rare cases the SO_2 can bleach out all the color.

Light yellow is the most common hue for young, dry, white table wines. This is not to suggest that there won't be numerous variations and depths of color within this chromatic range. Only experience can teach you the minute differences. For most wines in this category this will be their ultimate color achievement and they should be joyfully consumed at this point (one to three years of age).

Yellow/gold shades are most frequently associated with sweeter table wines, primarily during their youth—wines like Sauternes, the Beerenausleses from Germany, genuine Tokajs from Hungary, and the Vins Jaunes of France. A few drier white table wines will attain colors similar to this after three to four years of bottle age, especially if they've received some wood ageing.

Gold is the next stage of color development for these luscious sweet dessert wines as they quietly slumber decades or more in bottle. Some fine and great dry table wines will also approximate this shade after five to six years, with perhaps less depth of color.

Yellow/brown, for many authorities, signifies absolutely too much ageing for any dry table wine. Or, it could also be the tell-tale sign of early oxidation, that arch-enemy of wine. Bad storage and too much light can also be the villain. For those heavier, sweet varieties it could mark 20 to 100 years after their vintage and for them much remains to be appreciated by the most discriminating connoisseur. Fortified white wines exhibiting this tint may still be in good condition but have a *rancio* (see Glossary) character in smell and taste.

Rosé Wine

As with red and white, rosé as a color does not confine itself to describing a singular shade. Rosé wines vary widely in tint and depth of coloring according to the very different styles produced in various wine districts of the world. The better rosés are vinted from quality blue and black grapes, the skins remaining in contact with the crushed juice just long enough (five to forty-eight hours) to tint the wine to the desirable degree. Inferior rosés are occasionally the result of blending red and white grapes. But rarely do you find rosés that are simply a blend of red and white wines. This is the case not only because of the poor quality wine that can result, but because it's illegal in some lands.

To acquire a good, firm color for rosé it takes some very careful handling and judgment on the part of the winemaker. It is not always the "compromise" wine some believe it to be, nor is it simply a second-class red wine, as some also view it.

Since most rosés respond rather poorly to the march of time and most, if not all of their charm is in their vernal freshness, age is unquestionably their foe. They are usually bottled quite quickly (early in the following spring) with little or no contact with wood (ageing in barrel).

To wait longer than two years before drinking most rosés would be, with the rarest exception (e.g., some rosés from Tavel in France), too long. Chances are you will have missed their prime by a year or more.

A well-made, quality rosé attributes its color to the same two sources as red wine—the anthocyanin pigments (the purple, mauve, and lilac nuances), and to tannins (yellow, orange, and brown tints). As they age, the pigments combine with tannin molecules and can precipitate as sediment. Usually, the rosé has been happily consumed long before that.

The levels of pigments and tannins in rosés vary widely, depending on whether the winemaker has chosen to vinify it using a white wine technique (i.e., blushes) or more like a red wine (traditional rosé). As any rosé lover knows, there is a tremendous range of rosé colors. Grape variety can play a major role in the tint. Some examples of the variation:

Variety	Rosé Color
Cabernet	a raspberry touch
Carignan	a pomegranate tint
Gamay	a cherry tint
Grenache	leaning towards mauve and pinkish-orange

Rose, the standard rosé tint, is not just a weak, low-density red but a solid rose color. It should be a clear, firm shade. This is one indication of a quality rosé. The slightest tinge of orange or purple is forgivable, but it will still be a compromise from the standard.

Pink/orange is a common shade for several types of rosés made from grape varieties like the Grenache. This is especially the case if the fruit is grown in warmer climates. While producing pleasant wines, this shade is not indicative of better quality rosés.

Pink suggests a note of artificiality from too much winery involvement. A vivid pink color with blue or purple tinges may even indicate an unhealthy state, either high pH (low acid) or poor fining. Metal contamination can also cause a bold pink tint.

Salmon/pink can be another inferior shade. It may be caused by the grape being picked too late or our old spoiler oxygen has been at work again. Any hint of this brownish tint is definitely a negative factor and should be evaluated as such.

Color Sensitivity

Fortunately, most of us have no defects in our perception of color. But a significant portion of the human family have mild to serious problems when it comes to seeing color. Color blindness, whether complete or partial, is a complex ailment. It has a lot to do with those cone receptors in our eyes. See the "Eye" section in chapter 2.

Males are more affected with this deficiency. Estimates put the percentage of afflicted males at six to eight percent. Less than one half of one percent of females are affected. At times, this inherited deficiency may be so mild it goes unnoticed. If you suspect that you have a problem, a visit with an ophthalmologist will identify the problem.

※ ※ ※

Summary

It should be apparent at this point, there are some severe limitations in our ability to assess, with total accuracy, the visual aspects of wine. Again, this is true because we are employing the weakest of the five senses, our eyes, while trying to put into words the impossible—all the nuances and shadings of wine colors.

This helps us to appreciate the need for a total sensory evaluation of each wine. Exploring one or two facets is not enough. A complete, composite sensory profile must be made for each wine before you render a final judgment. But this does not have to be a long, complicated, and formal analysis. With a little practice you can use this method of wine analysis, step by step in a very casual manner, while you're drinking any wine. For the more formal evaluations you can bring out the rating sheets and all the other paraphernalia needed to make an in-depth investigation.

On the positive side of the visual coin, what we have been able to consider will most certainly go a long way to assist you in evaluating the general quality of the majority of table wines you'll come across, by both their color and appearance. In the final analysis you've made a few, significant steps forward and unlocked a few doors in your appreciation of this entire subject of wine evaluation, with several more to come.

CHAPTER 4

Nosing Around

AT last we put to use your most precise wine tool—your nose. Assuming that it's in fairly decent working order, minus any major obstructions, we can proceed with some of the most significant quality assessments you'll make in this whole evaluation procedure.

When you get to the more serious occasions for tasting wine, try to avoid situations that can hinder your nose from doing its phenomenal job. Smoke in the room, strong deodorants, perfumes, colognes, flowers, food smells, and so on can make your delightful task more difficult, certainly less pleasant.

Your awesome nose is used to explore three major wine facets: the **intensity** of wine odors, the **aroma,** and the **bouquet**. Its major challenges will be to both discover and evaluate the positive elements and to ferret out faults that will detract from the stature of the wine.

Wine odors derive from three major sources: the fruit—the grape itself (primary); the vinification process (secondary); and ageing the wine (tertiary). The grapes, of course, possess their own unique identity and pass this on, in varying degrees, to the wine. Vinification creates new odor compounds, by-products of fermentation and processing. With time will come additional fragrances that originate in wood and bottle ageing.

To give yourself the best opportunity to sense these odors, a glass that holds at least six to ten ounces should be used, one that is only slightly narrower at the opening than the body. This tends to funnel or channel the odors to your nose. Severe inward curvatures tend to direct the odors back into the glass and away from the nose. (See Figure 13 on page 155 for a recommended glass that performs consistently.) Glasses with "flared" openings tend to disperse the odors rather than focus them.

🐜 🐜 🐜

Swirling

It may be of some interest to smell a wine in the glass as it sits there on the table. But not much is happening. Some experts suggest this should be the first of three "nosings." Do it if you must, but don't expect a lot. When still, very few molecules rise from the surface. If they do it is very slow to be sure (see Figure 10).

Figure 10

There is 1,000 times more odorous substance in the wine in the glass than there is in the air above it.

"Swirling" increases the surface area of the liquid, forcing out more of the volatiles.

Several factors relate to the amount of volatiles that are released and can be "vacuumed" in by the nose:

1. the surface area of the wine;
2. surface tension of the wine (controlled by its structure);
3. relative volume of wine, compared to the volume of air in the glass;
4. vapor tension of the wine.

The solution to the problem of releasing more volatiles is "swirling." By swirling the wine in your glass you increase the surface area of the wine, while agitating and aerating it. This action actually forces out more of the volatiles, making your smelling job a little easier. The swirling action also coats the sides of the glass, evaporating even more volatiles. The agitation can serve to create a slight emulsion of liquid particles as well. Though different from volatility it does allow you to smell additional aromatics.

To keep your comparisons on that equal footing you may want to keep your swirling, in numbers of rotations, at a fairly constant count. This allows for more accurate comparisons of the "intensity" of the nose. Extra efforts to "bring out" the nose of a "shy" wine usually means inaccurate evaluations. And the simple fact remains: too much swirling and shaking can alter the very nature of that wine.

It may take some practice to achieve a smooth swirling motion, sans the spills that can occur. So for beginners, make sure there's nothing close at hand you don't want covered in wine. Try it first with the glass resting on the table. Gradually you'll find you can do it quite nicely without the table. Then, when you get really good at it, you can do it simultaneously, a glass in each hand. Show off!

※ ※ ※

Intensity

When it comes to wine smells there are a number of specific synonyms for intensity, words like strength, prominence, force, and if you want to be a trifle more graphic, terms such as power, muscle, and punch will suffice. A bit cavalier perhaps, but nevertheless they do help us to appreciate this particular quality. Intensity can range from being virtually non-existent to light to full to very intense.

The technical unit used to measure the intensity of smell is called the "olfactory potential." It expresses "the number of molecule-grams per liter of air at threshold concentration." To put that in some perspective, a forceful, aggressive odor would have an olfactory potential of about fourteen. The least intensive, to the human smell, would measure around four.

Wines soundly vinted from grapes of the more noble varieties often possess a more distinctive character. In one manner, this is detected by the intensity of their odors. The smell of very fine or great wine seems to linger in the glass long after the last desirable drop has stimulated the palate of some appreciative wine lover. Poorer quality grapes (for winemaking purposes) tend to have a very light odorous intensity (poor character) or they can be overly intense (e.g., some native North American and Muscat varieties). They're persistent, their aroma never seems to go away no matter how intensely you wish it would.

Often, vineyards that produce high yields per acre (too many grapes due to too little pruning) produce grapes of lower quality and character. They exhibit weaker color and flavor extracts, so it's little wonder they have diminished intensity.

Before you evaluate the intensity factor and rate it accordingly, you must discipline yourself to sort out several additional, potential complications. First, you must ask yourself, is what I'm smelling the maximum intensity of a fully developed wine—in other words, the best it's ever going to get? Or am I experiencing the same level of intensity from a wine that has yet to reach full maturity, the intensity of its nose increasing with time?

A little complicated, yes, but your visual inspection will have already helped you to determine the wine's approximate degree of maturity. Judging that the wine is not fully developed and has more to come, or that's it, as far as this wine is concerned, will assist your appreciation of this factor.

Additionally, a good wine judge must be aware of the masking potential of intensity. An intensely aromatic (aroma or bouquet) odor has the potential to conceal a number of defects. In the opposite direction, it would be unwise to ignore the fact that some wine odors (i.e., esters) can still affect our impressions even though they exist at levels below our ability to consciously smell them.

And on occasion, a wine can play "dead" on us. Early in its life a wine may lose virtually all of its fruit intensity. Racking, filtering, fining, and shipping can temporarily suppress all of its aromatics. But with rest it is often resurrected and re-invigorated (hydrolysis). This can all take place in a matter of months. Or the wine may be going through the infamous "dead zone" (see page 206).

✹ ✹ ✹

Assessing Potential

If you are going to score this wine using some evaluation system, you should assess it for what it is at this moment. You would certainly want to note whether you expect it to improve with age, though. Trying to guess at how intensity and other factors might improve with the passage of time is fine, even at times necessary. But these judgments should not be reflected in your rating at this time. As this and other factors improve they should receive an improved score, for if the wine is going to get better there must be room for the score to improve. So, while you may feel quite strongly that a certain element will improve, wait for it to do so before you give it the extra points.

There has been considerable debate and controversy over this issue for decades. And there are many notable winetasters who still feel you must reflect the wine's potential in your current scoring.

Certain clues will give experienced wine judges an idea of what a wine's future may be. It is difficult enough to assess the current status of a wine let alone guess at its future. But again, these vinous clues may be very strong and the judge quite certain. Yet, many wines, even whole vintages, fail to live up to some of these generous prophecies.

It becomes an even more questionable practice when a judge is asked to quantify his assessment of the wine's future and make it a part of his numerical evaluation. How strong is its potential to improve? If I score it for what I think it will become, instead of what it is now, when it does improve, does my score go even higher? Do I do the same on the downside? When a wine has passed its peak and is declining, do I still score it for what it once was? What happens when I feel the wine will only get worse with age? Do I guess at how bad that will be and score it for that, or stay with what it is now? What happens if it never achieves that potential? Do wine judges go back and rescind any medal it have been awarded? Or the reverse?

Thorny questions, indeed. For these and other reasons I feel strongly that we need to assess the wines for what they are now, not for what they may be in the future, no matter how forceful the indicators may be. Some judges fear that this would mean a significantly lower final score. Not really; with a few minor detractions (e.g., excessive tannins in youth) the inherent quality of the wine shows through. Approaching it this way allows room to advance the score when the real improvements actually appear.

Again, it is not the goal of this book to attempt to resolve these thorny controversies, but when the occasion demands, it must detail some of the processes that lead to the conclusions and views stated in these pages.

Although there are numerous potential faults in the nose of the wine, these are dealt with specifically under the heading "Bouquet." Our concern at this point pertains solely to the strength or prominence of the wine's nose. This does not mean if it has a fault that produces a strong odor you would therefore score it well. The intensity of the nose must be clean, vinous, without a major fault in either its bouquet or aroma, which brings us to that very topic . . .

🐞 🐞 🐞

Aroma

"Aroma" describes the group of wine odors that originate exclusively with the fruit—the fresh, mature grapes. This helps us appreciate why the term "aroma" is so often associated with the expression "fruitiness." A wine described as being fruity will possess an aroma strongly characteristic of its grape variety. Italian winemakers call it *fruttato*. It is also called "primary aroma."

Certainly the major part of a wine's aroma originates in the cells or tissues of the grape skin. They vary in their intensity, from grapes that have almost no aromatics to those that are extremely aggressive. On rare occasions the grape pulp has some odorous compounds, too.

Most other plants that have a "fruity" aroma will have the same compounds as their aromatic source. All fruits with pips or stones have a very similar volatile composition.

But some aromatic compounds stay very close to home, locked in the cells of the grape skins. Even crushing the berries into juice fails to release much of its aromatic elements. Fermentation plays a major role in extracting these compounds, and this partially explains why for some grapes their characteristic aroma is more pronounced after fermentation than it is from just the fresh, mature grapes themselves, or even the juice. This is especially true of classic grapes like Riesling, Chardonnay, Pinot Noir, Sauvignon Blanc, and Gamay.

Some aromatic compounds (monoterpene alcohols and oxides) pass almost unchanged through the fermentation process into the young wine. Of course, aside from releasing these primary aromas, innumerable new odors are created by the act of fermentation (secondary aromas).

Though the aroma is the simplest of a wine's aromatics it is not a simple odor at all. Often it is a compound, a rather complex blend of aromatics we essentially perceive as one smell. A simple variation in the amount or proportion of its constituents can create what appears to be a brand new odor.

The aromatic elements of wine belong to a variety of chemical families: alcohols, aldehydes, ketones, acids, esters, terpenes, and many more compounds. Esters are the main source of wines' fruity aromas (butyl, pentyl, hexyl), although some fruit aromas, like strawberry tones, are associated with other compounds (furaneol and lactones; see Figure 11).

Figure 11: Modified wine aroma wheel showing first-, second-, and third-tier terms

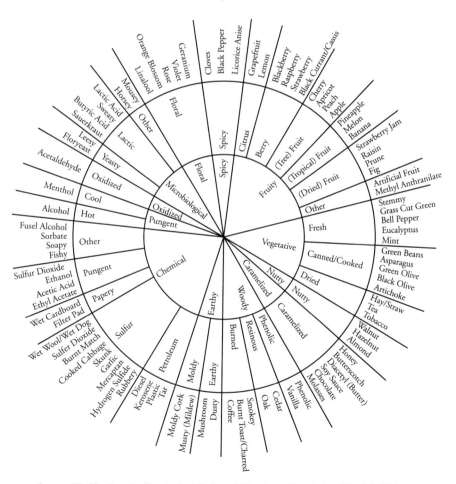

Source: "Modification of a Standardized System of Wine Aroma Terminology'" by A.C. Noble, R.A. Arnold, J. Buechsenstein, E.J. Leach, J.O. Schmidt, and P.M. Stern

More recent research is revealing a growing aromatic role for terpenes. Muscats, Riesling, Gewürztraminer, Sylvaner, and Müller-Thurgau owe much of their pronounced floral aroma to terpene alcohols (linalool, nerol, geraniol).

The aroma is more pronounced and distinctive during a wine's youth. As the wine matures the aroma declines in prominence to become a single, more moderate element in the developing bouquet of the wine. With quality wines of considerable age, the aroma may practically disappear, leaving only the complex odor of a mature bouquet. For "vin ordinaire" the only remaining smell may simply be vinous.

There seems to be a tendency of some wine authorities to rather downplay these primary aromas, even suggesting their continued existence after the fermentation stage almost suggests a flaw, referring to it more as grape juice than wine. Quite naturally these primary aromas should develop into secondary (fermentation) and tertiary (aged) odors. However, to expect all original fruit essences to be obliterated during the transformation from grape juice to wine is unrealistic.

I suggest a basic wine principle is: No fruit—no future! Wines that are rich in fruit aromatics (primary) will develop the most bouquet. When the fermentation odors (secondary odors) dominate the primary aromas in a young wine, it will likely be a short-lived wine that should be consumed at a fairly young age.

Aromatic Descriptions

When choosing words to accurately describe a distinctive wine aroma, drawing a relationship to the fragrance of another, more commonly known fruit or plant can be useful. It smells like fresh raspberries or violets, for example. You'll hear such expressions frequently in wine-tasting circles.

This is all well and good, as long as you keep it under control. At times these associations can evade the most experienced taster's repertoire. Some individuals begin to compare wine aromas to fruits and flowers so exotic you need to in turn compare them to other fruits and flowers for clarification. Even some of the most common smells require some practice before we can consistently identify them on their own. And our task becomes considerably more challenging when that aroma is only one part of a complex aromatic signature.

A friend once described the aroma of one wine as reminding him of the roses from his grandmother's garden—not just any roses mind you, but Grandma's roses. Other than Grandma, few people will ever have much of an idea what he was talking about—the proverbial "failure to communicate." So, do be judicious; you could easily end up on a horticultural tangent moving away from the subject at hand, wine.

Keep in mind many grape varieties possess identifiable and distinctive aromas of their own and should be described in terms of their own aromas, this being quite sufficient for growing numbers of winelovers to fully understand what is being described. On the whole, you are better off learning to identify these varietal aromatic signatures than you are searching for colorful synonyms.

Familiarity with nature's aromas is becoming increasingly rare in modern society. Let's face it, few have the opportunity to acquaint themselves with the infinite array of smells and fragrances this marvelous planet has to offer. In choosing descriptor words for wine aromatics you might conclude that some writers are of the opinion we all grew up with a glorious English garden behind the house. The reality is, a large part of the human population would be hardpressed to identify the fragrance of a rose, let alone an exotic array of fruits and flowers. Written communications should reflect that reality. Many wine writers need to write more for the consumer than for themselves or the "club."

This dearth of olfactory experience also means we need to broaden out our smell opportunities. Take every chance you can to smell a wide variety of fruits and flowers. Don't pass a flower shop, a garden, or a meadow without investigating its wealth of aromas. Greengrocers can help with a selection of herbs and spices. Rub, crush, and smell. You will be amazed at what you may have been missing.

Several transformations during the winemaking process will also have considerable influence on the level of fruit aroma. When left to ferment for a time on the skins, resulting wines will have more identifiable aroma (more aromatic elements are extracted from the skins).

Sugar can also play an additive role. Wines that have retained some natural grape sugar will usually exhibit a more prominent aroma than wines that are bone dry. This is well illustrated in wines such as the fragrant Asti Spumante with its high levels of residual sugar, as well as many white wines that have undergone prolonged, cold fermentation with varying levels of residual sugar.

A major point to remember under this heading is the pronounced difference between *aroma* and *bouquet*. They should never be confused with each other.

But how do you define *bouquet*?

❧ ❧ ❧

Bouquet

Aside from it sounding a little more distinguished and chic as a word, bouquet describes a more elaborate and sophisticated odor.

To state that "bouquet" is a "complex" odor is truly an understatement. It defines a level of complexity that still baffles modern science. It is completely appropriate to say that as we (tasters and scientists) peel away layer after layer of bouquet's complexity, we find only more layers. Yet this only adds to a complexity of pleasure, a depth of enjoyment. Whether or not we understand or can put a number to these intriguing aromatics is not the point; the fascination and pleasure remain.

For the purposes of this book we will follow the French lead and divide these incredible smells of bouquet into two distinct sectors.

1. Secondary Odors (fermentation bouquet)
2. Tertiary Odors (bouquet of ageing)

The factors that identify quality in perfume have many parallels in wine. Clarity, intensity, vigor, diffusive power, finesse, individuality, and length are common signatures of the top perfumes. The vocabulary may differ somewhat, but the picture is decidedly similar.

Secondary Odors—Fermentation Bouquet

The transformation of grape juice (must) into wine gives birth to the secondary odors. As the billions of yeast cells and bacteria act upon the grape sugars (approximately 200 grams per liter) they bring into existence a wide range of new compounds. Alcohol is certainly the major one, but a host of new elements are much more responsible for the new smells (see Figure 12).

Yeasts play an enormous role in the aromatic profile of a wine. Some 30 or more species of these monocellular molds are known and create their own unique aromatics. The modern use of cultured yeasts certainly gives more defined aromatics but less complexity. A mixture of yeasts often yields richer, more complex aromatics, although some wild yeasts can induce some rather unwelcome off-odors.

With a rich supply of vitamins and nitrogenous matter in the grape must, an amazing arsenal of yeast enzymes leads to the creation of a wide range of aromatic compounds. Research has shown that some

Figure 12: *The transformation of must into wine creates many secondary odors*

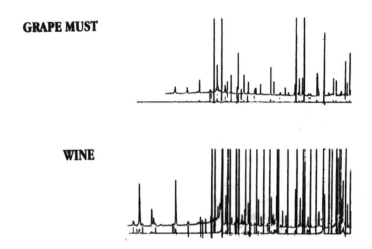

GRAPE MUST

WINE

yeasts' individual aromatic signatures are strong enough to transcend different fermentation conditions, even changes in grape variety.

Among the new aromatic compounds that contribute to the wine's bouquet are acids, alcohols, aldehydes, esters, fusel oils, terpenes, and ketones. Complex chemical reactions, progressive changes in the wine's tannins, and the odors imparted by wooden casks (and the changes resulting from the ageing of wood components) all add their individual notes to a blossoming, complex bouquet.

Many young table wines—red, white, and rosé—will for a short period of time (a few months, no more) possess a yeasty, sourdough, even banana-like odor as part of their fermentation bouquet. This would certainly help you identify the age of the wine, but this characteristic soon disappears, or should.

Surprisingly, even some fixed substances in wine (i.e., extract—soluble non-sugar solids) can affect the intensity of these secondary odors. And in some ways we even need to reverse what may appear to be common sense. Volatility is an example. As we've already mentioned, for any substance to even have a smell it must be volatile or in a gaseous state. We might logically assume that the larger and heavier the molecule, the more difficult it is to release it from the liquid to be nosed. Paradoxically, it is the lightest molecules that are the least volatile. Alcohols with the largest molecules (more carbon atoms) are more volatile and aromatic. Acids are the least volatile, so have the least smell.

Tertiary Odors—Bouquet of Age

The tertiary bouquet appears only with maturity, due to a combination of barrel (oxidative) and bottle ageing (reductive). It is then the summation of the three stages of wine evolution—primary aroma, secondary bouquet, tertiary bouquet—that creates the wine's unique aromatic signature.

The formation of the bouquet is the result of several complex chemical phenomena that can occur successively or simultaneously. Only superior wines make this journey. Ordinary wines travel from the vat to bottle to market at a rather quick pace. To do anything else would be a waste.

In the evolution of a superior quality wine the first stop is an encounter with the wine barrel, usually oak. From the wood is extracted a number of odorous compounds. One of the major components is lignin. But more than the simple extraction of wood components is involved. Once dissolved in the wine the oak components themselves age, like any wood does. Lignin oxidizes to four basic aromatic aldehydes; the most familiar aroma is vanillin, a highly appreciated, aromatic addition to the wine's bouquet.

This ageing step, involving the impact of oxygen in the barrel, is followed by bottle age, essentially without air contact (reductive). It is here that the greatest complexity is achieved. With time and proper cellaring, the wine begins to show its maturity on the nose. Some describe it as the smell of truffles and mushrooms. One of the bonuses of modern vinification methods is the retention of some of the primary fruit aromatics throughout the maturing process. It adds one more fragrance to an incredibly attractive and multi-faceted bouquet.

To be effective odor sleuths, we should also be aware of some of the odor interactions. Not everything is simply cumulative:

- Some odors in the same family, when combined, produce a synergistic reaction, a compound odor greater in intensity than their sum (i.e., some terpenes).

- When odors that are dissimilar in character but compare favorably in intensity are blended, they can be smelled individually.

- Some odors when blended together mask or neutralize each other.

- Our ability to detect some odors can be seriously diminished by the addition of another odor.

Some fortified wines (alcohol added) possess very distinctive bouquets at maturity. Certain sherries, for example, have a bouquet with a strong raisin-like odor. Baked wines like Madeira and some North American versions of sherry have a caramel odor (hydroxymethyfurfural) that is also easy to recognize once you have isolated it and cataloged it in your odor memory bank.

Several of the elements we have already spoken of have such a profound impact on wine odors they do need a little further consideration.

❋ ❋ ❋

Wood

Wood, whether it's used for ageing wine in large vats or in smaller cooperage (wooden barrels), introduces its own character to the wine. It is said to give complexity to a wine, as a number of constituents are actually extracted from the wood, evolve, and become part of the wine in both its bouquet and taste. Our wineloving friends from Germany call it *Holzgeschmack*. For red wines it is in most instances a plus factor, but if too prominent it can also be a fault.

By the very natural extension of this thought it's not too difficult to surmise that each barrel could easily add its own, very individual degree of character to the wine it contains. And indeed, this is frequently the case. Slight differences do become evident between identical wines taken from two separate barrels sitting side by side. You are not likely to experience this in the wines you purchase, as most producers, once the barrel ageing for that wine is completed, proceed to blend together all the wine of that type and vintage into large vats just before bottling, giving it a collective, consistent character.

But a certain reality must never be forgotten: Ordinary wines, those with poor aromatics and little body and structure, are unlikely to improve in small barrels. A brief stay in large vats may play a minor role in improving their short life.

Descriptive words used to identify the nuances and characters imparted by wood include vanilla, toasty, cigar box, smoky, sawdust, spicy, bacon, cashews, coconut, and olives. Distinctive smells reminiscent of different woods may also become noticeable, though oak is almost always the wood used: cedar, sandalwood, acacia, and chestnut are the most common woody nuances. Even the different types of oak can impart different aromatics to the wine (see page 124).

While some wine authorities express quite different, nevertheless civil, opinions about the degree of woodiness desirable in red wines, they more sharply differ in their views about any wood character at all in white wines. Some state categorically, no wood for whites; others make allowance for significant levels of this quality. Personally, I feel a certain touch of wood can enhance some of the drier, classic whites made from grapes like Chardonnay, Sauvignon Blanc, Sémillon, and Pinot Gris. For fruity, fresh wines that are best drunk in their youth, a woody character seems to be more of a negative influence. I'm thinking about table wines made from Chenin Blanc, Muscats, Colombards, and some members of the Riesling family. But do keep in mind these are the kinds of rules that are made to be broken.

A major concern over wood and white wine is its ability to deal with the oxygen as it infiltrates the wine between the barrel staves, through the bung hole, and through the pores of the wood itself. Red wines therefore have more of the natural constituents that can deal with oxygen, thusly preventing over-oxidation. More than just imparting a woody nose and taste, the barrel chemically alters the makeup of the wine.

Reluctance to mate white wine and wood is not quite so strong when it comes to actually fermenting white wine in barrique or barrel. The possibility of over-oxidation or excessive extraction of tannins is reduced because of the protective influence of the yeasts and the carbon dioxide produced during fermentation.

Although it became almost a nineties "right of passage" for winemakers around the globe to produce a "barrel fermented" Chardonnay, these wines often do exhibit greater complexity in both aromatics and taste. Barrel fermentation seems to knit closer together the primary and secondary aromas, along with the impact of the wood-based aromatics. Adding to the bouquet are even more complexities from the lees (spent yeast cells and fermentation sediment). Though the yeast cells in the lees are dead they can still absorb tannins and form new odor compounds through a process called "autolysis." This can add exciting new dimensions of smell and taste to some wines, if done well.

In the broadest of tasting terms, we can say then, white wines will exhibit more floral, citrus, tropical, and tree fruit aromatics, while reds lean towards berry, dried fruit, vegetable, woody, and caramelized odors.

✻ ✻ ✻

Oxygen, Oxygenation, Oxidative, Oxidation, Oxidized

These five words play an enormous role in the production of quality wine, or in its destruction. Despite their incredible impact on wine, these terms are frequently misunderstood, misapplied, and missing from some wine vocabularies.

From its birth onward, oxygen is part of a wine's life. When the grapes are crushed, then pumped, the wine racked, filtered, and bottled, oxygen comes into contact with it. Compounds like sulfur dioxide and a youthful lacing of tannins protect the wine from oxygen's damaging effects. But when the wine is not protected, high levels of a chemical called "acetaldehyde" are formed and can dominate every other wine smell. Its odor of apples, quince, almonds, stale oil, or rancid butter overshadows the primary aromas and secondary bouquet of any wine. The wine has become oxidized.

Most mature wine has some oxidative factors to it. When small amounts of oxygen slowly seep into a wine cask this is not necessarily oxidizing in nature; rather, it is a process of oxygenation. This extremely slow absorption of oxygen (aeration) is actually beneficial to the wine as it evolves towards maturity. In reality it is no longer oxygen at this stage, but tannins that are oxygenated. Oxidation involves two stages—the dissolving of oxygen through handling, wood and bottle ageing, followed by a slow combining of this oxygen with oxidative constituents in wine.

A simple exercise to create an oxidized odor is to leave a glass of ordinary red wine uncovered for several days or a week. Then smell and taste it. It may be an exaggerated example but usually effective enough so that you'll remember this fault for quite some time, even at low levels.

If allowed to advance far beyond remedy an oxidized wine can become *madierized*. This is a wine that is often too old or has been attacked by a massive invasion of air in barrel, or a severely "ullaged" bottle (see page 160). The term is applied because the aromatics it creates are reminiscent of Madeira wine, but of course, without its redeeming merits. It's cooked, caramel-like odor and dried-out molasses taste is obvious to amateur and pro alike.

✳ ✳ ✳

Bottle Age—Reductive

Wine finds its friendliest and safest environment in the glass enclosure we call a bottle. Here it develops more slowly and assuredly into its ultimate expression of quality. If allowed to make this journey in good health, whether red, sweet white, or rarely, a superior dry white, it develops the "bouquet of age." In the end, the wine has been transformed into an elixir so pleasurable we have written poetry about it for centuries.

While the wine slumbers in bottle an extremely complicated and mysterious series of aromatic chemical reactions is in process. Some odorous compounds are fading, some blossoming, still others are being newly created and added to a list that tops 700 in number. Researchers, using one of their most valuable investigative tools (a gas chromatograph or GC), know of over 600 peaks on a chromatogram (indicating individual compounds). Fewer than half have been identified, and perhaps only 60 have ever been measured quantitatively.

The understanding of our human "chemo-reception" abilities has been greatly increased by the invention of the GC in the United States nearly 40 years ago. The GC is really a mechanical version of the human nose, though our personal GC can sense many more aromatics than any mechanical version.

The GC can separate 200–600 vapor or gaseous compounds from one wine sample, representing perhaps only a few parts per million combined. Barely a handful may be strong enough to identify individually. Together they form a complex aromatic monograph that we sense as a whole.

Although the GC is enormously sensitive and able to separate these volatile substances it is far from being an aromatic identification. Since every compound has a characteristic pattern of ions (electrically charged atoms) an identification of the compound can be made using this pattern. This unique fingerprint is identified by a "mass spectrometer" (MS). When a means was discovered to link the GC to the MS, a powerful new tool was available to peer into the olfactory profile of wine. Our understanding of what our nose is telling us has as a result of the GC-MS taken a quantum leap forward.

The bouquet developed in bottle ageing is termed a "reductive bouquet." It is called reductive because it develops in what is essentially an airtight container. The opposite of oxidation is reduction (without air—anaerobic). Any oxygen left in the bottle after filling and corking will be consumed by the tannins in a matter of a few weeks.

In the reductive atmosphere of the wine bottle there is developed the most interesting and complex components of the bouquet. But problems can arise. If the effect of reduction is excessive, or the wine has been deprived of air too early in its life, smells can be created that can range from mildly unpleasant to stenches that could put you off wine for some time.

The wine trade has long debated the amount of oxygen that actually penetrates the modern wine cork, ultimately reaching the wine. Some assert that it is so little, essentially it cannot be measured. That appears not to be quite true. The variables determining the amount of air that gets into the bottle is the cork quality and how well it was inserted at the winery. Even imperfections in the neck of the bottle can be a factor.

However, assuming packaging problems are not a factor the amount of oxygen to reach the wine is truly tiny, but not completely insignificant. Some oxygen can also make its way into the bottle from the very cells of the cork itself, not to mention the amount trapped in the wine as a result of bottling. For each year of cellaring it is estimated an average of a fraction of a cubic centimeter gets past a sound cork.

Though cork is not a perfect seal, it's very close. And close is good. Perfection (completely airtight) in this case could create severe problems. When wine is totally deprived of oxygen and comes to be in the presence of sulfur dioxide (SO_2)—present in virtually all wine—it can be reduced to hydrogen sulphide (H_2S). As you may surmise, the dosage of SO_2 is critical.

Below certain levels (0.7 mg per liter), H_2S is really not perceptible to most human noses. Rise above that and we can get a faint stink of "ethyl and methyl mercaptans," an odor something like rotten eggs or sulfur springs. Most often, aeration of the wine will eliminate this level of H_2S and correct the fault. But a pronounced reductive bouquet can literally bury every other wine aromatic with putrid odors, at times onion and garlic smells. At this stage, the wine is irretrievably flawed, undrinkable.

While in bottle another danger exists: light. With prolonged exposure to direct light a photo-oxidation reaction can occur with some bottles (clear glass most often). The solution is obvious.

※ ※ ※

Sulfur Dioxide

As you've come to realize, sulfur can be both friend or foe to wine. Judiciously sulfuring the grape must can improve the color and the primary aromas in wine, by helping to break down the cells of the grape skins and by removing aldehyde smells.

An excess of free sulfur is definitely a negative aroma (burning match smell). With time this odor should decline and hopefully fall below the threshold of your being able to sense it at all. When sulfur becomes "bound" it is inactivated. However, you should be aware that individuals' sensitivity to sulfur varies tremendously. In an attempt to introduce a friend to a lovely California white varietal, the only response I got was his claim of a strong sulfur smell. I couldn't smell it, but I later learned he can smell sulfur as easily as a bloodhound can track a skunk.

If you have this unusual sensitivity you may have difficulty finding wines without a detectable trace of sulfur. Fermentation has as one of its natural by-products sulfur dioxide (SO_2). A small amount of SO_2 is a natural component in healthy wines. While sulfur negatives are quite real, the positive side of the SO_2 coin is so powerful even some producers of organic wines are convinced that it should remain in the winemaker's arsenal.

A list of the more common faults that can be identified by your nose alone follows:

Some Common Odor Faults

Odor	Source
acetone, nail polish remover	ethyl acetate
asbestos	odor of new or very old filter pads; gives wine a flat taste
asparagus	mercaptpentanone
banana	isoamyl acetate; frostbitten grapes; old wine in poor shape
bell pepper, excessive	methoxypyrazines
bitter almonds	poor fining (blue fining)
beer, flat	benzoquinone, or from a secondary bottle fermentation
bottle stink	trapped CO_2, SO_2, H_2S
buttery, strong	excessive diacetyl from malo-lactic acid

Odor	Source
corked	*see* moldy
crushed bugs	isoamyl alcohol
earthiness	geosmin
fatty, soapy	caprate, caproate, ethyl caprylate
garlic, onion	excessive H_2S
geranium	sorbic acid (preservative) attacked by lactic acid bacteria
grassy, excessive	*see* bell pepper
greenery, leaves	unripe grapes at harvest
horsey, leathery, sweat, ammonia	brettanomyces (yeast)
iodine	certain molds on rotten grapes
moldy	TCA (trichloroanisole)
mousy	2—ethyl—3, 4, 5, 6—tetrahydropyridine; yeast bacteria
nauseating mercaptan	ethyl sulfur
plastic	styrene
putrid, fermentation	isobutyric acid
sauerkraut	lactic acid
sherry-like	acetaldehyde
skunky, rotten eggs	hydrogen sulfide (H_2S)
sour milk, cheesiness	lactic acids
sulfur, burnt match	SO_2
vinegar	ethyl acetate

✻ ✻ ✻

Summary

Your nose, that protuberance on the front of your face, is a key instrument for judging wine—no doubt. But like any other faculty it needs exercise in a disciplined manner. Its talents are many and its sensitivity awesome, but it must be trained to focus on specifics.

There is no substitute for practical wine experience. Your written reactions to each of your experiences, filed away for future reference, will also help you grow and benefit from your wine-judging abilities. The task of distinguishing between aroma and bouquet is not a simple one. In fact, it may elude you for quite some time. But gradually, with time and practice, mixed liberally with a little persistence, each occasion you pour a glass of wine the differences will become more pronounced and your pleasure magnified.

Sniff on!

CHAPTER 5

A Touching Chapter

THERE comes the time when all this looking and smelling is simply not enough. Eventually you must put the wine into your mouth to feel, taste, and savor the rewards it has to offer. But what do you do with it when it gets in there?

Does it lie there like a stagnant pool of rain water? Or is there really anything to all this "sloshing and gurgling" carried on by wine-tasters supposedly in the know?

There's no question that some of the oral antics of winetasters at times appear to be rather quaint, to put it politely. The noise alone can call their social graces into serious question. But it all has a legitimate purpose.

The oral contortions, so clearly visible with experienced wine-tasters, usually coincide with their attempts to move the wine to various areas of the tongue and inner mouth. The reason, as you will discover in the following few pages, is to concentrate the wine on various groups of taste buds, as some are more sensitive to certain components than others. This movement also helps us avoid "adaption" on various zones of the tongue.

The gurgling results when the taster draws in air to mix with the wine. He does so to vaporize more of the wine, which in turn makes it easier to sense the various characteristics and components. There is definitely a knack to doing this without choking yourself or spitting up all over someone or something. Experience is the only teacher. The best way I can describe it is "whistling backwards." Of course, if you can't whistle frontwards you may have another problem on your hands.

At any rate, I'd suggest you practice with water or very cheap wine until you can do it reasonably well. Even though you may need a bib for the first few attempts, the dividends are well worth the effort.

And don't worry about the propriety of it all. In wine circles it's common, even anticipated. However, on occasions other than formal wine-tastings do make sure those in your company know what you're doing, lest they interpret your actions as a form of indecent oral behavior.

As our organoleptic examination continues, two major tactile (touch) sensations now deserve our attention. Your tongue is the primary instrument used to make determinations for both points—"body" and "astringency." We'll also take a closer look at "temperature," "tannins," and the "bubbles" in wine, to discover their contribution to the tactile experience.

✹ ✹ ✹

Body

This is one of the most difficult sensory assessments to make. Difficult because words fail to describe this sensation satisfactorily. So if you feel a trifle wanting at the end of this section, don't be too surprised. And I wouldn't recommend that you start an exhaustive search for more information; there's precious little to be had on this point anywhere.

The source of a wine's "body" or mouth-feel depends largely upon its content of polyphenols (tannins), alcohols, sugars, glycerine, and dry extract (soluble non-sugar solids). Without these components, or in diminished quantities, the wine would be watery, exhibiting a very thin consistency. The opposite, a wine with good body, would be termed full.

Some rather interesting and descriptive comparisons to body or the texture have been made using fabrics and their specific weave. Terms like silky, velvety, satiny, tightly knit, loosely knit, and so on, are appropriately applied to the feel of wine in the mouth and usually describe very positive stimulations. In the negative vein, we often apply words like grainy, coarse, and rough.

"Viscosity" is another word that helps us appreciate what is meant by body. Think of water and heavy cream. Their textures are quite descriptive of thin and full-bodied. Normal alcohol content ranges from seven to fourteen percent for table wines and fourteen to twenty percent for fortified wine (distilled spirits added).

Glycerine, usually formed during fermentation, can vary due to the length of fermentation, but ranges usually between six and ten grams per liter. However, grapes that have been affected by botrytis (noble rot, a beneficial mold—see page 213) can impart additional glycerine to the wine, sometimes creating ten or more grams per liter even before fermentation starts.

But we must ask, is being full bodied always a merit and anything less, respectively negative? For certain wines, yes! For others, definitely not! And here you thought this was going to be simple and straightforward.

A very full-bodied dry Riesling or Chardonnay table wine, in most cases, would be indicative of a poorly balanced wine. Wines produced from famous red grapes like Syrah (Rhône), Nebbiolo (Barolo), Pinot Noir (Burgundy), and the Cabernet Sauvignon (grown in California) as contrasting examples are expected to be wines that are more full bodied in style.

Dessert wines, high in sugar, fortified with alcohol, or just having a naturally high alcohol level, would be deserving of the term heavy in connection with their body. For table wines, heavy would most often represent a lack of balance.

Body You Can See

Sounds a little odd; however, two factors do give us a visual indication of "body," if you're paying attention.

Legs! We examine the legs or tears of a wine visually, so we have no choice but to abandon the tongue momentarily. We could have discussed this point along with the other visual aspects, but I felt it more appropriate to wait until we reached body. After all, it's easier to refer back to something you've already read than forward to an unknown.

Legs or tears—either term is suitable—are those clear, colorless little rivulets that frequently roll down the side of your glass. They are generated by the alcohol, water, and glycerine in the wine and provide you with a vague visual indication of the texture or body of that wine. By themselves they are a poor indicator of quality.

It's not the size or number of these legs that's significant, but the time before two or more tears formulate, become visible, and begin to slide down the side of the glass. Wines very low in alcohol and glycerine sheet off the glass very quickly, with perhaps only tiny droplets remaining, but no legs.

It's hard to get around that way, even for a wine, and obviously it can be the mark of a thin wine. The longer it takes to form the legs, the more significant the body, usually.

But we need to remember that legs can be generated in two ways, firstly, by swirling the wine in the glass. As it sheets off the sides, legs form in the process. Yet, a similar phenomenon can occur even when the glass is sitting quietly by itself, with no movement. Legs or tears seem to form miraculously on their own. It's called the "Marangoni" effect. The California duo of wine researchers, Amerine and Roessler, describe it best:

> Alcohol is more volatile than water; a thin layer of more aqueous liquid forms on the surface of the wine and on the sides of the glass moistened by the wine; this fine film has a higher surface tension. Capillary action causes the liquid to rise up the sides of the glass, and the increase in surface tension tends to form tears which eventually flow back down into the wine. The higher the alcohol content of the wine, the more tears there are.

Another visual component of body in wine is referred to by some experienced tasters as "fluidity." In a number of European tasting circles it is considered a significant quality factor. Essentially it's a visual assessment of the wine's consistency. A number of wine components make the wine more viscous. When swirled or poured in the glass each wine seems to have a unique way of flowing. These same wine components make the wine pour more slowly. In the laboratory these variations can be seen in how individual wines flow at different rates through a fine tube or filter.

❈ ❈ ❈

Temperature

Temperature may seem like a very separate stimulation, but in reality is very much a tactile sensation. Experts vary in the degree to which they assess the importance of this factor. Regardless of how important it is, we need to grasp the difference in the way we apply temperature to tasting wine:

1. tasting for evaluative purposes
2. wine drinking

Temperature has a physical impact on wine, as it does on us. For one thing, it slows down the wine ageing process. For us, fortunately, we seem to have fewer "warm receptors" in our mouth, which allows us to consume beverages hotter than we can hold with our hands

The simple truth is, the volatility of wine odors increases when the wine is warm, and is lower at colder temperatures. Professional tasters seek uniformity of temperature when serious tasting is involved. The critical range is usually 15 to 20°C (59 to 68°F), with 18°C (65°F) the temperature of choice. At serious wine competitions controlling the temperature can be a major challenge. The InterVin International keeps both preparation and the judging rooms at a constant 65°F (18°C) to avoid the reality that serving the same wine at different temperatures means you are serving two different wines.

The taster himself is sensitive to temperature. An environment too cold or too hot has predictable effects on judging performance. Serving temperatures applied to amateur tastings, and simply for drinking, are quite a different matter. In principle it is the level of tannins, acids, alcohol, and sugar that indicate the ideal serving temperature.

Wines rich in aroma, acid, and fruit are better drunk on the chilled side. Whites, usually with a lack of perceptible tannins, seem to fit this profile. Rosé wines, with a tad more tannin, can be a bit warmer, but certainly still on the cool side. Certain young, fresh reds with few tannins, wines that are light, with lots of fresh fruit (i.e., nouveaux), can also be happily consumed with a slightly chilly edge.

But wines that have achieved a complexity of bouquet and have significant levels of tannin are best at the warmer temperatures that release more of those mature, bottle-aged volatiles. Even a variation of 2°C can trigger arguments about perceived tannin levels!

Some Sensory Effects of Temperature

Less than 6°C (43°F)

- bouquet and aroma tend to disappear

- saltiness accentuated

- bitterness more evident

- acidity more prominent

- sweetness lowered

- body difficult to determine (thinner)

Less than 10–12°C (50–54°F)

- SO_2 sensitivity disappears

- bouquet almost neutralized

- acidity emphasized

- sweetness sensitivity diminished

- bitterness increased

- body perceived as thinner

Less than 18°C (65°F)

- bouquet remains prominent

- alcohol content mildly emphasized

- sweetness accented

20°C plus (68°F+) (higher in mouth)

- alcohol content strongly emphasized

- more body perceived

- sweetness becomes heavier

Temperature can also influence one of my favorite wine sensations—bubbles. The simple fact is, the solubility of carbon dioxide is affected by temperature. As the temperature rises more of the carbon dioxide (CO_2) is released.

✻ ✻ ✻

That Sparkling Feeling

The human threshold for CO_2 in a wine is about 500 mg/l. It's also true that some CO_2 in wine is "invisible" even though we may sense it as a light prickle on the tongue (best down the center). Some refer to it as a "petillant," "vivace," or "spritzig" feeling. But what effect does temperature have on our sensitivity to CO_2 in wine?

Quite profound, actually! For example, look at what happens to a wine with only a slightly perceptible bubbliness of 700 mg/l. At

20°C (68°F)—obviously perceptible;

below 12°C (54°F)—barely noticeable;

below 8°C (46°F) —it disappears.

The bubbles in wine bring us such pleasure it's no wonder sparkling wines are referred to as the "wines of celebration." We also need to consider some additional CO_2 influences and what they can mean to our pleasure and assessment of wine quality.

Few things you put in your mouth can be more stimulating or tactile than bubbles. Some sparkle (usually artificial) can be so intense it can even trigger a mild pain reaction. In its softer form we love it. Aside from its obvious tactile (haptic) impact, CO_2 can alter our perceptions of a number of important wine components.

Few wine pleasures are more internationally appreciated than the fizz of a sparkling wine—from its anticipated implosive pop, to the festive froth that breaches the rim of the glass, to its foamy collar (cordon), this is one wine quality we really do see. Or do we?

The visual sparkle in a glass of "bubbly," with its streaming necklace of golden pearls, is certainly a traditional part of the sparkling wine experience. But bubbles are meant to be felt. So the question remains—are they all that relevant in their visual form to the genuine quality of a wine?

So often I've listened to assessments of sparkling wines that included such determinations as "the number and rate at which the bubbles stream upwards," "the nature of the froth that breaks the surface of the wine," and "the importance of the size of the bubbles," and so on. After 25 years of tasting wine as a profession, the visual importance of the sparkle still evades me. One of the best sparkling wines I ever experienced lay suspiciously still in the bottle after the cork was removed; barely a bubble even in the glass. But in the mouth it exploded, not only with the flavors and bouquet of an excellent wine, but the foam was absolutely scintillating and soft, all at the same time. It was unquestionably a memorable wine.

Carbon dioxide only becomes visible as bubbles in wine as the result of an active point on the surface of the glass. It could be something as simple as a particle of dust or lint, an organic substance, a germ, even a scratch or unseen flaw on the surface of the glass. In a perfectly clean glass, with an absolutely flawless interior surface, few if any bubbles would be seen. To some that would be disappointing. And tragically, to some wine judges it would be devastating to their evaluation of the wine.

Some wine competitions take extra care to open and pour the sparkling wines in front of the judges, so they can see how the wines fizz and incorporate that visual into their evaluation. But is that truly an important factor in assessing a wine's sparkle?

The act of professionally judging wines demands an "even playing field" for all samples. Though well intentioned, opening and pouring a "bubbly" in front of a judge is not enough. If a visual assessment is going to be equal for such a fragile factor as a wine's visual sparkle, you would have to also ensure that each glass was identical inside and out; that the lint and dust inside was precisely the same; that it was poured with exactly the same speed and fell from the same height into the glass; and on and on.

Sound absurd? Absolutely! That's why the only fairly level playing field for judging a wine's sparkle is inside your mouth. Visual evaluations of sparkling wine are tenuous at best. Approach them with great care and suspicion.

The very structure of the "mousse" in sparkling wine depends on a number of factors:

- the constitution of the base wine (its colloidal factor)

- the sparkling technique employed (e.g., Methode Champenoise)

- the length of time it was aged on the lees

- the temperature of the wine

If a wine releases its bubbles too quickly, it may well have undergone too rapid a fermentation or been stored improperly (too warm or affected by vibration).

Carbon dioxide in wine only becomes visible as bubbles when the wine's CO_2 saturation point is reached (about 1.5–2.0 g/l). Below that level, CO_2 is there, we just can't see it, because bubbles are not being formed. However, we can feel it, down to about 0.5 g/l, below which we no longer discern it well. But it's there, and it can still have an effect on important wine components.

There are several terms used commercially to identify various levels of CO_2 in wine. The lightest sparkle (no need even for special corks and wire hoods) is *perles* wines or *perlant*, then *petillant*, followed by *cremant*, leading to a full sparkling wine or *mousseux*.

The sparkle of wine (its pressure) is also measured in atmospheres:

1 atm. = 14.69 lbs./sq. in.

Perles wines = approx. 1 atm.

Petillant = approx. 1.5–3 atm.

Cremant = approx. 3.5–4.5 atm.

Mousseux (sparkling) = approx. 5–6 atm.

Production laws in various countries may allow for differences in these distinctions.

We also need to look past the fizz of a sparkling wine to its many other merits. I feel this is an important point, too often overlooked with bubblies. A fine Champagne for example, with or without bubbles, is still a fine wine, or should be.

There are three basic methods you can employ to make a wine sparkle. The cheapest and fastest method is simply to inject the wine with CO_2 as they do with soda pop. The bubbles are characteristically large and coarse in a tactile and visual sense. Wines made in this fashion are usually ordinary to start with and the sparkle flattens fairly quickly.

Charmat Methode or *Cuvée Close* are the terms used to describe a "bulk fermentation" system that creates sparkling wines in large, closed tanks. The bottling is then done under pressure. Wines made with this process are certainly better than those injected with CO_2, but I've come across few appraisals for this method from any wine authorities that could be called "glowing." The subsequent filtering these wines receive before bottling can remove some of the sparkle, causing the wine to flatten sooner. Top-up CO_2 injection is often used.

The superior method, recognized unanimously as such, is the *Methode Champenoise*. This time-honored process employs a second, individual "in-bottle" fermentation. It takes longer, is more expensive, but the results are well worth it all.

On pouring a glass of sparkling wine made from this process (many wines other than Champagne use it) you will immediately note two visual characteristics that often separate it from the imitators. First, you will notice that after the first layer of foam has died away a tenacious collar of tiny bubbles (cordon) will often remain around the edge of the wine next to the glass. It should become apparent the bubbles themselves are different, too. They are smaller, fine bubbles that often appear slowly and last longer than either of the other two processes, especially when compared to the wines that are artificially gassed.

A "transfer" system is used, as well. This allows for the second fermentation to take place in-bottle, but the now sparkling wine is then removed to large tanks for filtration and then re-bottled. The processing and handling often causes a small loss of effervescence, which is topped up with a little "hit" of CO_2 gas.

Now if we could just convince some governments that bubbles in wine do not constitute a legitimate reason for an added levy of tax . . .

Winelovers should also be aware of invisible CO_2. Below visual and tactile thresholds CO_2 can actually cause a wine to feel thinner in the mouth; it accentuates acidity; reinforces the effects of tannins; and diminishes our sensitivity to sweetness.

At its birth wine is practically saturated with CO_2, some of which it will retain into old age and senility. Through handling and storage much of it evaporates before it reaches the bottle. Here its loss is negligible. Unless the CO_2 is visible in bubble form it is, unfortunately, a part of wine even professionals rarely consider.

★ ★ ★

Astringency

No doubt about it—astringency is a tactile impression. Although astringency and bitterness originate in the same family of wine components (polyphenols), bitterness is a true taste sensation, while astringency is more tactile. In laboratory language we are considering "stypticity."

The astringency in all fruits and vegetables originates with the same polyphenols. Cooking diminishes the astringency and perhaps explains why cooked vegetables gained such popularity.

In wine, there are two sources of the tannic cause of astringency, the grape skins (three to six percent of skins), and the wooden casks used to age wine. Though different in sensation their tannins both belong to our polyphenol family. The tannin molecule is a polymer containing two to ten smaller molecules.

Not all tannins are equally astringent. Wood tannins appear to be softer and less aggressive. Grape tannins are called the "backbone" or spine of wine. With sufficient grape ripeness, fruit, sugar, and alcohol, their aggressiveness is moderated somewhat. Excessive acidity can make them feel harder still.

At proper levels tannins contribute significantly to the body of the wine, giving it structure and a "mouth-filling" sensation. In excess, it makes the wine feel hard, coarse, austere, and green. By drying out the surfaces of the tongue and mouth a feeling somewhat like a chafing occurs when the surfaces contact each other.

You should have little difficulty identifying astringency. It leaves a rough, gritty, "furry" feeling on your tongue, teeth, and on the inside of your cheeks. A wine without an appreciable level of tannin, thus virtually no astringency, would be described as smooth. If you've ever had a cup of tea that has steeped too long on the leaves or chewed fresh grape skins you will have some idea of the tactile quality of astringency.

Red wines have by nature more tannins (from their skins) and are therefore expected, early in their life, to be more astringent than whites. And because tannins accentuate acid perception reds seem balanced with less acid. This single element also accounts for much of the reason why reds generally look forward to longer lives than whites. The tannins that cause astringency act as a natural preservative. Many modern white wines have become too thin. Often the reason is an insufficiency of tannins. This results in their reaching maturity much too quickly, as well.

Some researchers are convinced that tannins also play a role in flavor perception. Others attribute an individual taste to tannin, even suggesting that an aromatic character develops with time. There seems to be little available evidence to support this idea, but the tannins certainly can heavily influence other components and their sensations.

When tannins are green, from unripe grapes, or are at aggressive levels in a wine that is fairly young, and the wine is acidic and thin, a metallic taste can easily be generated. Though no metals are involved, the wine can actually become "tinny" to the taste. As already mentioned, some tannins by themselves are said to have a very mild bitter taste. That may be true, but when incorporated into a wine, that flavor can be dominated or hidden quite easily by other taste components. Even a light tactile astringency can all but disappear.

Tannins have a tremendous impact on the health of a wine. Because they combine so easily with other components, especially oxygen, it is a major factor in the prevention of spoilage. Wine would have a very difficult time ageing gracefully without those astringent tannins. The more tannins, the less need there is for acid. Acids also play a vital, protective role in wine's ageing ability. If the theories become practical reality most of the tannins will combine or link up with its close relatives, those anthocyanin color pigments, and precipitate together as sediment. This leaves the mature wine smooth, round, and a pleasure on the nose, the taste buds, and our tactile sensors.

Levels of Tannins in Popular Beverages
(grams per liter)

coffee	2 g/l
tea	1.6 g/l
white wine	0.5 g/l
rosé wine	1-2 g/l
red wine	3-8 g/l
beer	0.1-0.15 g/l

If you've ever had the opportunity of tasting a series of red wines, making use of a spittoon to get rid of the excess wine, you may have seen tannins in action. When the tannins of red wine come into contact with the protein in our saliva, the color pigments and tannins will often precipitate. You'll see them as stringy filaments floating in the spittoons, or even feel them in your mouth. When several, very tannic young wines have been tasted in a row the coating on your tongue can be so thick you can literally scrape it off with your teeth. It's not hard to understand, then, that the viscosity of your saliva can be severely reduced by this tannic assault. Remembering how important that saliva is to lubricating your tongue and oral membranes, the experienced taster will factor this into how much he may need to rinse, despite the fact that rinsing too often can present its own problems.

In assessing its overall value to a wine, you can see we're dealing with a two-edged sword here. Generally, if a white wine is even mildly astringent, much longer than six months or a year it can indicate a fault and may be rated that way.

But for red wines a very different scenario is enacted. Early in its life most red wines should have a respectable level of tannin and be noticeably astringent. If you know it to be a young wine then this will be a positive factor for that wine, for the astringency can be a promise of good years ahead and a wonderful reward at maturity. Again, you have to evaluate the wine for what it is now; and with all that youthful astringency, it is not in the most pleasant shape for consumption. So you rate it for now, noting that it will improve, gaining in points as well as stature. But as the wine ages the tannins begin to link or combine and drop out. The wine softens with each birthday, reaching an ideal stage where it is no longer an astringent wine, but smooth and silky. At least that's the way the scene should play for fine and great wines.

However, if this softening with age does not occur, you may have to count it as a negative. It may be "green" tannins from grapes harvested before they were fully ripened. The rate at which a wine softens with respect to its tannins will be unique to that wine and that vintage. However, when it becomes obvious the wine is indeed deteriorating in several respects (i.e., no fruit), with yet a pronounced astringency, the future of this unbalanced wine is determined. It will never soften.

Grape Tannins

- coarse, rough feel

- more noticeable on the teeth, lips

- can be hard, green, bitter in youth (grip)

Wood Tannins

- softer, more "dusty" character with a spicy warmth

- more evident on the cheeks, near the rear of the mouth

The ancient oak cask is as much a part of modern winemaking as the most sophisticated computerized wine press. French oak (Quercus Rober and Sessilis) has dominated the cask scene for generations. American oak (Quercus Alba), now using French coopering techniques, is beginning to take its place alongside the French.

Though they are all oak they impart different aromas and flavors to the wine, based largely on the tightness of the grain. This determines the amount and speed of the extraction. Each type of oak, grown in different forests, imparts to the wine its unique character.

The initial levels of tannins—and color pigments—have a great deal to do with "maceration," the amount of time and manner in which the crushed grape skins remain soaking in the juice. Most of the red color pigments are extracted in the first few days. However, growing numbers of winemakers are experimenting with and using an "extended maceration," often extending it a month or more after the wine has fully fermented. An odd series of changes seem to affect the tannic and bitter perception of these wines.

Some Popular Oaks

Origin	Grain	Common to Varietals	Imparted Character
Allier (France)	tight	Gamay, Pinot Noir, Chardonnay, Pinot Gris	flowery, perfumed
American (Missouri, Tennessee, Arkansas)	average	Cabernet Sauvignon, Zinfandel, Sauvignon Blanc, Petite Sirah	vanilla, herb-like, spirity
Limousin (France)	open	Brandy, Port, Sherry, Cabernet Sauvignon, Syrah	vanilla, a touch of lemon
Nevers (France)	average	Chardonnay, Sauvignon Blanc, Gamay	buttery, citrus
Troncais (France)	medium-tight	Pinot Noir, Pinot Gris	earthiness
Vosges (France)	tightest	Chardonnay, Pinot Noir, Pinot Meunier (Champagne), Sauvignon Blanc	light vanilla, neutral

In the first few days of color and tannin extraction the young red wine is rough, somewhat bitter, and astringent. This is largely due to the bitter and astringent nature of the small, extracted tannins. A youthful purple tint dominates.

Yet with extended maceration those initial rough edges seem to soften. It is suggested that as more and more tannins are extracted they link together (polymerize) as long tannins, which are decidedly less bitter and astringent. Some link further with some of the color pigments, becoming so large they fall out as a sediment. The color then stabilizes as a more mature red.

Aromatics of cinnamon and vanilla increase as the wine softens and becomes more approachable at a much earlier age.

CHAPTER 6

A Matter of Taste

TRUE, we've been talking about taste all along. But finally we're ready to consider, not the broad sense of the word, but the four more specific true, taste functions differentiated solely by your tongue. These are the sensations we earlier identified as sweetness, acidity (sourness), bitterness, and saltiness.

However, in advance of tackling these four elements, one at a time, it's the ideal time for us to consider very briefly the word "threshold." You have many, you know.

⁂ ⁂ ⁂

Thresholds

There's your threshold of hearing, the point below or above which you can no longer hear a sound. For the average person their hearing threshold is approximately 50 cycles on the low end to 15,000 cycles on the high end. Beyond either threshold, sounds are audible only to the exceptional human ear.

You have a personal threshold of pain, too, a threshold most of us don't really care to experiment with, not even in the interest of science. These two rather simple examples help us appreciate that each person's threshold varies for every sensation. This is also true for all the different sensory stimulations we've discussed to this point, and for the ones yet to come.

Technically, there is more than one threshold. Our threshold of perception or recognition is generally defined as "the minimum quantity of a product required for it to be recognized, the sensation to be identified." But there are two other thresholds we need to understand:

Detection Threshold: the least energy capable of producing a sensation; the absolute threshold.

Difference Threshold: the least amount of stimulus needed to change perception; differential threshold.

Thresholds will vary considerably depending on which sense we're using. At times our senses will demand a 30 percent change before we ever detect the alteration. Individual sensitivity can vary profoundly when it comes to perceiving a particular stimulation (e.g., SO_2). Yet apply another stimulation and the sensitivities between the two individuals could reverse. So, for each odor, for each taste, and for each sensation of touch, you have a personal perception threshold, a point beyond which you lose the ability to sense that particular stimulant.

A few simple taste experiments such as those described in chapter 9 will help you determine if you have a threshold that will act as a serious impediment to your judging wine fairly accurately. Most of us don't, but should one become evident you can simply make use of a friend who doesn't have that particular drawback.

Finding a group of wineloving friends whose strengths and weaknesses inter-relate, compensating for each other, can be great fun and quite rewarding. By combining your strengths in a composite rating, your accuracy and consistency will be greatly improved. Professional tasting panels often function in just this manner.

Obtaining the sensory maximum from any stimulation is going to make your perceptions and judgments easier and more accurate. Few tasters would find much to debate with in this fundamental tasting principle. But this introduces us to a controversial topic involving winetasting technique.

☙ ☙ ☙

To Swallow or Not To Swallow

It's common for most wine experts during a tasting to spit (expel) some of a wine sample into a spittoon, or some such receptacle, after tasting it. This action is not a demonstration of how they felt about the quality of the wine. There's sound reason for it. After tasting and swallowing a few dozen wine samples you can appreciate how a taster's accuracy may decline in direct proportion to the number of samples.

Some writers have expressed great concern about the impact of this amount of alcohol. Some employ rather humorous and suggestive warnings, but they all seem to imply the same thing—spit out all of the wine if you're going to be tasting a great many samples.

Other writers have suggested that you don't even have to swallow the wine to ingest enough alcohol to cause you problems. They point out that alcohol absorbs into the bloodstream as it's being swished around in your mouth, right through the mucus membranes lining the oral cavity. While this may be true, the critical issue is, how much do we absorb in this manner?

Are these concerns warranted? Are there any hard facts to support these dire warnings? There is evidence, but it makes the case in the other direction. A number of wine competitions have had their judges submit to a breathalyzer following a full day of tasting. The number of individual samples consumed by each judge ranged from 50 to 130.

The results of the InterVin International Wine Competition are typical. For judges that consistently swallowed some of each wine sample during the tasting day, a range of .005 to .04 was registered by the breathalyzer. The average was about .02 (.08–0.10 indicates legal intoxication in most jurisdictions). The number of samples consumed that day by each of the 51 judges was 60. The judges also enjoyed a luncheon that day—with wines. The bottom line is, swallowing a small amount of each wine sample does not present a problem with blood/alcohol levels, nor do blood/alcohol levels reach the numbers that are likely to impair judgment. At such slow rates of ingestion the body metabolizes the alcohol quite easily. It will likely be eliminated in the first pass through the hepatic system. Of major concern is that the competition be well organized and of an impeccable professional caliber.

Having removed the negative implications, there are a number of factors that suggest that if you were not to swallow, but rather spit out all of the sample, the quality of that judgment would then be impaired. Sounds almost heretical, but it's true. That taster would miss a number of important stimulations.

From a pure taste perspective, we need to recall that the "bitter" stimulation is best perceived on the rear surface of the tongue, using those circumvallate papillae. You may remember that they are served by a different nerve that transmits these stimulations to the brain. If swallowing does not take place, many of these receptors will not be involved, so will not transmit their message to the brain. In addition, taste papillae are located in the pharynx (the tube connecting the oral cavity and the throat), and on the tonsils and epiglottis. These would be totally missed. In addition, these bitter-sensing papillae are "trough-like" and require a more determined effort to get the fluid to inundate them. That means swallowing is almost a necessity—unless you've become extremely adept at gargling.

You may also remember the tremendous significance of "retronasal" smelling, the odors reaching the olfactory zone via the "back door," so to speak. This presents us with another powerful reason to swallow.

The mouth has a connecting channel to the nasal passages. At the beginning of the swallow this channel and the one to our lungs, is closed. You may have experienced the rather unpleasant, choking results when this "misfires," or when your nose turns into a double faucet.

But when the wine has been swallowed the respiratory circuits are reopened. The movement of the pharynx then creates a gentle internal pressure that forces the vapors up into the nose, increasing the depth of our olfactory impression. Immediately following this swallowing action we usually exhale. This expelled air will then rush along the wine-moistened surfaces of the pharynx and oral cavity, becoming impregnated with the wine volatiles, and headed straight for that awesomely sensitive olfactory patch. All because you swallowed.

Of course, you can make some assessments without swallowing. But why? They will invariably be short-changed for no sound reason.

Let's move on to something a little more palatable—how sweet it is!

✽ ✽ ✽

Sweetness

This factor alone causes more differences of opinion than perhaps all the other factors that determine the quality of a wine grouped together. Most people are quite adamant about their personal preferences when it comes to sweetness. So much so that this offers for us a major hurdle to surmount. It's the "one teaspoon of sugar in my tea and that's it! I'll never change" type of attitude we're faced with. Far too often it's this strong preference that clouds judgments. So if the sugar (crystalline carbohydrate) content of a wine is not in tune with our personal taste the rating of that wine could suffer as a whole.

It's a tough tendency to overcome, especially for new wine drinkers, and I have no easy formula for defeating it. At least, to be forewarned is to be forearmed, or something like that. It's not surprising that almost all sweet substances have a similar molecular structure.

To further complicate this situation, sweetness levels do not dogmatically define a virtue or a fault. Much depends on the type of wine and what the winemaker was trying to accomplish in the first place, and how the sweetness level relates to other facets of the wine. There was a time when you could list varieties of grapes, related to a region, and arbitrarily state that wines made from them should ideally have only a specific sweetness. And few authorities at that time would have disagreed.

It's no longer that simple. Producers around the world do experiment with consumer preferences by producing wines from the same grapes with different residual sugar levels. Even some traditional wine producers from the traditional wine regions are finding that if they are going to sell their product on the international market they are pressured by the preferences of that market to alter their products to meet local tastes, especially where sweetness is concerned.

With red table wines we are still primarily talking about wines that are normally quite dry. Only occasionally do we see red table wines coming to market with a touch of sugar (one to two percent). For these wines, quite often the term "mellow" will be marked on their labels to identify this characteristic. Because of the masking effect of red wine tannins you need over one percent residual sugar (10 g/l) for it to be readily detected.

Sweetness has traditionally been more pertinent to white wines and rosés. Because of their simpler nature and broader sweetness range, whites and rosés are the bridges by which many make the transition from other alcoholic beverages or soft drinks to the wine world.

Individuals vary considerably in their ability to detect sugars. The average sweetness threshold is about 0.7 percent (7 g/l). Any less and for most of us the sweetness seems to disappear altogether.

We find two natural sugars in wine, glucose and fructose. There are more, but these two are by far the most significant. Interestingly, we are all more sensitive to fructose than to glucose.

And just about the time you're telling yourself you're a pretty good judge of sweetness and that assessing sugar content in wine should be fairly simple, consider this before you take any bows: Several constituents in wine create the illusion of sweetness, while other elements will confuse your ability to judge the legitimate sugar level accurately.

Alcohol, glycerol, butanediol, aldehydes, amides, ketones, esters, and certain yeasts can actually make you think you are sensing a certain level of sweetness. Super levels of fruit aromatics and a fruity taste can also create a sensation of sweetness. And it's the acidity, astringency, and bitterness that can seriously confuse your awareness of sugar levels. If, for example, the wine is overly tart or even bitter, will you be able to accurately judge the degree of sweetness, in comparison to a wine of equal sugar content, but having little tartness or bitterness? These and other elements can mask or enhance your perception of sweetness. But don't be disheartened. It may be a little difficult at first, but with some practice it's "do-able."

About this time you're probably wondering, where does all this residual sugar come from? Doesn't all the natural grape sugar get processed, used up, during fermentation, like I've been told?

Most frequently for table wine, yes! All the natural sugars are normally transformed into alcohol and CO_2 during fermentation, leaving us with a totally dry wine. There are, of course, several unfermentable sugars that remain in wine, but they are not at levels we can taste.

Several doors are also open to the modern winemaker to arrest fermentation at various points, leaving natural, residual sugars to act as sweeteners. The most natural method of accomplishing this is simply to use grapes that have super amounts of fruit sugars. During fermentation the yeasts and sugars start making alcohol. But yeast is somewhat human in one respect: it can stand only so much alcohol. When the new wine achieves a certain level of alcohol (12 to 14 percent) the remaining yeast cells just roll over and die, so to speak, and the wine stops fermenting. But because you've used these super-sweet grapes you'll end up with sugar left over and a wine with a certain degree of sweetness.

This can be carried only so far. Many grapes that do produce high levels of sugar do not produce wines of quality. But there are some grapes that are late-picked (*Spätlese* in German), therefore developing additional sugar content, and are super-ripened to the point they have so much residual sugar they naturally produce true dessert wines (Sauternes, Beerenausleses, Tokajs, ice wines, and so on.).

But how do you get any residual sugar from grapes having only normal sugar levels and when all you want is a touch of sweetness left in the wine? Modern technology has the answer, several in fact.

With modern equipment, especially filters, centrifuges, and pressure-controlled tanks, fermentation can be halted at almost any point. First you select the desired alcohol/residual sugar ratio and when that point is reached during fermentation, the wine is then centrifuged and/or filtered, removing the remaining live yeast cells. This leaves a wine with the exact balance you want. But at the same time, the wine could be lacking in any number of other desirable characteristics.

This is obviously a gross oversimplification of the whole procedure, as there are innumerable factors and technicalities that a professional winemaker must evaluate before taking any of these steps. But for our purposes it gives us an overview of what can take place.

Descriptively, you could use terms that range from "dry" to "medium dry" to "medium-sweet" to "sweet" to "very sweet" to describe residual sugar levels. Some wine authorities use different terms to express the same sensations, but the ones we've selected are as descriptive as any.

Notable by its absence in these pages is any consideration of extra or additional sugar being added at the fermentation stage ("chaptalizaton"). To get into this discussion would take too many pages and perhaps be more confusing than enlightening. For our purpose, perhaps it will suffice to simply say that for table wines sugar is added from outside sources only when there is a legitimate need, such as when the grapes fail to produce enough natural sugar in poor harvests. As grape sugars increase so do aromatic and flavor components, usually.

But sugar is not added to sweeten the wine. Basically, any sugar that is added (cane or beet sugar usually) is done so during fermentation to aid in the achievement of proper alcohol levels. The sucrose sugars (sucrose = 1 molecule of glucose + 1 molecule fructose) invert enzymatically during the process to fructose and glucose, so essentially act as would natural fruit sugars.

Common Wine Sugars

- glucose
- fructose
- sucrose
- galactose
- arabniose
- xylose
- lactose
- ribose
- maltose

Sweetness Levels (10 grams per liter = 1 percent sugar)

Description	Residual Sugar
dry	1–6.0 grams/liter
medium dry	7–1 5 g/l
medium sweet	18–30g/1
sweet	30–50 g/l
very sweet	60+ g/l

Some Typical Sweetness Interactions

sweetness + *acid* = masking effect for each

sweetness + *saltiness* = masking effect for each

sweetness + *strong fruit aromatics* = possible reduction of fruity aroma

sweetness + *strong fruit aromatics (terpenes)* = increased fruity aroma

bitterness + *sweetness* = delay of bitter sensation but not diminished

While interactions between sweetness and other wine components are part of the wine experience, the individual sensations can be separated. It takes a good deal of concentration and a focus on the tongue's receptor zones most sensitive to those individual stimulations. Developing this concentration skill means it can be applied to olfactory sensations, too.

But do be aware of a similar combination sensation. More than a blend of sweet and acid, it is a "sour-sweet" stimulation that can be the result of lactic bacteria spoilage. This is not an auspicious introduction to wine acids, but it is an introduction.

☙ ☙ ☙

Acidity

Acidity is the pucker power, the zing in wine, that tartness that gives the wine a certain crispness and bite to it. Without discernable quantities of acid the wine would be the opposite—dull, flat, insipid. Both extremes are negative factors. A healthy balance is what we're looking for.

In much of Europe it's referred to as "nervosity" or nervousness. It's confusing in direct translation, but think of it as its "nerve," as in English colloquial terms like "backbone" or "spine."

In laboratory language acidity is called sourness. Again it's an unfortunate choice of words since sour has come to mean a spoiled wine in the language of the English-speaking consumer. Oh well, some day a universal wine language . . . But one thing we do know for certain—all sour or acid tastes are caused by hydrogen ions. Even as the grapes ripen and gain sweetness their acids fall due to the loss of hydrogen ions.

Acidity, or the lack of it, is usually more important to white wines. That's not to suggest it makes no difference at all to red wines. But because whites have fewer tannins, as well as fewer of several other constituents, acids are more significant to the overall character of white wines.

Part of the youthful roughness and harshness of a wine is frequently the result of the stronger, more active nature of that wine's tartaric and malic acids. However, with age some of the tartaric acid transforms into insoluble potassium bitartrate and drops out (precipitates) as those tiny, harmless crystals we spoke of earlier. Malic acid can also be transformed to the softer lactic acid in a bacterial fermentation.

But wouldn't you know it, there are more acids to consider than just tartaric and malic. (Is nothing ever simple anymore?) The principal wine acids are tartaric, malic, lactic, citric, acetic, and succinic. All of them can influence your judgments.

To get a more complete understanding of the role acids play there is need to introduce and briefly explain, five different wine terms used in connection with acid levels: fixed acidity, volatile acidity, total acidity, real acidity, and pH. It's to your benefit to know the differences.

Fixed Acidity is defined as the combination of all the normal organic, fruit acids found in the grape and subsequently in the wine (acids like tartaric, malic, lactic, citric, and so on.). Together they range around four to twelve g/l (grams per liter).

Volatile Acidity (VA) is a technical term that describes acids that can be removed by distillation. For our purposes we are primarily concerned with only one of several acids that fall into this category—acetic acid (vinegar), found generally at 0.3 g/l to 0.5 g/l

In these small amounts it is said (erroneously, I feel) that acetic acid adds a note of complexity to a wine. But in excess of that (0.8+ g/l), it is beginning to be identifiable as that negative vinegariness of a spoiled wine, more in taste than smell. An associated ester (ethyl acetate) gives us more of the sour, acrid, pricked smell at levels of about 0.15 to 0.18 g/l.

Total Acidity (TA) is the overall acidity (more properly, the "almost" total acidity, because not all acids are represented). It's the fixed acidity plus the volatile acidity and is frequently the acid count for wines, expressed as so many "grams per liter tartaric." The French express total acidity as "sulfuric" (conversion: succinic g/l x 1.531 = tartaric g/l.).

Real Acidity expresses the wine's pH factor (acid/alkaline balance). In case you're not up to date with your shampoo commercials, seven is neutral pH, below seven is acidic, above seven alkaline. It's a common term used in the wine industry. For every drop of one unit of the pH, the acid strength increases by a factor of ten.

pH is not the easiest concept to master. I'm still not completely certain I do. What helps me to remember: p = power, H = hydrogen (as in hydrogen ion concentration). It is an extraordinarily important consideration for winemakers and grape growers alike. It often indicates how mature the grapes were at harvest. pH can make or break a wine. As tasters, we're concerned with it as an after-effect, how it influences the wine we may be sampling.

pH is really a measurement (by a pH meter) of exactly how acidic the wine is. At low pH levels (3.2–3.6) the wine has greater protection from bacterial spoilage. Low pH (high acid) also affects color, especially in reds. High pH (less acid) often means a less brilliant color, leaning towards purple. Low pH usually indicates a more intense and lively red.

All wine is acidic (below seven pH) but at a pH of 3.8 to 3.9 wines are dull, flat and flabby. Some grapes can have identical TA (total acids) but vary in acid strength with just a minor difference in the pH number.

Some Typical pH Measurements

completely acid	= 0
limes	= 1.0
pure lemon juice	= 2.2
orange juice	= 3.0
German Riesling	= 3.0+
crisp Chardonnay	= 3.1–3.3
soft Chardonnay	= 3.4–3.5
good Cabernet Sauvignon	= 3.4–3.
soft Cabernet Sauvignon	= 3.8+
dessert wines	= 3.5-3.8
distilled water	= 7.0 (neutral)
alkaline	= 7.0+

In terms of the "total acidity" measurement, a figure below five or six g/l is leaning towards the flabby side. As we approach seven or eight g/l TA tartaric the wine is gaining crispness and bite. At nine to twelve g/l we have a very acidic wine. However, when balanced out with residual sugars of three to five percent (30–50 g/l) an extremely pleasant and savory experience can be created.

Wines contain six principal organic acids, three inherited directly from the grape, and three formed as part of the fermentation process. These acids are generally more complex and tart. Other mineral acids (i.e., sulfuric, nitric, hydrochloric) are present in trace amounts, along with small amounts of other organic acids.

Most Common Wine Acids

Acid	Source	What To Look For
Tartaric	grape	hard, tart acid; highest level of wine acids; has aftertaste in back of the throat
Malic	grape	green apple (most acidic assertive taste) fresher, fruitier; converts to lactic acid during malo-lactic fermentation; Germans call it apfelsauer
Citric	grape	fresh, citrus character; very little in wine; has a sweetish touch; lingers
Acetic	from fermentation	vinegary taste &smell; acetic acid bacteria forms ethyl acetate that has stronger sour smell
Lactic	mainly from fermentation & secondary malo-lactic fermentation	buttery, cheesy aroma; important to body and flavor
Succinic	during fermentation	stable, "winey" acid; can be bitter & salty at the same time; also contributes to body & flavor

Malo-Lactic Fermentation

There is no more appropriate place than in our "acid" section to introduce you to another love/hate relationship experienced by wine-makers world wide—malo-lactic fermentation (MLF). This intriguing process adds yet another love/hate element—diacetyl. Winelovers can be entranced by the complexity added to a wine by a MLF or, if it goes astray, the wine can be a write-off.

Using the word "fermentation" can be a bit misleading here, because MLF is a bacterial fermentation, not yeast-driven, as in a normal alcoholic fermentation. And as you might expect, the two acids—malic and lactic —are the major players involved. Citric acid plays a small role, as well. Most often, MLF occurs naturally, as a secondary fermentation, stimulated by a bacteria (*Leuconostoc Oenos*). In essence what results is the transformation of some of the more aggressive, harsher malic acid to the softer, creamier lactic acid.

Sounds good so far, especially if you have a wine that is a bit too acidic in the first place.

In addition, tasters suggest that a greater aromatic and taste complexity is added to the wine. Still sounds pretty good. One of the by-products of MLF is a compound called diacetyl, a buttery aromatic found in many of California's rich, oaky Chardonnays. Sounds too good to be true. That's the problem: sometimes it is. Not all is perfect with MLF or diacetyl.

MLF is almost universally accepted for red wines with decent levels of acid. In the exchange from malic to lactic acid, some 30 percent of the malic acid is transformed to lactic acid. This accounts for a softer acid perception, but the overall acid level literally drops by about one gram per liter and the pH goes up a bit as well. Low-acid wines simply can't afford this. Such wines are usually from warmer climates. In cool-climate wine regions it is most often a boon, because acids are normally higher.

MLF is less desirable in white wines where acid is more critical and off-odors more easily detected. Because MLF is often a naturally occurring, secondary fermentation, winemakers sometimes do little to prevent it, or actually encourage it in vat, before the wine is bottled. This is almost an act of self-defense. If the MLF takes place in bottle, disaster is frequently the result. Better to get it over with while the wine is still in large vats, where you can control it to some degree. Blending a wine that has gone through MLF with one that hasn't could also cause problems in bottle.

The Two Sides of the Malo-Lactic Coin

Positive
- reduces acid and softens its sensory perception
- adds to a more complex bouquet
- adds buttery, butterscotch aromatics (diacetyl)
- adds to bacteriological stability of the wine

Negative
- reduces fruitiness
- MLF in bottle causes off-odors (i.e., cheesy), haze, and gas that can break the cork seal, which endangers the wine
- causes some flavor components to precipitate as sediment
- the lowering of excessive acid levels can be accomplished in less problem-prone ways.

Diacetyl (the chemical added to margarine to make it smell like butter) has become a "buzz word" among Chardonnay producers. When balanced, and if the bacteria is only allowed to be active for a limited period of time, it adds that positive buttery, caramel note to big whites like California Chardonnays. If kept below about 1.5 ppm, it seems to be a hit with consumers. Winemakers are not fond of its results with too many other white varietals.

In consumer blind tasting tests, however, the diacetyl touch was not highly favored. When three options were presented to the consumer groups, their order of preference was:

1. wines with no MLF
2. wines with properly controlled MLF
3. wines with spontaneous (in bottle) MLF

When consumers speak, winemakers would be wise to listen. It would be worthwhile to expand this diacetyl sampling to further identify winelovers' preferences.

✳ ✳ ✳

Bitterness

Unlike the ease with which we accept, even lust after, sweetness, bitterness takes a little work. But a great many people accomplish the task. It is an acquired taste, no matter how early in life we are exposed to it. Perhaps many of those who claim to appreciate it have simply learned to tolerate it.

This aversion to bitterness has probably served us well, as most poisonous plants and chemicals have a bitter taste. It has at least made us a little cautious in accepting bitter food and drink.

We have no problem identifying bitter tastes. Caffeine in strong coffee, tonic water (quinine), Aspirin (acetylsalicylic acid) are common examples. We even court the appetite-stimulating effect in bitter drinks such as vermouth, Campari, gin and tonic, and the enormous popularity of after dinner "bitters" throughout Europe. We find bitter components throughout nature—in vegetable extracts and chemical salts.

In wine, bitterness originates with that family of chemicals we've talked about so often already—polyphenols—found in the condensed tannins in the pips, skins, and stalks of grapes, as well as in some compounds we're not even sure of yet. Not all phenol compounds are bitter, though. The anthocyanin red pigments seem to have little taste.

In a young red wine tannins account for about 1 to 3 g/l—in whites much less, measured in milligrams per liter. As tannins mature they link up with themselves and the pigments and precipitate, leaving the wine with barely a hint of bitterness, if not well below our threshold of sensitivity.

Bitterness is frequently confused with astringency. That's only fair since both bitterness and astringency originate from these same compounds (polyphenolics or tannins). But remember, astringency is a tactile or touch sensation, while bitterness is a true taste stimulation.

One of the first things we come to realize about bitterness is the difficulty we have in properly describing it. You sense it best on the rear, upper surface of your tongue. It's more prominent in the finish or aftertaste of the wine, where it is one of the properties that seems to linger awhile on the palate.

Bitterness can be quite normal for a short time in many very young wines, especially reds. But for sound, well-made white wines it should disappear soon after bottling. For reds it may take a year or two to lose this quality. If it doesn't, it will probably remain somewhat bitter for the better part of that wine's lifespan, and forever stamp it with at least one negative quality.

A very faint touch of bitterness is characteristic of some red wines even at maturity, and there are those authorities who feel this is not a fault. But it should be so faint you would perhaps have to taste the wine twice to notice it. Anything more and we're back to our negative considerations. Bitterness quickly becomes offensive.

Some white wines known to be low in tannins have still exhibited a certain bitterness to them—dry Muscats and Gewürztraminers, for example. Why is a mystery yet to be unravelled. Even though we don't have the answer it still remains a negative factor when it becomes too pronounced. White wines that are fermented too long on the skins can also have a bitterness about them, as do wines with a high sulphate content. With reds having low acid, it can also reveal a bitterness. Acids tend to mask bitterness at all stages except the finish.

You would describe a wine, in terms of bitterness, as having no bitterness, to being very bitter. You can fill in the middle graduations with your own expressions.

As we said, some winetasters and connoisseurs appreciate a touch of bitterness in certain styles of wine, usually reds. But generally it is not a positive factor, even less so with whites. And very definitely it's a fault if there is sufficient bitterness to remind you of caffeine or quinine.

✠ ✠ ✠

Saltiness

In the original *Winetaster's Secrets*, published in 1981, I summarily dismissed salt in wine by stating, "For our immediate purposes we can ignore saltiness, as wine contains little salt, certainly not usually at levels you can sense, unless you count those cooking wines that have salt added to them."

I was in error, and have truly repented from my wayward path. I also extend my apologies to those I've led astray.

It's not that there is some profound new revelation that identifies salt in wine. Wine contains about two to four grams per liter of salty compounds, primarily potassium bitartrate. This and other mineral salts, though below our threshold of distinct perception, do have an effect on what we taste.

This is where I made my error. I forgot what every chef knows—that that dash of salt, though not enough to taste directly, highlights and enlivens other flavors. It does just that in wine as well. In sweet wines, along with acids, it prevents the high sugar levels from becoming cloying and unpleasant to have in your mouth. With the acid and that almost imperceptible dash of salt, sweet wines finish clean in the mouth, without that sticky-candy aftertaste.

CHAPTER 7

Getting It All Together

TO this point we've examined in detail separate wine factors to determine their individual merits and what they add to or take away from the quality of wine. The following subjects deal with aspects of how well a number of these elements combine or marry. If some elements, even in a fine wine, are at odds with each other the wine as a whole suffers. Yet, wines that may be quite ordinary by nature could have their component parts so well in tune with each other they give to the drinker a very pleasurable overall experience. Such a wine would be called "harmonious."

* * *

Flavor

We've already examined individually several flavor factors with our nose and taste buds. But under this heading of flavor we attempt to interrelate all these constituents, arriving at a general impression that defines that wine's flavor. Here the nose and taste functions work as a team, in tandem, complementing each other, the sum greater than the parts, a kind of synergistic function. Neither the nose nor our sense of taste can individually master this depth of stimulation. They must collaborate.

Flavor will be perceived only when we bring together our assessments of smell, touch, taste, and our common chemical sense. But this is more than mental addition work. The wine needs to be evaluated for this composite factor alone. A separate sip may be necessary to consider it as a whole, more than the sum of its parts.

There have been attempts to produce a combined flavor measurement, just as we can technically quantify specific flavor components. It has met with little success. Conventional measurement systems lack the sophistication to be able to accomplish this delightful task. The human bank of sensory recorders remains the only set of instruments capable of such complex inter-related assessments.

The intensity and attractiveness of that flavor is a vital component of its quality. That intensity is often judged by its length. Winetasters use words like "persistence," "finish," "aftertaste." "Persistent Aromatic Intensity" (PAI) is a phrase used often by European tasters. A flavor's length, its ability to persist, is vitally important to its quality.

Persistence—Finish

Great wines are distinguished by their length of finish—that lingering, overall characteristic impression left by the flavor. A wine with a poor finish (aftertaste) will not only lack intensity, but be short-lived in your mouth, its impression fading quickly once it is swallowed.

Some have likened it to an echo. A pleasurable but fading memory of sensations that were so clear and evocative at their beginning, but have departed with a lingering farewell, not a terse, abbreviated retreat. In France, they use words such as *fumet* for this aromatic aftertaste. *Remanance* is a synonym we can use.

The ideal is a comfortable, lengthy reminder of the composite character of the flavor. Just the opposite is a wine with a short finish, the flavor disappearing quickly. However, should it linger too long, wearing out its welcome, this too would be a fault, every bit as negative as if it disappeared before you had a chance to really get to know it.

Some experts suggest the flavor impression should last so many seconds precisely (caudalies), and you should count it off to determine this factor. If you choose to do so give yourself considerable latitude, as there are any number of factors that can affect the consistency of such a practice. Make sure what you're sensing is not just a lingering bitterness, tannins, acid, or sweetness. When any one of them is out of balance individually, they can persist longer than the true composite flavor.

❦ ❦ ❦

Typicalness

This is perhaps my least favorite wine word. I'm not sure I wouldn't vote for its abolition, if it ever came to a vote. Yet to be fair, it does have some rare, legitimate applications.

Some wine authorities remain convinced that "typicity" is an important factor in wine quality. It must be, as they say, "good of its kind." At the risk of sounding blunt—*who cares?* That's a little like being introduced to a stranger and worrying about who his or her parents are rather than what kind of person this individual is.

There is a new wine reality some seem reluctant to adopt—wine has truly become international in its personality. Modern consumers are interested in the inherent quality of a wine, not so much about where it comes from or what it's "supposed" to be like.

While typical regional characteristics may be important to some, other regions in the world can produce wines equally unique, but have some very similar characters. That is neither good nor bad! It's not imitation! It is a quest for quality.

Fortunately, I'm not alone in this view. This word upsets many in the wine trade. They quite rightly feel that the word "typical" is abused and that you cannot stamp out wines as if using a cookie-cutter. Each wine is an individual.

Though I agree with them in principle, I still feel the occasional, judicious use of this term can be justified. It can also help you become a better judge of wines, if kept in proper perspective. You are, however, cautioned against misuse of the word, trying to fit wines into slots they don't really belong in. A good example: those who insist on comparing the character of fine Cabernet Sauvignon varietals from California with the noble red Bordeaux wines of France. This can be a fascinating assessment and challenge, but too often some non-qualitative but typical factors are allowed to reflect in the judging procedure. In many non-qualitative respects the two wines can be very different and comparisons on this basis can be unfair to both. It's a pity to see so many get caught in this trap. Even professionals, who should know better, do so on occasion. I reluctantly include myself in this group.

At best, typicalness is a touchstone, a reference point. When the grape variety is known there are certain basic (our apple vs. orange) qualities that should be apparent and are certainly comparable. This reference point helps us to relatively evaluate wines made from the same grape variety, but grown in different regions, for example. I use the term relatively because certain grapes develop markedly different characteristics when grown in different regions, characteristics that are not necessarily related to quality. There are still a number of factors that can be legitimately compared, but you should limit it to these alone.

Most important, this standard, if I can use that term, becomes valuable when judging different vintages from a known region and/or producer. They certainly should possess many typical qualities.

However, when you're judging non-descript wines (wines made from non-distinctive grape varieties) typicalness becomes almost impossible, as a factor, to apply, except in the most general vinous terms.

※ ※ ※

Balance

Few things in life are more important than balance. In the end, it is balance that often reveals quality. Harmony is defined as "coherence between the parts of a whole." In the context of wine, that is precisely what is meant when its constituents yield a rich marriage of flavors and pleasure.

It is here too where human senses are master. At the present state of technology, human tasting ability surpasses the best the laboratory can offer. In fact, the technological advances we've made in laboratory analysis seem to be leading us further away from any profound understanding of wine balance. It is deeper knowledge and insight into our sensory perceptions that have increased our grasp and appreciation of wine.

But do keep in mind, balance is not a quality reserved for the elite of the wine world. Balance is desirable in all wines, from the most humble vin du pays to those that genuinely aspire to greatness.

For a wine to possess balance, all its individual elements will be in tune with each other, allowing even ordinary wines to demonstrate this virtue. So, a wine that exhibits a fine nose but has poor or excessive taste qualities would be assessed as unbalanced. Consideration, however, must be given to that wine's maturity, for a wine may take several years, even decades, to achieve this balance and harmony.

Of course, you will have to score it for the degree of balance it demonstrates at the moment of tasting, if you're doing an evaluation. This leaves room for that score to increase, if indeed the wine's balance does improve. In some instances a wine may even become less harmonious with age, as one element may develop some attributes too aggressively, throwing the wine out of balance.

※ ※ ※

General Quality

When we reach this heading we've come full circle. For the past 140 pages or so I've been inviting you to carefully dissect a wine step by step. Now I'm asking you to put it all back together and assess it as a single entity with "quality" in mind.

The overall impression you receive, swallowing more of the wine at this point, will relate the total richness of the wine's character. In a sense it's the marriage of all those points we've considered individually—the appearance, the color, aroma, bouquet, the four true taste sensations, and so on. How does the wine affect you? Is it a memorable wine?

You are tasting the wine as a single entity now, assessing its character as an individual wine. You may even discover that two faults you had previously identified could, in effect, cancel each other out, by acting as a counter-balance to each other (acid/sugar excesses) producing a wine that is generally very pleasant.

So, this is not a regressive step but a final and necessary component of your total evaluation. But take care not to use this category to correct previous individual evaluations or to express your personal likes and dislikes. If need be, go back and alter your first impression, if you have modified your judgment on a certain point. As stated earlier, evaluating or judging wine is not a contest. It's an honest attempt to understand and accurately assess the merits of a wine. Reviewing the elements that define "Quality" in chapter 1 will help you clearly see how and why this factor must be assessed as an independent evaluation.

❧ ❧ ❧

Hedonic—I Like It

If you want another way to express how much pleasure you derive from something, *hedonic* is not a bad word to use.

Since it seems impossible for any human to be totally objective, my purpose in introducing a hedonic factor into your evaluations is an attempt to at least contain this element to one section of the process.

There are any number of environmental influences that play a part in creating a person's individual taste. Cultural, family, and religious are but a few of the more obvious influences. So this is the place to express them. You've been struggling to remain as objective as possible to this point; now's the time to let it all out. You're encouraged to express a flat-out like or dislike opinion. Be opinionated—just don't let your previous, more critical analysis influence the expression of your gut feelings.

Some taste experts will object to the inclusion of the hedonic factor in wine evaluation. If it bothers anyone that much, ignore it. But in the end, this is very likely the major determining factor that will direct you to the wines you drink.

CHAPTER 8

Putting It Into Practice

The Approach

Whether it's a glass of wine shared with a friend or mate, or a flight of wines to be tasted with a group, you're taking part in one of the most enjoyable social exercises possible. Wine was created with us in mind, for our pleasure and relaxation, a balm to our good health. Wine is truly a social lubricant.

Yet, wine challenges more than our physical senses. It tests our faculties, our deepest perceptions, our ability to think and reason. All in a little glass you hold in your hand. But this is a voluntary function, one we must be intent upon sharing. For it will all slip past our notice if we fail to focus our perceptive powers on this marvelous product of the vine. Winetastings can be arranged with a wide variety of purposes in mind. From a simple gathering of friends, to a comparative tasting by a wineloving group, to a technical evaluation by winemaker, marketer, laboratory technician or researcher, the goal is much the same: to gain a better understanding of wine.

If your winetasting affair is more casual in nature, a few friends and a few bottles of wine, a wine sampling more than a tasting, you may not desire to be all that critical. And there's nothing wrong with this arrangement. In fact, it can be very enjoyable just getting to know a little more about a few wines and a few friends, in a more relaxed and casual atmosphere. It's a legitimate type of winetasting that is rewarding and satisfying in a way no professional tasting could be.

But if you're looking for a more practical, learning experience, perhaps even keeping a record of your evaluations, you will want to pay a little more attention to detail. You may also want to provide your tasters with some type of evaluation sheet. While some might prefer to simply rank the wines for that tasting, that can be a bit shallow and unproductive when compared to an evaluation of the wines.

The advantage of using one of the evaluation systems is your ability to relate the ratings from one tasting, to wines scored at another tasting, weeks, months, even years apart. Simply ranking a series of wines at one tasting, from the best to the worst, may indeed have some value, if that's what you want to do. But that fails you as a taster when you desire to relate those wines to anything outside of that particular tasting event.

An evaluation system, to work to your ultimate benefit, must disclose to you, the taster, the essence, the nature, the stature, the intrinsic value of every wine, regardless of when or with which wines it was tasted. Each wine should be approached and assessed as an individual, and should be evaluated in relationship to consistent standards—not another wine.

☀ ☀ ☀

The Setting
Depending on the type of winetasting you desire at the time, the setting, your tasting environment, may strongly influence your wine judging abilities. We spoke earlier of outside influences that could alter your judgments. Lighting, background color, sound—all can have a distinct effect on your sensory impressions.

First, the lighting. If it's completely impractical for you to provide indirect, natural lighting (an evening tasting is a good reason), the most accessible and economical alternative is clear, incandescent bulbs. Small desk or student-type lamps equipped with such bulbs, sans any frosted covers, are excellent for this purpose. They will influence the natural wine color the least. Most available fluorescent lighting will not only alter your color judgments but can, quite surprisingly, distort your sense of taste, too. So do stay away from them.

Try to provide as white a background as possible (walls, tablecloth, and so on.). Your room's color scheme may be the talk of the decorating set, but it could seriously upset your color and taste judgments. So do your best in this respect.

Since it's been claimed that music can sooth the heart of the savage beast, it shouldn't be all that surprising that it has the power to influence your wine ratings. This has been well-documented and the effect is quite consistent. So turn off the stereo and politely remind your more vociferous co-tasters to "belt up" during the actual tasting. Even casual remarks can throw you off. "Oh, isn't that marvelous, George!" has got to start you wondering which point was so marvelous. Your objectivity can go out the window with one simple comment.

Participants in the winetasting shouldn't be part of the problem by disturbing others' ability to concentrate. It is not out of place to make a polite request of attendees to be aware of the interference personal grooming items can cause—perfumes, aftershave lotions, shaving creams, deodorants, some cosmetics, lipsticks, hand lotions, even clothing like leather and suede have their own distinctive aromatics and a definite impact in a room full of people.

And don't forget a spittoon for expelling wine. If you don't have an official spittoon-type bucket for this purpose anything that's visually not too unattractive and doesn't leak will do. Sparkling wine buckets do well. Very effective and hygienic are foam drink or food cups. With a plastic lid they can be closed and disposed of easily.

And don't overdo it, please. Professionals are accustomed to tasting 20, 30, 40, 50 or more wines at a sitting without becoming inundated or inebriated. Try to keep your sampling down to six or eight wines at the most for one event. Not only can it be less expensive, but the impression and insight you do get from one wine will not then be washed away in a tide of too many samples. One of our objectives is to build a taste memory, not to set a world's record for the most wines tasted in one sitting.

❋ ❋ ❋

Smoking

As an ex-smoker I sincerely wish I could state that smoking will seriously impair your ability to taste wines well. Aside from it appearing to be a logical assumption, it remains just that, an assumption.

Hard evidence simply isn't there to support either view. Research on this situation is scarce. Some claim that tests have been carried out with results coming down in favor of the smoker. I haven't seen these tests, nor am I aware of anyone who has. However, it does support my own experience.

Having directed panels of tasters in international wine competitions for over 10 years I've watched, logged, and computerized the lasting results of both smokers and non-smokers. I find no differences.

I wish I could. But they don't exist. Why? I'm not sure. It seems to defy logic. No doubt there is a change or difference between the palates of smokers and non-smokers. But the difference appears to have no effect on how well they do their job.

If any real differences exist the smoker has learned to adapt—not consciously—but his innate senses have made the necessary adjustments. The wine industry is saturated with anecdotal stories, even legends, of smokers who have retained their tasting prowess despite a butt hanging from one side of their lips and a wine glass approaching the other.

It may be that the only advantage that non-smokers have is that they'll be around a little longer to taste a few more wines. That, we have the facts to prove. It also appears that in general, smokers find unpleasant odors less offensive and pleasant odors not quite so pleasant.

However, allowing cigarettes to be used in the same room where a tasting is being held is out of the question.

No Smoking! Post this sign prominently and don't shy away from reminding offenders. As little as two cigarettes smoked in a closed, average-sized room is sufficient to distort both visual and olfactory senses significantly. If someone can't possibly go that long without a butt, serve them a glass of something else and ask him or her to do whatever it is they have to do in another room. This is not intended to offend any smoker. As an ex-smoker I can't recall ever taking offense at no smoking regulations at a winetasting; it's the expected thing. Not only is it expected, it is reasonable and considerate.

🐞 🐞 🐞

Palate Refreshers

Anyone who has consumed wine with food—that should include most of us—knows from personal experience that different foods change the taste of wine. The pairing of food and wine has become almost a science—well, a ritual anyway.

With this awareness firmly programmed into your PC—I mean the one between your ears—why should anyone be surprised that food items served during a serious wine evaluation will seriously distort sensory impressions? It might actually improve the wine you're tasting, but it will still be distorted.

A panel of tasters has a wonderful Premier Cru Burgundy to evaluate. They don't know what the wine is—it's code #837. Judge Mary is nibbling on a cracker as she is about to sample the wine; Harry has just swallowed an ounce of decent cheddar; Bill, a little more famished, has just laid waste to a strip of rare roast beef. Why would anyone be surprised when their evaluations are only vaguely related? Some professional wine competitions continue to offer this fare during tasting sessions.

Most proteins will fix the tannins in wine. Even the most astringent, monster red seems civilized with enough cheese to polish its rough edges. Meat will push back our sensitivity to sweetness and acidity, while bringing out more salt and bitter sensations. Green vegetables reverse the distortions. The list of foods and their distortive effect is a long one. The point is—avoid them.

Even water is not problem-free. Some waters are well endowed with mineral salts which definitely impact on your tasting accuracy. The solvent effect of distilled water can also lead you astray. Neutral spring water seems to work best. But not too much.

Rinsing after each sample is a bad practice. Your mouth builds up a wine awareness—a programming or conditioning, if you will. Constantly rinsing with fresh water after each sample interferes or prevents this sensory "set-up," requiring a constant readjustment. If the water is meant for thirst or for its alcohol-diluting ability, drinking—without gargling or rinsing—causes little change inside your mouth. Too much water, as in rinsing, also alters the composition of your saliva, affecting its function.

If your event includes food as a reward for your tasters, after their task has been performed, keep in mind the smells that can invade the tasting environment. Such enormously different aromas, especially from hot foods, are immediately sensed, even at very low levels, and from considerable distances. One panel of tasters at our InterVin competition could tell the time at least once every morning and afternoon without looking at a watch. They could smell the coffee being prepared three floors away in the hotel.

If what you have arranged is a casual affair, a wine and cheese party, just ignore everything we've said here, and in the past seven chapters.

✹ ✹ ✹

Blind Tastings

It's difficult to forget some images. They're so vivid and full of meaning. One such mental image will remain with me forever. The setting—an international wine event in Frankfurt, Germany. Media coverage was quite extensive, with news teams vying for an angle, a different slant. One team consisting of a newsman and a cameraman decided to re-create their own version of the international "blind" tasting that had taken place earlier that afternoon. The "on-camera" personality sat at a table in a popular local restaurant. It was covered with glasses and wine samples. As the brilliant camera-light flicked on and they went live to air, the newsman, blindfolded with a heavy black scarf, gave his version of the results of the blind tasting of that afternoon, the one he had not attended. So much for relying on general opinion.

Blind tastings are, of course, very much a part of serious wine evaluations—an absolutely vital part, some feel. I tend to agree, as long as the goals of such tastings are in keeping with what can realistically be expected in this environment.

Opinions vary widely concerning the efficacy of such tastings. Part of the problem is that blind tastings are not always succinctly defined. There are now "single blind" tastings, "double blind" tastings, even "triple blind" tastings. And here you thought blind was blind.

In olden days a true blind tasting meant that you knew nothing about the wine you were about to taste, other than what your own senses allowed. Today, such deprivation would qualify as a "double blind" tasting, or is it a triple? At any rate, a single blind tasting allows the tasters limited information about the wine. Perhaps it's a tasting of a specific grape variety from various parts of the vinous globe. Only the variety is known, everything else is "blind." Or, the single piece of known data could be a vintage, a region, even a property. I suppose our news friend would have replicated such an event with just one eye covered.

Some noted tasters are of the opinion that a single blind tasting is more informative and rewarding. Very often that view is taken because the goal of such a tasting is more to identify which wine is which, and not necessarily the difference in quality. In reality, single blind tastings can expose the tasters to regional, varietal, even vineyard biases.

True blind tastings (double blind) avoid most prejudices. They explode myths. When the mind is relieved of such biased data it is forced to think about and focus on sensory impressions, not pre-conceived notions. To me, the best of all worlds is to taste double blind first. Then, if a common factor exists among the wines, repeat the tasting revealing that single piece of information. Comparing the two results can be quite revealing.

If you are arranging a blind tasting remember not to allow the bottles in the same room as the tasters, not even covered. A quick peek even at the top of a bottle or a vague shape behind the wrapper can defeat the challenge at hand. Serve the wine to the tasters in glasses already poured in another area—the glasses in each flight must be identical and the pours equal.

Blind tastings can be a genuine education, and a challenge to your growing sensory acuity. Any sense of humiliation from making erroneous guesses will be lost in the benefits and pleasures. Besides, how do you humiliate a humble person?

❋ ❋ ❋

Glasses

First things first. When it comes to selecting glasses you need to keep firmly in mind the purpose of the wine event at hand. Is it a more serious, qualitative evaluation, a casual wine appreciation event, a wine, food, and friends gathering, or just you and a glass of good wine? In all cases, the glasses should be of basic, sound quality. They should be uncolored, crystal clear, and minus any of those lovely cut-glass patterns. They should be large enough (holding six to ten ounces), stemmed (to keep your fingerprints off the bowl), and tulip-shaped (the opening slightly smaller than the bowl), which acts to funnel the aroma and bouquet to your nose. That's the basics.

If you're doing a deliberate, qualitative assessment there are several important factors that need your attention:

1. the glasses used should be identical; different shapes emphasize different aspects of the wine;

2. if practical and affordable, use thin crystal glasses for clarity and feel;

3. the rim of the glass should be thin and not "rolled";

4. ample size, six to ten ounces, stemmed;

5. pour size: about one third of the glass volume; allows for adequate swirling and aeration;

6. the bowl of the glass should not be too tall; when shorter it allows your nose to get closer to the wine;

7. not a lengthy stem; better balance and stability;

8. the opening should comfortably allow your nose to enter the glass, but not be so wide that it allows a lot of "outside" air to be breathed in as you inhale the aromatics.

153

Glass Design

The wine glass has come a long way from the earthenware and pewter goblets of the 16th century. With the advent of crystal in the early 1800's the appreciation of wine seemed to explode. A greater awareness and appreciation of colors, aromatics, and clarity became possible.

Since the mid 1980's a handful of wine glass producers have created a mild stir within the wine trade and among connoisseurs. Glassmakers have commercialized a fairly new idea (it began in the 1950's with Claus Riedel).

By altering the shape of the glass, it is claimed, you can accentuate, even change, the character of the wine, theoretically producing a vessel which is "best" for that wine style. Others claim that glasses shaped in such a way enable them to spotlight the merest shadow of a fault. Do these claims hold water, or better yet, wine?

Many sectors of the wine trade could be heard "oohing" and "aahing" as they discovered that yes, glass shape can alter our perceptions of wine, sometimes profoundly. When the impact of this revelation dies down somewhat, a few more pertinent questions will become apparent, such as, Is this really good or bad? How does it impact on consistent wine evaluation, so necessary for qualitative tasting? Is it fair to assess wines— whose very structure and character may be so different—when the glass accentuates one wine more effectively than the other? If glasses are so capable of "improving" a particular wine's aromatics, even its taste profile, does this mean each wine should have a uniquely designed glass to uplift its character? When so many differences in wines exist, why so few of these new, superior glass shapes? How can so few of these new glasses work so well with so many different wines?

Some of the claims made by these glassmakers border on the absurd. The bowl shape and lip of some of these vessels are said to be able to direct the wine to various parts of the tongue, so creating profound differences in taste. At first, that might sound almost reasonable, but try it yourself—try to hold any liquid on one part of your tongue for anything more than a fraction of a second. And, of course, you will discover upon reflection, people actually drink differently. Some seem to suck liquids in, others pour it down; there's the "sipper," the "guzzler," the "swisher," and you name it. Perhaps a line of glassware could be created to accommodate or get the best out of how we drink so individually.

Because this is a facet of wine that has not generated a lot of thought in the past, and I include those in the trade, we have been a

Figure 13: Glass design optimized for wine tasting

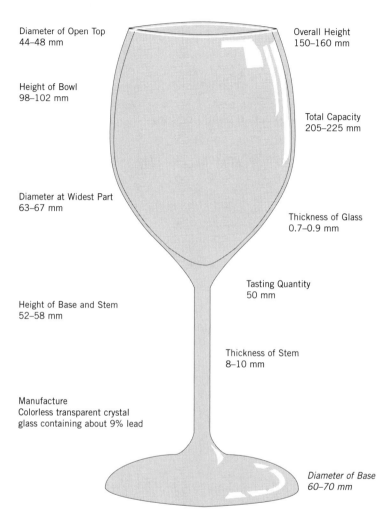

Diameter of Open Top
44–48 mm

Overall Height
150–160 mm

Height of Bowl
98–102 mm

Total Capacity
205–225 mm

Diameter at Widest Part
63–67 mm

Thickness of Glass
0.7–0.9 mm

Tasting Quantity
50 mm

Height of Base and Stem
52–58 mm

Thickness of Stem
8–10 mm

Manufacture
Colorless transparent crystal
glass containing about 9% lead

Diameter of Base
60–70 mm

Source:Based on International Standard ISO 3591-1977. Reproduced with permission of the International Standards Organization. Full details can be obtained from the ISO.

little more receptive to the "hustle" effect of some of these half-truths. Remember, these are glass salesmen talking.

There is no question that if you alter the shape and size of a wine glass you will have your perceptions changed. But temperature can do the same thing, even more forcefully.

To evaluate wines fairly and consistently, professional judges insist all wine be served at the same temperature. This uniformity should also be true of glasses. In test after test the glass that has accomplished this task most admirably has been the ISO or INAO glass (see Figure 13). It is the "level playing field" in the glass world. Not that it can't be improved, and I'm sure it will be in the near future, but it's the best we have for consistent wine evaluation, for now.

But when we turn to "drinking" wine, we obviously adjust the wine's temperature to accentuate the characteristics we personally like. That can also be true of glassware. Specific glasses will alter our perceptions of each wine, and that's fair. But keep in mind, the desirability of such changes will reasonably vary according to personal preference. Maybe we've discovered a new research exercise—have we taken all these new glass shapes and evaluated their effects on the same wine, but at different temperatures? Is nothing ever simple anymore?

Promoters of these marvelous and often fairly expensive drinking vessels frequently put to their audiences this rather loaded question: "Can one glass shape serve all wines equally?" Common sense might suggest, "of course not." However, when serious wine evaluation is the task at hand, there is only one answer: "It must!" If a variety of glasses are used, it is now the message bearer that has become more important than the message.

A Little Housekeeping

Purists suggest that washing crystal wine glasses should be done without any detergent. But after a while things won't stay very pure. To remove greasy fingerprints and lip marks (including lipstick) a little detergent is necessary. But several water rinsings should follow immediately, before any soap can dry on the surface. Dry and polish them with a lint-free cloth (linen, and so on.). Some authorities prefer to air-dry their glasses after the final rinse.

The purpose of all this fuss is to ensure there will be no taste or smell from residual detergent or soap. Some experts even go to the point of rinsing their glasses only in distilled water to avoid odors from some of the chemicals in tap water. Excessively hot water for washing or rinsing can needlessly stress fine crystal, even crack it.

If you use an automatic dishwasher, *beware* of some dishwasher detergents. That ingredient that makes the water sheet off the glasses so nicely, avoiding all those spots, can remain to create off odors and tastes. If you can, put the glasses through a couple of extra rinse cycles, minus the soap or rinse agents.

It is commonly thought that crystal glassware is too fragile to put through the automatic dishwasher. Most crystal producers say, "no problem." Indeed, good crystal is a lot tougher than we think. It is often stronger than plain glass. The real problem can often occur because of the weight of the glasses; they're so light, at times the pressure of the dishwasher's jet spray can bounce them around more easily. Keeping them a distance from the spray jets can solve that problem.

If you find yourself running short of glasses and it's not very practical to wash and dry them between samples, there is an alternative solution. Pour a half an ounce or so of the next wine to be tasted into the used glass, swish it around and pour it out. The glass is now conditioned for that wine to be sampled. Of course, you'll have to calculate if the wine loss may be enough to justify the purchase of additional glasses.

✹ ✹ ✹

Breathing

Opinions over "breathing" a bottle of wine certainly vary widely Discussions on the subject can get a trifle hot, as they say.

Experience has taught many winelovers that something changes in a wine that has been allowed to "breathe" awhile after the cork has been pulled and before you pour. Innumerable anecdotal experiences have been recounted in vivid detail, about the wine becoming so much "better" after several hours of breathing. "It was obvious," they say. "Everyone could tell the difference."

Wine researchers and scientists will invariably respond, "Rubbish! There's not enough air that can get to wine in a bottle after several hours of 'breathing' that could make any difference to the wine." In fact, that is true. Estimates put the rate of oxygen being dissolved into a wine breathing in bottle at about a milligram per liter, far from enough to make any appreciable change, they say. Twice as much oxygen is absorbed with the simple act of pouring it into the glass.

Yet, we would be unwise to totally dismiss what many a winelover has observed over a few centuries of wine-in-bottle experience. Something changes. It does! But the most salient question is, does it improve or lower the quality of the wine?

Most of the claimed improvements generated by "breathing" a wine is that it is "softer, less aggressive, having reduced the greenness and acid edge of the wine." Expressions of this nature are common. But again, is this better? Tasters who sit on the other side of the fence worry, with good reason, about what happens to mature wines. After perhaps years in bottle, developing the intricate and complex qualities of reductive ageing, could some of that be lost in those few hours of breathing? For me, I want to experience as many nuances in the aromatics as possible. If they "aerate" away they're gone forever.

So often the "wine improves with breathing" viewpoint is expressed without the benefit of direct comparison to the same wine tasted immediately after the cork has been pulled. So, what happens when direct comparisons are made?

The Same Wine

No breathing:
- a series of aromatics were more strongly noticed in the glass
- in the mouth it was livelier, fresher; more finesse and elegance

Allowed to breathe:
- less pronounced, more faded aromatics
- in mouth—less lively, more common; fuller and fleshier

Even among aficionados of breathing wine there is acknowledgement that aerating venerable, old wine is a no-no. Too many have sadly stood by and witnessed the decline and crash of an old wine. Some have even logged the experience by frequent taste evaluations completed every few minutes. Sometimes the nose-dive can be so rapid, it's over in a matter of minutes. Exposure to air can weaken and destroy these senior citizens so quickly. I once watched a 50-year-old Barolo collapse in glass in 15 minutes. When another glass was poured from the same bottle (which had been re-stoppered) it was still in marvelous shape.

But does this mean there are no legitimate reasons to breathe any wine? If you prefer the effects of the "Allowed to Breathe" list above, by all means go ahead. However, there are some other reasons that have to do more with correcting faults, or at least trying to. You may remember our mentioning earlier that unpleasant "reductive" odors (H_2S—hydrogen sulfide) can develop in bottle; a light gassiness (from a trace fermentation or a partial malo-lactic fermentation) can also occur. Aeration from breathing may help, even correct the fault.

※ ※ ※

Decanting

Certainly allied to the breathing issue is the practice of "decanting." Practitioners share a common belief in the power of air to somehow transform a wine from mediocrity to a higher realm. In the case of some not so pleasant, rather coarse and harsh wines, there may indeed be a case to be made. With those harsh edges peeled away, including a lot of the aroma and flavor (probably not so great in the first place), the wine may be a little easier to swallow.

Some winelovers have even suggested that exposure to air is a means of speeding up the maturation process. "While not exactly the same," they say, "it gives you an idea of what the wine will be like when it reaches maturity."

The error in this logic is trying to equate oxidative ageing (air contact) to reductive ageing (without air when in bottle). In reality they are completely different. To generate that exposure to air, decanting (pouring it from bottle to decanter) is prescribed. Even more radical treatment is advocated at times—pouring the wine back and forth between containers several times. I guess the objective is to "force-feed" the wine some oxygen.

While some evaporation certainly occurs there is no chemical reaction taking place that would account for any alteration to the wine, other than getting rid of some "bottle stink" (SO_2, H_2S, and CO_2 odors). Since wine doesn't oxidize that quickly, certainly not the "hefty" reds that are the very wines so often said to need this treatment, such views are on shaky grounds.

Again, tests using laboratory conditions have been applied to a wide range of wines varying in stature, variety, and age. Wines freshly opened were paired in blind tastings with wines that had been exposed to various contact times with air. What did the tasters conclude?

Identical Wine

Aerated/Decanted:
- changes were noted
- some intensity of aroma lost; bouquet gone
- soft to dull tactile sensation (variations noted due to exposure times)
- in a rare few wines the loss of nose was more than compensated for by the softer mouth-feel
- was generally disliked by the tasters

Freshly Opened:
- retained fruit and bouquet
- no change in body or structure
- you have to live with what you sense when the bottle is freshly opened
- strongly preferred over almost all aerated wines

The legitimate reason for decanting any wine has remained the same for a few centuries—sediment. A number of wines, as already discussed, will have a sediment that can detract from the pleasure that wine has to offer. The decanting procedure may even require a fine gauze to act as a filter. But the results are worth the time and effort.

One other sound reason can justify the procedure known as decanting: esthetics. Some decanters are breathtakingly beautiful. They grace a table as no wine bottle ever could. If you prefer wine poured from a decanter, do it. It offers a gracious note of civility, too often lost by a generation in pursuit of the "casual."

If you're going to decant, do so just prior to serving the wine. Not only for the reasons we've just outlined, but a health factor could be involved. Research in the late 1980's raised a cautionary note concerning the lead content of both lead crystal decanters and glasses. With time, dangerous levels of lead can be leached from the decanter into those precious liquids we savor so appreciatively.

But there's no reason to panic. It takes time. Unless you were to leave the wine in the decanter for days or weeks, there's no worry and no reason to discard or relegate what may be a family heirloom to the status of curio. As for lead crystal glasses, they're of even less concern. Though many have a 24 or 30 percent lead content, wines spend such a short time in contact with the glass it's of no significance. So, there's no need to pass your china cabinet with a suspicious glance at the crystalware.

Crystal can be produced without lead, and more and more glassmakers are doing just that. Some of the world's most renowned crystal producers are now making lead-free crystal. With a little care and attention to detail, the lead crystal you may now own can be used just as safely.

☙ ☙ ☙

Ullage

When experienced winelovers purchase, or select from their own collection, wines of advanced age, the word "ullage" is of major concern to them. Perhaps more than any other single factor it can indicate the health of that wine, without the need to actually pull the cork.

Figure 14: Ullage in Bordeaux-style bottles

Figure 15: Ullage in Burgundy-style bottles

Ullage is the space between the bottom of the cork and the surface of the wine. It can vary considerably. It can range from almost "cork tight" to being several inches away from the cork.

The causes of poor ullage can include low-quality cork, which loses its elasticity and its tight seal; a natural contraction of the original fill level; poor cork insertion at the time of bottling; temperature changes that cause the cork to expand and contract; low humidity, allowing the cork to dry out and shrink, breaking the seal; a bug called a cork weevil boring holes in it.

For whatever reason, as the wine either evaporates or seeps out, air is pulled in to replace the loss of liquid. The wine, depending on its vigor, will oxidize eventually and will, with enough time in this state, turn to vinegar. Wines 50 years and older can typically present this range of ullage.

Ullage in wines sold in high-shouldered, Bordeaux-style bottles are easier to judge. High-fill: Excellent. Top shoulder: Good. Mid-shoulder: normal fill at this age. Low shoulder: risky business.

The slope-shouldered, Burgundy-style bottle is not as easy to judge. It's more difficult to assess how much wine has been lost. To make it even more challenging, the modern reality is that there are many bottles "like" Bordeaux and Burgundy that have longer or shorter necks and different slopes to the shoulder. It takes a practiced and experienced eye to judge well.

Evaluation Systems

As you may have surmised by this point wine is a field of endeavor, a topic of interest, an avocation (in both of its definitions) that is riddled with controversy. I'm not suggesting that it's negative, destructive controversy, because generally it is dialogue that is constructive and beneficial to an increased understanding and appreciation of wine as a part of life. Granted, the debates get rather heated at times, but rarely bitter.

We are about to enter a corner of the wine arena that generates great emotion amongst connoisseurs of wine, among the wine media, educators, marketers, and winemakers—in other words, with almost anyone who has more than a passing or casual interest in wine. Numerical wine evaluation systems—scoring systems! For some, only a verbal description will do. They charge that putting a number to a wine (whether out of 20 or 100 points) is misleading.

Viewpoints seem to be sharply divided about this subject, with little middle ground. I will not attempt to be a mediator, for I am firmly of one opinion. However, I have noted that many of the differences seem to be based on a misunderstanding of the basic terms of reference.

Often—too often, sad to say—opponents of numerical evaluation systems seem to know little about how or why such a system is supposed to work. This results in absurd claims and charges against all such methods of evaluating wine, at times even against the tasters who use them. Commenting on the issues involved can't be avoided, but it would be good to first understand some of the various approaches to wine assessment.

Depending upon the source you use, there seems to be a variety of approaches to the variety of approaches. There are "discrimination" assessments, "descriptive" judgments, and "affective" approaches. There are different scales to be applied—"nominal," "ordinal," and "ratio" scales. There are highly "empirical" philosophies and purely "analytical" judgments. And there are "flat out" "hedonic" approaches, the "I like it or I don't like it, and how much I do or don't" systems similar to those methods used to assess manufactured foods. This is based on the theory that quality is founded on popular opinion. With wine, of course, there is no such given relationship to popularity. Statistical analysis is then applied to most of these systems to eliminate the possibility of chance.

After reviewing so many of these approaches I was drawn to how an eminent French scientist and wine researcher, Professor Emile Peynaud, expressed it:

> I have examined a wide range of literature in great detail in an attempt to discover just what statistical calculation could contribute to the work of a wine-taster. I would be the first to be interested if it improved my work or made my task any easier. But this method has few possible applications in daily winetasting because the problems posed by comparisons between wines are simple and can generally be resolved by common sense.

Somewhere in between the "empirical" and the "analytical" there must be a way to apply the analytic and descriptive in a manner that both measures and assesses. I believe there is, and that that balanced approach is expressed in a number of numerical evaluation systems. But of course, that comes nowhere close to settling the arguments. What kind of numerical system works best?

A quick look at just some of these systems (see Appendix B) will give you an idea of the diversity of approaches employed, even within the context of using numerical scoring systems. However, I believe it would be an error to view these approaches as just expressions of preference.

Sensory evaluation is every bit a scientific discipline. Using human sensory tools is much like using any other instrument. It has a methodology, a means of measurement (how intense is it, how sweet is it, and so on.), and the most powerful computer known (your brain) to do the analytical work. Referencing these perceptions to numbers is really codifying the relationship between humans and wine. It requires a unique approach.

There's no question about it—translating sensory impressions into numbers is a tricky job, not for the faint-hearted or indecisive. Popular systems include point scales of 0–5 (Germany), the 9-point "Quartermaster" scale recommended by the ASTM, the Beverage Testing Institute's 14-point system, University of California Davis's 20-point method, and the increasingly popular 100-point evaluation systems. There are several more in between the 20- and 100-point scales. Yet, it's not the numbers that are so important but the way in which you reach those numbers.

I will not, on this occasion, even attempt to critique the various evaluation systems. However, I will happily confess to being an ardent supporter of a 100-point system. You may have discerned that I said *a* 100-point system—not *all*. There are 100-point systems, and 100-point systems. It has taken over 20 years of constant revision to establish the current 100-point InterVin Numerical Evaluation System (see Appendix B). It is the one I use as a private winetaster and the one used for the InterVin Wine Competition.

Regardless of which system you use, there are a few, very basic, fundamental principles that must drive any system of numerical evaluation. When those who challenge the numerical concept pressure you for some justification, start by reminding them that it is highly unlikely any numerical system would ever have been developed if words had proven to be sufficient for the task.

The basic principles behind any numerical evaluation system should

1. follow the natural sequence our human senses dictate— *visual—olfactory—tactile—taste*;

2. avoid large numerical ranges for one evaluation—it's impossible to consistently assess a range of 20 or 30 points, as some systems assign to one element such as taste, for example;

3. not assign any element in a wine only a "0" or "1" value—no factor is so simple that it's either good or bad;

4. eliminate as many subjective judgments as possible;

5. recognize that not all elements are of equal "weight"—for example, the value of acidity to a wine is of greater weight than the "surface condition" in our visual assessment;

6. acknowledge that assessments that judge the intensity of an element (sweetness, body, and so on.) are not linear (the more the better approach)—allowance must be made for the style the winemaker has chosen (i.e., light, elegant vs. big, assertive);

7. not allow the imposition of regional criteria upon a wine—some wines would be "typically" great, if they're of typical poor quality.

Despite all of the human variations in taste, sensitivity, and perception, a good numerical system can extract an amazing level of harmony from its users.

The 100-Point System

Perhaps no other wine evaluation system has come under greater fire than the 100-point system. One of its strongest proponents, the internationally known taster Robert Parker, Jr., has certainly borne the brunt of the attacks in the wine media.

So, what are the common complaints from those who prefer to use only word descriptions to assess wine? I don't include among this group those journals that employ such subterfuge as three- or five-star evaluations. This is obviously a numerical system; it's a shame they don't have the spine to put the number there. But it does seem to satisfy a great many who think numbers should not be used.

Let's address some of the popular objections and accusations.

The 100-point system identifies and measures only the faults of the wine under scrutiny. I have problems even understanding this complaint, let alone the fact it's so far removed from the truth. The vast majority of the assessments in a "century" system measure the positives. Of course, faults have to be identified and factored into the equation.

This kind of system adds up all the individual ratings to reach a score. What this can do is allow a really bad element to be hidden and go unidentified. You could never tell by just a number. Wrong! Any good 100-point system will allow any single factor (e.g., oxidized) to completely halt the evaluation, if it is serious enough. A wine with such a fault wouldn't be given a final score.

The focus on numbers diverts attention from the true appreciation of the wine's quality. I don't agree. The way the number is achieved is the important factor. The number simply places it in perspective.

Numbers shouldn't be the guide used to purchase wine. This is usually a recommendation from someone who is selling wine. Though many wine merchants have highly respected tasting abilities and reputations, and despite the fact we are reminded that in making their choice of wines to sell means they have to "put their money where their mouth is," we also need to remember that once a merchant has "put his money where his mouth is" he is tempted to then "put his mouth where his money is." Also keep in mind that numbers alone should not be used to guide your purchasing decisions. They are an indication of the general quality, but may have little or nothing to do with whether or not you will like the wine.

The 100-point system doesn't take into account the price of a wine. Fortunately not! And when you think about it, it shouldn't. A numerical assessment is the result of a detailed evaluation of the innate quality that exists in that bottle, something that is determined by sensory analysis alone. Price is determined by the marketplace. Price is a business strategy based on economic realities, at least that's how it's supposed to work. Value is extremely important to consumers today, and is perceived as a relationship between cost and how much you enjoy a wine. On the other hand pricing is often an expression of how much someone else thinks you'll enjoy it. Consumers can quickly perceive the value of a wine. When two wines rate closely in numbers, but are divided by several dollars on the price tag, it doesn't take a mental giant to perceive where the value is.

To get higher scores you have to make wines that are big, tannic, oaky—monster wines. Nonsense. Any well-thought-out system is not linear. Bigger doesn't mean better. The system makes allowance for stylistic variations—from elegant and restrained, to powerful but balanced. In fact, excesses would cause a loss of points.

Rating systems like the 100-point approach encourage an homogenization of wine styles. Unless wines fit the

judges' formula they suffer on the point scale. Really, the opposite is true. Again, a good system gives no points for typicity. Minus the regional biases and tradition, winemakers are considerably freer to express themselves, without being fettered by standards that can only serve to stifle their creativity. What such an evaluation system does not do is allow regional tradition to substitute for quality.

Such systems do not encourage wine consumption or enjoyment. It puts wine on a numbers pedestal. To evaluate any wine you must take it off the pedestal and taste it. That's the only way it can work. I can't even imagine someone who is guided through his local wine shop, the score charts of the pundits in hand, who buys all that wine and doesn't drink it. Though consumers are missing so much when they buy only by the numbers, at least they're buying.

One thing we must realize about numerical systems of this nature is that they are not new. Humans have been evaluating things with numbers for a long time. Ironically, many of the experts and wine writers who have railed so long and loud about "the numbers" in essence use numerical systems in different guises all the time. The numbers may not be printed, but that's what is really being expressed. Whether it's a chart or stars, it's numbers.

After all, what is the alternative? Word descriptions, they say! It is true, words can detail some things numbers cannot. But having read so many of these written wine descriptions for 20 years or so, I dare say the numbers often describe more reality than the words. If we have problems relating to numbers in terms of precision, try to draw a consensus with words. After listening to some long and windy pontification on what a wine tasted and smelled like, I've often wanted to stand up and shout, "But how good is it?"

The simple fact is, when you assess a wine numerically you are not simply pulling numbers out of a hat. To do it correctly you must use your complete sensory abilities to reach a numerical conclusion. Winetasters long ago discovered a need for something more than a ranking of wines (setting a single flight of wines in order of preference or perceived quality). Unless a wine was in that flight you have no idea of its comparative stature. So there was a need for a system that possessed a means by which the taster could transpose the results of one tasting to another—and that's precisely what a numerical evaluation system does.

He wasn't speaking of wine, but Lord Kelvin's learned view certainly applies. He observed, "When you can measure what you are speaking about and express it in numbers, you know something about it, but when you cannot measure it, when you cannot express it in numbers, your knowledge is of a meagre and unsatisfactory kind; it may be the beginning of knowledge, but you have scarcely, in your thoughts, advanced to the stage of science." Remember, the number is only a symbol, a reference to what you have learned from a detailed sensory evaluation.

☆ ☆ ☆

Wine Competitions—Their Value and Goals

Statistics vary, but give or take a few thousand labels, some 500,000 wine brands seek your financial support. And that doesn't count the different vintages of the same wine that may be on the shelves at the same time. That's fair! That's free enterprise. But which labels will you choose? How will you decide to spend your wine dollars? Personal experience is invaluable. But individually sorting out the great, the ordinary, and the undrinkable is an awesome prospect, delightful but highly impractical.

There is, of course, no shortage of "expert" opinion that can be tapped. New wine books flood the market each year. Most major newspapers carry a wine column, even a handful of wine magazines are making a go of it.

Very much a part of all this vinous journalism are wine evaluations, the judgments of experienced tasters. Although the experts are occasionally at odds in their assessment of a given wine, it is rare for a truly "great" wine to be controversial with regard to its quality. Wine writers, as it turns out, are generally pretty good winetasters. But they're human! They're influenced by such variables as the time of day, ambiance, personal mood, their health, the nature and number of the wines to be sampled, and their individual palate bias. Illustratively speaking, what is presented by the expert's individual wine judgments is a series or collection of different snapshots, spanning a period of time. Fair!

But what is really more desirable is an opportunity for a "group photograph"—the tasting and evaluation of many wines, at the same time, under identical circumstances, by the same group of experts. This scenario should present a more balanced, insightful, and accurate evaluation. Not perfect, but few things are.

This is no doubt, the guiding principle behind most modern wine competitions. Different philosophies will vary the goals and to some degree the results. There are regional, state, national, and international wine competitions. They are all, in essence, qualitative tastings, an attempt to identify wines that excel, wines that demonstrate that something extra, either in sheer quality or in good value.

The Goals

The objectives of a wine competition are quite simple:

1. to fairly evaluate the wines consumers will be exposed to in the marketplace;

2. by its healthy competitive spirit to stimulate winemakers to strive for ever greater accomplishments whether simple and ordinary, quality affordable wines or those rare treasures we squirrel away to savor at just the right moment.

Who Enters Wine Competitions?

As the director of an international competition (InterVin International), I can assure you virtually every quality level conceivable enters wine competitions. The suggestion that truly fine and great wines ignore such "mundane" events is simply untrue.

There are, of course, some estates that have a policy of not entering any competition. The reasons are best defined by themselves. Many of the truly great wines do, in fact, participate in wine competitions. They will, quite naturally, want to be assured that the event is well run and fairly judged. If that is genuinely the case, there is little chance that their quality will be overlooked or misjudged.

Wine competitions certainly appeal to wineries that have yet to establish their credentials with the consumer or within the trade. Wine medals go a long way to achieve recognition with both. If the competition has a trusted reputation, an indication on the bottle that a medal has been won has an interesting effect—it sells wine. When a shelf of Chardonnays faces a weary shopper, that publicized medal may indeed be the factor that determines the choice of purchase.

A Competition Secret

Gold medals are usually the major award in most wine competitions. They identify the "top rung" of the wine ladder, so to speak. Very close behind are the silver and bronze medals.

At times the marks between these award levels is quite narrow. But as some winery people admit, it's tough to market a silver or bronze medal. We live in a society that believes in the "go for the gold" principle. Rarely are second and third place winners remembered, no matter how close they were to winning the gold.

However, in terms of wine winners, a great many bargains can be found among the ranks of silver and bronze. The line that differentiates them can be marginal. The smart wine buyer can at times obtain truly fine wines at very reasonable prices by searching for the silver and bronze medal winners. In reality, the silver or bronze award may distinguish a wine that is simply too young; its potential may be enormous, yet to be realized.

Chapter 9

Tuning Up Your Senses

SENSIBLE exercise tones up the muscles, increases your stamina, and generally improves your physical well-being. At least that's what it's supposed to accomplish; for some I'm not always certain that's the case.

At any rate, tuning up your senses can be even more rewarding when it comes to winetasting, as there are some very simple, basic exercises well worth the effort.

We are, to a degree, limited in exercises here to those that are practical for home use. Color evaluations are limited to our identifying different color intensities, not tints or hues. All the other facets of tasting will have to be gained by direct experience with the wines involved. Novice and seasoned taster will both benefit from these exercises.

I am purposely going to keep this as simple as possible, as much for my benefit as yours.

Please note: These exercises are not intended to represent an experiment of a laboratory nature. They are simply home experiments designed to test and improve your wine senses.

※ ※ ※

Triangle Test

Our sensitivities are affected, positively and negatively, by a great many outside influences. Some days we just don't function very well, our sensory acuity seems to have taken a vacation. How can we know when this happens, preferably without finding out the hard way?

A simple triangle test can often let us know if our senses are flashing the green light, or telling us, "Try again some time." Two glasses of one wine is poured, a single glass of another wine closely related is added to make the third. Identify which is which with tape or stickers placed underneath the foot of the glass. You are now required to identify which is the odd sample. Sounds simple, but it can usually tell you if your general level of sensitivity is low or if you're "hot." If you flunk, you may want to think seriously about whether you want to continue with the tasting exercises ahead of you or wait for a better time.

Sweetness

To test and exercise your sensory ability to detect residual sugar levels purchase a dry red wine that is fairly ordinary in nature, not overly strong in taste or price. You can repeat these tests using similar quality white and rosé wines.

Using granulated cane sugar, dissolve two teaspoons in six ounces of your selected wine. This will act as your base sweetener, so keep it in a separate container.

Now, pour two ounces of your selected red wine into four identical glasses. To one glass, add one teaspoon of the base sweetener, to the second glass add two teaspoons, to the third add four teaspoons. The fourth glass remains unadulterated.

At this point mark the glasses in some manner to identify which is which but in a way that is not evident while you are tasting. A simple method is to number pieces of masking tape 0 to 3 and stick them underneath the foot of the glass. Label the pure wine 0 and the others 1 to 3, from the lowest to the greatest amount of added base solution.

Now, while none of the tasters are watching, have some non-participant in the tasting re-arrange the glasses in a different order. By sampling each you are expected to place the glasses in their respective order of sweetness, from the one with no added sweetener to the sample with four teaspoons of the base sweetener solution.

To keep the fluid levels the same in each glass you may find it advantageous to mix up a large batch of each solution in a separate container, pouring equal amounts of each into the four glasses.

You can apply the same methodology to detect total acid, acetic acid (vinegar), and tannin to sharpen your sensory talents for these three elements.

❁ ❁ ❁

Acids

To achieve your base solution in a test for total acid, dissolve $1/4$ teaspoon of citric acid (available at your drugstore) in five ounces of your selected wine. Again, with four sample glasses of wine (two ounces in each) add one, two, and four teaspoons to three of the glasses, the fourth nothing, and repeat your attempts to arrange the glasses in proper order, from no additional acid to highest acid content, by tasting the samples.

To test your sensitivity to acetic acid, make a base acid solution from one tablespoon of red wine vinegar added to five ounces of wine. Once more, using four sample glasses of wine (two ounces in each), add one teaspoon of the base acid solution to one glass, two teaspoons to a second, and four teaspoons to the third glass. Now, once more into the breach to see how your senses react.

❁ ❁ ❁

Tannins

This test for tannins has a CAUTION to it. DO NOT make your base tannin solution for this test too far ahead of time (do it just before the test). Tannic acid can hydrolyze in time to a TOXIC acid. A further precaution would be to ask your tasters not to swallow these samples.

If the foregoing hasn't frightened you off, the test goes much the same as the others. To get your base tannin solution dissolve $1/4$ teaspoon of tannic acid (available at your drugstore) in nine, repeat *nine* ounces of wine. To the four glasses of wine, this time each having three ounces of wine in them add one teaspoon to one glass, two to a second, and four to the third; the fourth as is, of course.

A safer, but less effective solution uses a $1/4$ tsp. of grape tannins (available at home wine supply stores) mixed with neutral-grain spirit or vodka, about one ounce. Add it to about nine ounces of wine for your base.

It becomes very obvious you can alter the selection of these dosed glasses in a variety of ways to make a more complex test. Selecting a sample from each different test (with the exception of the one for tannin) to see if you can distinguish which was dosed with which provides an added challenge. We'll leave all the potential combinations to your imagination and adventuresome spirit.

We've already discussed the interaction of wine components. They can mask, neutralize, enhance, multiply, and alter one another. To help you experience some of these effects you can mix the samples already prepared in a variety of instructive ways. Try sweetness and acid by adding a drop or two of alcohol (neutral vodka) to the sweetness samples. You will discover the role it can play in our sweetness perception. Avoid using the tannic acid solutions.

To identify your mouth's individual taste geography you can use cotton swabs soaked in each solution. Touch them to various spots on your tongue and mouth and note your various sensitivities.

🐜 🐜 🐜

Visual

For a color density test simply cutting the wine with increased amounts of water will give you sufficient exercise in this area.

🐜 🐜 🐜

Olfactory

A rather elementary test for aroma can be made using concentrated apple juice, the type you find in cans in the frozen food section of your supermarket. Using a white wine add one teaspoon of undiluted apple concentrate to one glass containing three ounces of white wine, two to the second and four to the third. One glass remains unadulterated, of course. Now, after confusing the order using only your nose, re-arrange them in the correct order from zero to three.

To set up for a sulfur test create a base solution of water (one liter) to ¼ teaspoon of potassium metabisulphite (available at winemaking supply stores). To glasses with six ounces of wine add ⅛ teaspoon, ¼ teaspoon and ½ teaspoon of the base; one glass at zero, of course. Sniff on!

🐜 🐜 🐜

Further Tests

It is uncertain whether a winetaster's talents are inborn or learned. We might reasonably suspect a little of each. Whichever, these exercises will quite definitely tune up your senses, and most important will give you a better idea of what you are looking for in normal winetasting. They can also help you to identify any personal disfunction that would seriously affect your winetasting endeavors. Quite naturally, depending upon the number of tasters sharing these experiments, you'll have to expand your quantity of basic test material.

There are also a number of additional, very simple tests you can set up for yourself and a few wineloving friends. Learning to identify grape variety is one very important exercise.

By purchasing several bottles of varietal wines (wine made exclusively from one variety of grape), like Cabernet Sauvignon, Pinot Noir, Merlot, Gamay, Chardonnay, Riesling, Sémillon, Sauvignon Blanc, Chenin Blanc, and so on, you can group similar types together and practice identifying the individual types.

Label the glasses again under the foot and have a neutral party arrange the order. From this simple test you will begin to appreciate the qualities that identify the classic wine-making grapes. Be certain to make notes.

From this point you can progress to identifying some of the famous wines that are blends of two or more grapes, like some of the wines from Bordeaux, Chianti, Châteauneuf du Pape, Côtes du Rhône, Valpolicella, Spain's Rioja wines, Graves, Soave, and so on. Then, break them down by countries of origin to see if you can identify certain regional and national characteristics.

Remember, try not to do this alone—invite some friends to join your experiments. It's much more rewarding and pleasant to share the experience. Sharing the cost is not a bad idea either.

With each experiment and each wine, your sensitivity and love of good, honest wine will blossom. The dividends are myriad.

Chapter 10

A Few Grapes and a Little Wine

AN estimated eight thousand grape varieties are currently under cultivation. Fewer than twenty are considered classic.

To attempt to provide a comprehensive description of all these grape varieties and their wines is a monumental, a life-time undertaking. The following guide is obviously not such an attempt. (You might want to obtain a copy of Jancis Robinson's *Vine, Wines & Grapes.*)

However, to limit our considerations to just those classic jewels of the vineyard would be to shortchange winemaker and winelover alike. So, I have added a few more ordinary but popular types and a special section on hybrids.

My description of the characteristics for these wines is in the broadest varietal terms. Winemakers from region to region often have very different goals in mind when they select a particular grape. And many varieties offer the vintner the needed flexibility to allow them success in a number of directions. So we must be flexible to the same degree in our judgments.

And neither is this an attempt to establish the "pecking order" for the top winemaking grapes. Many of the wines you will make acquaintance with in the years to come are duly represented here, but not in any suggested or intimated order of merit.

Don't stop here, though. Carry on with your personal wine investigations. Vintage variations, lands of origin, soils, climate (macro and micro), winemaking philosophies, clonal selection, fermentation technique, and age all exercise enough influence on each wine to make it profoundly different.

Get to know as much as possible about each wine you drink by additional reading. You'll be a better judge and a more knowledgeable lover of wine.

❧ ❧ ❧

Varietal Freedom

A great many voices have expressed concern about the world-wide proliferation of the "big four"—Cabernet Sauvignon, Chardonnay, Pinot Noir, and Sauvignon Blanc. Fears are often expressed that lesser known varieties, particularly some rare, virtually unknown ancient, regional varieties, will be washed away in a tide of Chardonnay and Cabernet.

The concerns are legitimate, but need to be refocused. Expectations that a small producer in an old, traditional wine zone should ignore the popularity and profits connected with the big four is unrealistic and unfair. The big four are so popular, not only because of fickle, international trends and the intensity of promotion on their behalf, but because of quality. They are at the top of the varietal sales ladder because they can be so good.

Economically, it is a tempting situation for a small, unknown winery to rip out vines that may indeed be unique and distinctive and replant them with varieties that are better known and sell. And the simple reality may be these older vines yield poor quality, difficult-to-sell wines. From a winemaker's point of view, to continue making barely marketable wines so that a few jaded palates can try something different once in a while is not sufficient reason to go bankrupt.

A compromise should be encouraged. Allow producers the privilege of making whatever wines that can sell, without condescending, sarcasms such as, "Oh, not another Chardonnay!" When such enterprises remain financially viable, they can be encouraged (with the resources now available to them) to preserve, even promote, ancient regional varieties that truly possess not only unique character, but have the framework of genuine quality to support them.

Please note: The term "Wine Colors" used in this list refers to the normally expected color range influenced by style and/or age.

✳ ✳ ✳

Vinifera White Varieties

Grape Variety: Albarino

Wine Colors: pale, silver/green.

Nose: intense floral with pear, apple and citrus with mineral undertones.

Taste: light to medium-body, brisk, high-tartish acidity, with unusually long finish.

Wines: Riax Baixas and other regions from Galicia in north-eastern Spain, and from the Vinho Verde region of northern Portugal.

Comments: Increasingly important and expensive white wines in Spain now finding a large market in North America. Some link its origins to the Riesling grape as it has similar characteristics.

Grape Variety: Aligoté

Wine Colors: pale yellow to faint gold

Nose: pleasant, undistinguished, nutty at times

Taste: dry—good acidity—moderate length

Wines: appellation whites in France's Burgundy region—varietals

Comments: probably a native of Burgundy—not usually much body—losing ground in France—planted in Bulgaria, Romania, Russia, and Canada—quite prolific

Grape Variety: Chasselas

Wine Colors: light yellow to full yellow

Nose: low, undistinguished, faint smokiness

Taste: neutral—some fruit—lots of alcohol

Wines: Fendant in Switzerland, Gutedel in Germany

Comments: perhaps the oldest cultivated variety known—sometimes petillant—grown also in New Zealand—also known as Viala

Grape Variety: Chardonnay

Wine Colors: pale yellow/green to yellow to golden

Nose: smokey, fruity bouquet—difficult to describe—butter—tropical fruit, appley, nutty, vanilla (from oak contact)

Taste: austere, steel-like, dry, rich mineral flavor—pineapple, tropical fruit, melon—nice long finish and pleasant acidity in quality versions—occasionally buttery, nutty in richer versions—lean to full bodied

Wines: famed white Burgundies like Chablis, Montrachet, Meursault, varietals in California and now most wine-producing countries

Comments: medium-bodied wines that change character from region to region—not a true Pinot grape—blended with other grapes to produce real Champagne, Beaujolais Blanc, Macon Blanc, and many simple Bourgogne Blancs—popular and excellent varietal in California—grown also in Australia, Canada, New Zealand, Romania, South Africa, Russia—can age well—also known as Beaunois, Weisserburgunder

Grape Variety: Chenin Blanc

Wine Colors: pale yellow/green to pale yellow to old gold

Nose: fruity, berry-like aroma, peaches, melon—light bouquet —waxy, lemony, ripe pear

Taste: thirst-quenching, fruity and spicy flavor—good sugar/acid balance—both dry and sweeter types—with age, a taste of almonds—moderate structure

Wines: white wines of Vouvray, Anjou, and Saumur in the Loire Valley of France, varietals, sparkling

Comments: often a full-bodied wine that does well in cooler climates—when produced by a cold fermentation it creates additional fruitiness—also grown in U.S.A., Ukraine, with small plantings in Australia and New Zealand as well as South Africa—can be aged—also known as Pineau de la Loire in France and as Steen in South Africa

Grape Variety: Colombard

Wine Colors: medium full yellow, occasionally greenish hints

Nose: apples, limes, melon, flowery

Taste: good alcohol and acids—light to moderate body

Wines: grown in Côtes de Blaye in Bordeaux area, Gascony, California, South Africa

Comments: blended in California generic "Chablis" and in South Africa's Stein (Colombar)—also used for brandy distillation in cognac and Armagnac

Grape Variety: Folle Blanche

Wine Colors: greenish yellow to yellow

Nose: some floweriness—moderately fruity

Taste: lean, light, acidic dry whites—light to medium body

Wines: Gros Plant in Loire, Picpoul in Southern France

Comments: superior variety for brandy distillation (disappearing)—some used in California white blends

Grape Variety: Furmint

Wine Colors: light to deep golden yellow

Nose: appley to honey with age

Taste: good alcohol level in table wines, tart—rich, old apple and honey with age

Wines: dry table wines to rich, viscous Tokaji in Hungary

Comments: a major component in Hungary's most famous white Tokaji (Tokay)—grown in small amounts in Austria and parts of former Yugoslavia (Dalmatia)

Grape Variety: Gewürztraminer

Wine Colors: pale, to medium yellow, to golden

Nose: intensely distinctive nose—grapey, herb-like aroma—flowery bouquet of roses and jasmine, lychee fruit, peach

Taste: distinctive spicy flavor with a touch of bitterness—soft, velvety and full-bodied—dry to sweet—decent acids—long flavors

Wines: varietals

Comments: Gewürztraminer is the more pronounced, distinctive, and aromatic strain of the Traminer grape—shows a tendency towards a lower acidity than Riesling, but often has some residual sugar—one of the oldest vines known—Alsace sets the standards for this type—known as Tremino Aromatico in Italy, the Formentin in Romania and Hungary, and is grown in France, Italy, Germany, Austria, Spain, Australia, New Zealand, Hungary, Romania, U.S.A., and Canada

Grape Variety: Grüner Veldiner

Wine Colors: light greenish yellow to yellow to gold

Nose: spicy, earthy, aromatics of green beans, lentils—bouquet of red pepper, nutmeg, honey

Taste: good fruit, dry, good acids—medium body

Wines: Gruener Veltliner (Austria), Veltlini (Hungary)

Comments: usually meant for early drinking—sometimes "spritzig"—almost always good, with some rare, great wines in dry and late harvest styles—small quantities grown in Czech Republic, California, and Hungary

Grape Variety: Marsanne

Wine Colors: straw, yellow, which deepens to gold with age

Nose: floral, spicy, somewhat tropical fruit scents, like lichee or starfruit. Often anise-like nose. With oak aging, smoky and vanilla notes are added

Taste: full-bodied, quite soft and rich in texture, with low acidity and higher alcohol. Powerful, long-finish and very complex

Wines: Hermitage (Rhône Valley), Varietal Marsanne wines increasingly from the Languedoc, the Goulbrun Valley in Victoria, Australia, and California

Comments: Growing rapidly from its home base in Northern Rhône Valley where historically it was blended with Roussane and barrel-aged to produce some of the longest-lived white wines of France. Age-worthiness also proven in Australia when produced from old vines and low yields.

Grape Variety: Müller-Thurgau

Wine Colors: pale yellow to gold

Nose: clean, fresh, fruity bouquet—spicy, floral, herb-like, but not as distinctive as Riesling

Taste: fruity, with a touch of Muscat flavor with a hint of nutmeg—not high in acid, a soft wine—dry to medium dry to very sweet

Wines: used in many German whites like Liebfraumilch with other grapes or by itself—varietals

Comments: one of the most widely grown grapes in Germany—grown in Alsace, Switzerland, Italy, Austria, Hungary, the Czech Republic, Slovakia, Slovenia, New Zealand, probably a self-cross of the White Riesling—does not generally take ageing too well, but will improve as yields are reduced and the vines are matched to ideal soils and micro-climates—also known as Riesling Silvaner and Rivaner

Grape Variety: Muscadet

Wine Colors: light greenish yellow to golden touches

Nose: light, floral—not complex

Taste: lean body—dry, acidic, musky flavor—moderate alcohol

Wines: Muscadets (or Melon) of Loire Valley

Comments: much of what is called Pinot Blanc in California is Muscadet—also called Weisserburgunder in Germany and Alsace.

Grape Variety: Muscat Blanc

Wine Colors: pale yellow to gold with occasional greenish tinge

Nose: floral, fruity, musky aroma often related to roses—intense, rich bouquet in some dessert versions

Taste: very pronounced musky flavor, a grapey overall characteristic—from very dry to very heavy dessert wines

Wines: Asti Spumante (Italy), Setubal (Portugal), Muscat d'Alsace, and the Muscatels of France, in Banyuls, Rivesaltes, Beaumes-de-Venise—extraordinary Australian dessert versions (Liqueur Muscats)

Comments: best example of the very large and ancient Muscat family of grapes—makes very dry table wines to quality dessert wines—grown in France, Spain, Portugal, Italy, Africa, South America, Australia, Greece, Russia, U.S.A., and Canada—also known as Frontignac, Moscato Bianco, Moscato D'Asti, Canelli, Muskateller, Brown Muscat

Grape Variety: Pinot Blanc

Wine Colors: pale yellow/green to yellow

Nose: flowery, fragrant aroma—bouquet, from light to fairly intense

Taste: subtle but distinct character—vivacious often tannic flavor, very difficult to describe, you'll just have to experience it—dry to sweet

Wines: varietals, Pinot D'Alsace, Pinot D'Alba and Borgogna Bianco (Italy)—sparkling wines—doing well in parts of Germany, Italy

Comments: a mutation of Pinot Noir—grown in most major wine countries—not to be confused with Chardonnay—adapts better to cooler climates—low in acid when grown in warmer regions—smooth, good body, ready soon—also known as Klevner, Pinot Bianco, Beli Pinot, Fehrburgundi

Grape Variety: Pinot Gris

Wine Colors: pale yellow/green to full yellow

Nose: pleasant, distinctive, flowery aroma and bouquet, but not very intense

Taste: smooth, fruity taste—slight bitterness in the aftertaste, some claim a hint of almonds; dry to medium dry; good alcohol; medium acid

Wines: varietals, Terlano and Pinot Grigio (Italy), Tokay D'Alsace (France), Szurkebarat (Hungary), Rulander (Germany)

Comments: distinctive, full-bodied wine, often lacking delicacy, but mellows when mature—genuine member of the Pinot family—occasionally a little dull from low acidity—grown in France, Italy, Germany (largest producer), Hungary, Switzerland, Austria, U.S.A., Canada

Grape Variety: Sauvignon Blanc

Wine Colors: pale yellow to gold

Nose: clean, fruity aroma of black currants, sometimes a distinctive grassy bouquet—often a touch of wood, asparagus, bell pepper, celery

Taste: often a pungent, spicy, almost vegetative taste—can be quite acidic at times—usually quite dry—some excellent late-harvest versions with hints of peach and apricot

Wines: white wines of the Loire such as Sancerre, Pouilly-Fume, the Fume Blanc of California, also a part of the blend for Graves, Sauternes, and Barsac in the Bordeaux region of France—varietals from New Zealand to Canada and everywhere in between

Comments: a very distinctive wine with a good long finish to it—somewhat coarse at times—often a crisp, acidic dry table wine—Barsac also known as Blanc Fume, Muskat-Silvaner, Fume Blanc.

Grape Variety: Scheurebe

Wine Colors: light yellow/green to golden

Nose: grapey, blackcurrant aroma; honey, some spice when mature

Taste: very fruity character; good acids, medium to dry to very sweet;

Wines: varietals in Germany, California, Canada

Comments: Sylvaner-Riesling cross; better when fully ripened and used in Auslese styles; among most successful of German crosses (1916, G. Scheu)

Grape Variety: Sémillon

Wine Colors: light yellow to deep golden

Nose: soft, herbaceous; a touch of tropical fruit and citrus; good alcohol, low acid; waxy, orange at maturity

Taste: soft, medium acids—good body and extract

Wines: varietals; major part of Graves and Sauternes, Barsac, Loupiac, etc.; also known as Chevrier, Green Grape (in South Africa), Hunter River Riesling (in Australia)

Comments: outside of Bordeaux does well in Australia's Hunter Valley, Washington State, bulk table wines in South America, New Zealand, Hungary, Romania—being appreciated more as a separate varietal

Grape Variety: Sylvaner

Wine Colors: pale yellow/green to yellow

Nose: bouquet and aroma similar to White Riesling but not as pronounced

Taste: similar to Riesling but more earthy, not as distinctive—lacks crispness—dry, to softly sweet—characteristic short finish (some exceptions)—is more distinctive when grown on chalky soils as in the Franconia district of Germany—medium dry to very sweet

Wines: varietals—blended in many Germany white table wines, occasionally labeled simply "Riesling" in California

Comments: best drunk young—a major variety in Germany (sometimes called Franken Riesling)—planted in Alsace, Hungary, Slovenia, Czech Republic where it changes character significantly and is called Zirfandler—also grown in northern Italy and U.S.A.—also known as Franken Riesling in U.S.

Grape Variety: Trebbiano

Wine Colors: pale lemon to pale gold

Nose: saffron-like aroma—not an intense bouquet

Taste: faint taste of almonds—medium-bodied, slightly astringent—dry to medium-sweet—good acids

Wines: a prominent part of the blend for Italian whites: Orvieto, Frascati, Marino, EST! EST! EST!, Gambellara, Lugana, Soave—also blended in Chianti—White Shiraz in Australia

Comments: the major white variety in Italy—grown in Southern France (Ugni Blanc)—now in small plantings in California—primary cognac and Armagnac grape— also known as Clairette in Southern France

Grape Variety: Viognier

Wine Colors: pale to deep golden yellow

Nose: rich, peach-like aroma—complex, herbal bouquet

Taste: crisp, herb-like—full-bodied, good extract

Wines: Condrieu, Château Grillet—allowed in red Côte Rotie—varietal in California, Australia, France's Ardeche, and Rhône

Comments: late ripening, low yield—northern Rhône—also now in Italy, U.S.A. (California, Colorado, Utah, Virginia)—in many ways lacks precise description

Grape Variety: Welschriesling

Wine Colors: pale yellow/green to pale yellow—golden in late harvest style

Nose: some very faint White Riesling floral characteristics— medium aromatic intensity

Taste: light, Riesling-like flavor with some bitterness in the finish characteristic short finish—dry to medium sweet—light body—solid acidity

Wines: varietals—Welschriesling (Austria, Romania), Riesling

Italico (Italy), Laskiriesling or Grasevina (Serbia, Slovenia), Olaszriesling (Hungary), Vlasky Riesling (Czech Republic)

Comments: not related to genuine White Riesling—thrives in Austria and Eastern Europe—better than its reputation (a common, ordinary wine) when handled properly—of unknown origin despite some theories

Grape Variety: White Riesling

Wine Colors: from very pale yellow/green to deep golds

Nose: fruity aroma (not grapey), clean, flowery, citrus—bouquet; very distinctive, honey, white truffles, peaches

Taste: crisp fruity acidity—good long finish, some claim a taste of orange blossoms with a touch of cinnamon—dry to very sweet —light to full-bodied

Wines: the classic white of Alsace, Moselle, Rhine—varietals in almost every country that grows grapes

Comments: The classic Riesling grape—light to medium body—from the very dry Alsatian varieties to the famous German dessert wines (Beerenauslese, Trockenbeerenauslese)—not usually high in alcohol (9–11 percent)—planted in almost every major wine land, where it retains some of its basic varietal character, with perhaps a unique regional character—does better in cooler climates like Germany, Alsace and northern California—has many imposters like Grey Riesling, Missouri Riesling, Italian Riesling (Welschriesling) which are not true Rieslings at all—many good crosses of this grape such as the Sylvaner (Franken Riesling), Müller-Thurgau, and the California cross, Emerald Riesling (with Muscadelle)—also known as Weisser Riesling, Rheinriesling, Klingelberger, Johannisberg Riesling, Rhineriesling

✳ ✳ ✳

Vinifera Red Varieties

Grape Variety: Barbera

Wine Colors: light to deep purple and ruby red

Nose: aroma of violets and cherries—distinctive berry-like bouquet

Taste: medium body, good acidity, prominent fruity flavor, dry

Wines: varietals primarily from Italy and California

Comments: best examples come from the Piedmont district in Italy—can be aged to a soft full wine in good years— good alcohol levels (12–13 percent)—a fruity wine maturing at 2–3 years of age—also grown in Argentina and Brazil

Grape Variety: Cabernet Franc

Wine Colors: dark red/purple to red/brown

Nose: more herbaceous than the Cabernet Sauvignon aroma—bouquet of violets, raspberries, blackcurrants, black pepper, cherry

Taste: similar to Cabernet Sauvignon, but not as distinctive— good acid content, astringent in youth, dry, can be both more and less tannic than Cabernet Sauvignon—but generally less body than Cabernet Sauvignon

Wines: Chinon, Bourqueil, Champigny of the Loire, many of the better rosés in that same French valley (e.g., Cabernet D'Anjou), a major grape used in Bordeaux especially for St. Emilion—varietal wines—also known as Breton, Bouchet, Carmenet

Comments: often stands in the shadow of the more reputed Cabernet Sauvignon—the finest rosés in the Loire come from this grape—not heavily grown outside of France—developing well in northern Italy—also grown in Eastern Europe and California

Grape Variety: Cabernet Sauvignon

Wine Colors: red/purple to mahogany (with age)—can reach great depth

Nose: pungent aroma of blackcurrants and cedar—full, complex bouquet, herbaceous, cassis, green pepper

Taste: warm, rich, often very tannic and harsh when young—a complex taste that improves with a touch of wood—dry—smooth, velvety texture at maturity with a long lasting flavor

Wines: major component of many of the great Bordeaux Chateaux, Clarets, varietals

Comments: greatest red wine grape—does best in Bordeaux and California—also grown throughout Eastern Europe, Italy, Spain, South Africa, Australia, New Zealand, Canada—varies in character somewhat from country to country, but keeps its basic qualities and nature—can be very different wines due to much blending with other wines (Merlot as an example)—often tremendous ageing ability (decades)

Grape Variety: Carignan

Wine Colors: deep purple

Nose: neutral, vinous, faint peppery fruit

Taste: harsh, tannic, some bitterness in finish

Wines: rarely a single varietal—bulk and jug wines—also known as Carinena and Mazuelo (Spain)

Comments: needs to be blended—major quantity varietal in Southern France—grown in California, North Africa, South America, South Africa, Israel, Spain, Sardinia

Grape Variety: Cinsault

Wine Colors: red/purple to brownish/red

Nose: light floral aroma that develops a better, more complex bouquet with more spice to it with some wood and age

Taste: soft and full-bodied—dry to medium dry—fine varietal character

Wines: important component in many wines from the South of France, like Châteauneuf-du-Pape, Minervois, Corbieres, Côtes du Rhône—the Hermitage of South Africa

Comments: a quality grape growing in importance in Southern France and South Africa (Hermitage)—also made into Roses and Ports—good depth of color

Grape Variety: Gamay

Wine Colors: light red/garnet to full red

Nose: fruity, aromatic berry aroma, cherry, raspberry

Taste: soft, fruity, refreshing taste—little or no bitterness or astringency—good acid balance—dry to medium dry

Wines: Beaujolais, rosés, varietals—Anjou Gamay

Comments: light, fruity red wine—not high in alcohol or extract—doesn't generally age well—best when young and slightly chilled—the Gamay-Beaujolais vine is actually a member of the Pinot family—both it and the true Gamay (Gamay noir a jus blanc) are grown in the Beaujolais region of France, California, Canada and in Eastern Europe—also found in the Loire, Switzerland, and in Valle d'Aosta in Italy

Grape Variety: Grenache

Wine Colors: purplish rose to pale brownish/red

Nose: perfumed, somewhat spicy aroma, can be light to very pronounced bouquet, often wood aged

Taste: medium body, not usually tannic or acid—fruity, grapey flavor —very dry to medium sweet

Wines: Tavel and other rosés of Southern France—varietals—Cannonau of Sicily

Comments: often a major component in many reds from Southern France (i.e., Châteauneuf-du-Pape) and Spain (Rioja and Navarra)—low pigment level is a major fault—native of Spain (Garnacha) used in many Rioja and Penedes wines—blended in Châteauneuf-du Pape, Côtes du Rhône, Fitou, Corbiere, Minervois and the famous dessert wine, Banyuls—grown in France, Spain, North and South Africa, Australia, Italy and California where it does particularly well

Grape Variety: Kadarka

Wine Colors: light to deep garnet red

Nose: spicy, fruity, leathery

Taste: good levels of alcohol, tannins—dry to sweet versions, solid body

Wines: light, dry table wines to sweet—varietal, Gamza, red Aszu

Comments: grown throughout Eastern Europe, some in Austria—from rosés to late harvest reds—called Gamza in Bulgaria, can age well

Grape Variety: Malbec

Wine Colors: deep, ruby garnet

Nose: fairly intense, plum and black cheeries, earthiness

Taste: full-bodied, fairly tannic, with fruit undertones

Wines: major red grape of Argentina where it is bottled solo and also used as a blend, and Cahors, France, and other southwest France wines

Comments: in Europe it is mainly a blending grape with Bordeaux varieties because it adds body and texture to the blends. Known as the Cot grape type in southwest France

Grape Variety: Merlot

Wine Colors: ruby red (occasionally slight orange reflections) to red/brown

Nose: fruity aroma of strawberries, cherries plums—herbaceous bouquet, good intensity, floral

Taste: a soft round flavor, a little thin but it has individuality—dry with good acid balance

Wines: important blending grape in Bordeaux—varietals in Italy, California, Eastern Europe, South America, Australia, New Zealand

Comments: does better in cooler climates—used in blends for its intense bouquet and softness—more important in the St. Emilion district of Bordeaux than in the Medoc—used widely in Pomerol—grown in France, California, Italy (5th most important vine), and in small amounts in most wine lands in the world—also known as Medoc Noir

Grape Variety: Mourvedre

Wine Colors: deep, opaque purple to black colors

Nose: intense, floral, with undertones of lavender, blackberry, black pepper and anise

Taste: very full-bodied, quite tannic, medium-long finish, can become more earthy and leathery with maturity

Wines: Bandol (Provence) where it dominates the blend, and in the reds of the Southern Rhône and Languedoc where it blends with the Syrah, Carignan and Granache

Comments: also called the Monastrell, the second most important red grape of Spain. Also labeled Mataro in California, and increasingly being bottled as a single varietal wine.

Grape Variety: Nebbiolo

Wine Colors: dark ruby red (with orange/yellow reflections) to mahogany

Nose: spicy aroma—aggressive bouquet, violets—tar-like tones—truffles

Taste: some say of olives, and mushrooms (I suspect they got too close to their antipasto)—full-bodied—tannic in youth, dry, velvety-smooth when mature—high in alcohol and acid—good, long finish

Wines: Barolo, Barberesco, Gattinara, Carema, Roero, Inferno, Donnaz. Ghemme, Valtellina reds—(the who's who of Northern Italian red wines), varietals in Uruguay, Switzerland, California

Comments: one of the truly superior red grapes—grown primarily in Italy—produces classy, well-balanced high quality red wines of great ageing potential—also known as Spanna and Chiavanesca

Grape Variety: Pinotage

Wine Colors: deep purple/red to garnet

Nose: assertive, spicy aroma—developing good complexity with age—some say "nail polish" nose, but is really amyl acetate

Taste: full-bodied, big wine—good acid balance—fruity, Cinsault-like taste—some bitterness in the finish—medium to long flavor

Wines: varietals

Comments: a cross of Pinot Noir and Cinsault (called Hermitage in South Africa)—the Pinot element removes some of the "hot climate" characteristics—developed and primarily cultivated in South Africa—Australia, New Zealand, Germany, and California are now experimenting with this variety

Grape Variety: Pinot Noir

Wine Colors: pale to deep burgundy red

Nose: aromas vary: raspberry, strawberry, beetroot—pronounced but elusive, difficult to describe, perhaps due to true grape aromas being so light they are overpowered by yeast aromatics and malo-lactic odors

Taste: elegant fruity quality—a distinctive penetrating flavor, not as tannic or dry as Cabernet Sauvignon—great breed and power—silk like smoothness when fully mature—full-bodied, dry—alcoholic

Wines: Burgundy—varietals worldwide—rosés—Champagne and/or a component of

Comments: does not age as long as Cabernet Sauvignon, varies depending on producer, vintage and storage—grown in France, Germany, Canada, Switzerland, Austria, Hungary, Romania, Bulgaria, Italy, South Africa, Australia, U.S. (Oregon, New York, California) where it is often heavier in color and flavor—also known as Spatburgunder, Noiren, Pinot Nero

Grape Variety: Sangiovese

Wine Colors: light to intense garnet/red, orangeish rim

Nose: fruity, strawberry—raspberry aroma—earthy, complex bouquet

Taste: bone-dry, a touch of bitterness, good length—moderate alcohol, good acids and tannins

Wines: Brunello, varietals—major component in Chianti, Carmignano, Vino Nobile, Torgiano

Comments: can be found as vino novellos, to light vin ordinaires, to some of Italy's most serious reds—great variations often due to clonal selections—a.k.a. Sangioveto, Brunello, Prugnolo

Grape Variety: Syrah

Wine Colors: pale ruby to garnet and deep almost black/red to red/brown

Nose: aroma of raspberries, blackberry, cassis, and pepper—distinctive bouquet at maturity, cedar-like, full, smokey

Taste: very tannic in youth, matures quickly—truly a big wine, good acid balance, dry—mellows to a smooth full-bodied rich wine at maturity

Wines: Hermitage, Crozes Hermitage, Cornas, St. Joseph, Shiraz of Australia, some true Syrah varietals, major part of Côtes Rotie

Comments: rough, coarse, tannic in youth—one of the 13 grapes used in Châteauneuf-du-Pape—now grown in Provence, Midi, California, Argentina, South Africa— a.k.a. Sirah, Hermitage, Shiraz

Grape Variety: Tempranillo

Wine Colors: medium-depth to full deep ruby red

Nose: slightly perfumed fruit aroma—more complex, flowery, cedary bouquet, a touch of licorice

Taste: medium soft structure, low acidity—solid tannins, mod alcohol—good length

Wines: Ribera del Duero—major component in Rioja, Navarra, Valdepenas, Pesquera, Vega Sicilia—varietal in California

Comments: a major quality red grape variety of Spain, but often blended with other varieties—now grown in France, Portugal, Argentina, California—a.k.a. in Spain as Ull de Llebre, Tinto Fino, Cencibel, and Tinta Roriz and Aragonez in Portugal

Grape Variety: Zinfandel

Wine Colors: pale yellow, to rose, to deep ruby/red, to inky garnet black

Nose: prominent fruity, berry-like aroma—some claim aroma of bramble, wild blackberry—full distinctive, complex bouquet, raisiny at times

Taste: full-flavored, can be very tannic, with the berry-like flavor—dry to very sweet

Wines: White Zinfandel, Zinfandel Rosé, red varietals—late harvest dessert wines and Port style fortifieds

Comments: known in old Yugoslavia as Plavac or Plavina— California classic—Primitivo of Italy—varies widely in nature and quality in different regions—from the rare rich white to the fresh, dry and fragrant roses and blushes, to light and big reds—better quality reds take ageing well—late-harvested Zinfandel may carry on for decades—few, other than the lands mentioned cultivate this vine—experimental in South Africa, Australia, New Zealand

❋ ❋ ❋

European Hybrids

Grape Variety: Baco Noir

Wine Colors: red/purple to soft red/garnet

Nose: herbaceous aroma, some say similar to some clarets— some Labrusca noticeable

Taste: rather neutral but a bit spicy—good alcohol and acid—full-bodied with a medium-long finish—very mild Labrusca character —dry

Wines: varietals, blending wine

Comments: usually develops good color depth—early ripening grape—grown in France and Eastern North America—Baco (No. 1) hybrid of Folle Blanche and Riparia

Grape Variety: de Chauna

Wine Colors: red/purple

Nose: fruity aroma similar at times to Gamay and some Pinots— mild Labrusca character—little bouquet development

Taste: some qualities of Gamay—light to medium-bodied Labrusca mildly evident—medium to high acidity—dry

Wines: varietals, blending wine

Comments: early ripening grape—does not improve a great deal with age—Seibel 9549 hybrid—not very successful in France but grown in Canada and eastern United States

Grape Variety: Marechal Foch

Wine Colors: red/purple to red/brown

Nose: herb-like aroma, very vinous—when well made can have little or no Labrusca evident—develops complexity with age

197

Taste: an earthy wine with a Burgundian/Rhône character—spicy, with full round body—good acid levels—dry but not austere

Wines: varietals, blending wine

Comments: good color depth—takes moderate ageing well—a Kuhlman 1882 hybrid of Riparia/Rupestris by Goldriesling—very vigorous vine—grown in France, Eastern U.S.A., and Canada.

Grape Variety: Seyval Blanc

Wine Colors: pale yellow

Nose: slight honey-like aroma, mildly fruity—very mild to no Labrusca—develops some bouquet

Taste: delicate fruity taste—light to medium body—good acidity medium to long finish—dry to medium sweet

Wines: varietals, blending wine—used in some sparkling wines

Comments: a golden yellow grape grown in France, Britain, and eastern North America—a well-balanced wine with a good future—Seyve Villard (5276) cross of two Seibel hybrids

Grape Variety: Vidal

Wine Colors: pale to intense yellow/gold

Nose: neutral to spicy aromatics—develops mango and raisiny bouquet in late harvest and ice wines

Taste: medium to full viscous body—dry to extraordinarily sweet—good alcohols and length—good acids

Wines: dry table wines, to late harvest, to ice wines, some used in sparkling wines

Comments: superior hybrid (Vidal 256)—if cropped back can yield complex dry whites—proving to be a great ice wine grape—grown primarily in eastern North America

※ ※ ※

Early North American Hybrids

Grape Variety: Concord

Wine Colors: purple/red

Nose: musky (fox), grapey aroma, very persistent

Taste: heavy grape flavor, overly prominent, lacks subtlety— quite acidic at times—dry to medium sweet

Wines: North American Kosher wines, Pop wines, varietals

Comments: typical native North American slip-skin grape—the back bone of eastern North American viticulture for generations—other native Vitis Labrusca varieties possess similar characteristics to lesser or greater degrees—foxiness is partially caused by an ester (methyl/ethyl anthranilate) not present in Vinifera— characteristically low in sugar and high in acid—makes great jams and jellies

Grape Variety: Delaware

Wine Colors: pale to medium yellow

Nose: grapey aroma—distinctive spicy bouquet

Taste: delicate grapey flavor—slight muskiness (foxiness)

Wines: varietal

Comments: a pink grape—one of the finest early North American hybrid grapes—makes a fruity, soft wine with good body—pleasant without too much Labrusca foxi- ness—usually some residual sugar

Grape Variety: Dutchess

Wine Colors: pale to medium yellow/green

Nose: spicy, flowery aroma, can have very little Labrusca noticeable

Taste: crisp in youth, but develops a soft, round full body with time—very mild, pleasant Labrusca taste—pleasantly dry to medium dry

Wines: varietals, often a major part of Canadian and New York State sparkling wines

Comments: superior, distinctive early North American hybrid of Labrusca and Vinifera—late ripening white grape— grown primarily in eastern North America—a unique, very pleasant wine

Chapter 11

Age: Its Effect on People and Wine

WHEN we think of ageing and winetasting we automatically think of the age of the wine, and perhaps the glorious complexities of smell and flavor that comes only with maturity. Yet what about the taster?

❋ ❋ ❋

The Taster and Age

It doesn't take much personal experience to understand that with age comes diminished capacities. So why should we be surprised that our winetasting skills—our senses of sight, smell, touch, and taste—are also affected? Our body organs progressively weaken and we perceive stimulations less clearly and less quickly.

The weakening of our vision is probably the most noticeable. As we approach the fifth decade of life many of us begin to have some difficulty observing objects close up. The intensity of light that reaches the retina is reduced, making it more difficult to distinguish objects in the dark and requiring more light in order to read.

Our ability to see suspended material in the wine and perceive the luminance accurately requires more effort and closer scrutiny. Fortunately, we have sufficient visual aids—lenses and lighting—to compensate. We just need to remember to do so.

Our olfactory acuity declines somewhat as well. It seems to take more of the volatile substances to trigger the necessary responses in the brain. By way of compensation, our experience and memory banks are filled with a wealth of sensory data upon which we can draw and compare.

Our loss of taste can be quite profound, yet we rarely notice it. Our increased desire for more spicy, strongly flavored foods may be the only clues. If we haven't assaulted our taste buds with too many years of spicy hot foods we will retain about a third of our taste buds into the eighth decade. As our mucus membranes become slightly less efficient, our saliva supply seems to decrease and we need to compensate for that dry mouth with a bit more liquid.

Whether our tactile sensors become less efficient or we pay less attention to them is not clear. But it appears a little more concentration makes up for the loss.

As we have learned in earlier chapters all of these sensory stimulations must reach the brain before we make any sense of them. This generates perceptions. The pathways and the speed at which we recognize the signals are diminished as well. It appears that the velocity at which the signals travel the nervous system to reach the brain declines by about two percent each decade. So, we may be a little slower, but we get there.

Fortunately, with our wealth of experience we seem to more than compensate for some of the effects of age by understanding more about all those subtle and complex nuances. Besides, we simply enjoy the sensations more.

The moral of the story: make way for the young when accurate evaluations are necessary. Impart to them the benefits of your experience and share with them the pleasures and joy of wine.

※ ※ ※

Ageing Wine

As the ancient wine cliché so succinctly puts it—"all wine gets older, but few wines get better." The "getting better" part has a lot to do with how the wine is aged, especially in oak barrels.

It has also been said that "the art of graceful ageing is that of prolonging the virtues of youth." For wine there is some truth in this expression. Some of the qualities of wine (i.e., a portion of its fruit) should be carried on through to maturity. However, the fascinating quality of a ripe, mature wine at its peak of perfection comes partly from what happens to it in the cool darkness and tranquility of the wine cask.

The practice of ageing wine in wooden barrels is ancient. The Gauls were probably doing it over 2,000 years ago. But ageing in wood is not a magical potion. The truth is, you cannot put a poor quality or mediocre wine into a cask and remove a truly fine wine months or years later.

Some simple wine truths have become self-evident over the centuries. A truly fine wine will increase in quality, a poor wine will only get worse from its visit *en barrique*. Without an intense flavor and aroma and an ability to deal with oxygen, you only put the wine at risk in wood.

With so many ageing options available to the modern winemaker the debate has become, how long do you leave it in wood, new and old? The formula, if there is one, is enormously complicated. It involves the choice of woods (limousin, alliers, nevers, American or Russian oak, for example) and the percentage of the wine to stay in new wood, as compared to used, more neutral barrels. The answer is very often one of an extremely personal nature, an expression of style and taste. And the only reliable instrument to judge this blend of time and materials is the human sensory computer. You have to taste it!

The wise use of wood is part science, part art, part intuition. More does not mean better. Wines over-aged in a barrel assume an unpleasant woody characteristic, which dominates the other flavors and aromatics. For some though, this is a blessing—wood can cover a multitude of sins.

But what about wines like sherry, which may spend decades in wood before they reach the bottling line? Sherry is, of course, a wine that has been slightly fortified. A small amount of alcohol (three to six percent by volume) has been added to the wine's natural alcohol level of 12 to 15 percent.

At 16 to 18 percent alc./vol. most bacteria don't make it out alive. This allows the wine to be safely kept in a somewhat oxidative environment (barrel). Sherry is aged in partially filled barrels where oxidative ageing takes place for several years. Without the spoilage-bacteria messing things up the oxidative bouquet of aldehydes (quince, dried nuts, butter and rancio) develops unimpeded. Aldehyde levels can be 10 times those found in table wines. The sherry becomes almost immune to air. Even after you open a bottle it will not deteriorate for weeks.

The timing is individual, too. For some quality wines three to four months in new wood is sufficient, for others six to eight months, for yet others even longer. The end result of this slumber in cask is an increase in color intensity, a decrease in the coarse young tannins, and an unquestionably positive bouquet of new and intensified aromatics.

But what actually happens to the wine while it's in contact with wood? In general terms, here are some of the fascinating changes that transpire:

- very slowly the barrel allows air into the wine (oxygenation) which also loses two to five percent of its volume each year to evaporation (further concentrating flavors and aroma)

- in a dry cellar more water evaporates causing a concentration of the components with a slight rise in the alcohol content; a humid cellar allows more alcohol than water to evaporate, so a slight drop in the alcohol levels

- the extraction of aromatic compounds from the wood itself

- an increase of volatile acidity (not solely acetic acid, but other acids)

- a form of self-fining takes place through a fall-out of sediment and tartrate crystals

- an increase in body because large molecules from the wood dissolve in the wine increasing the viscosity

The oxygenation of a wine in barrel, so vital to this phase of the ageing process, is painfully slow. The variation in the amount of O_2 that reaches the wine depends on the porosity of the different oaks Nevertheless, it is an extremely small amount. More air gets through the bung hole when the wine is topped up than seeps through the wood. Some casks are so tight they even create a vacuum.

Oak woods are composed largely of cellulose, hemicellulose, tannins, and lignins. It is the latter two that do most of the interacting with the wine, injecting a wealth of new aromatics. These are the major compounds that are extracted or diffuse into the wine.

- *Lactones* impart a very subtle and fragile aroma of coconut

- *Aldehydes* increase if barrels receive a "toasting" when new; the primary aromatic aldehyde is vanillin, giving us that familiar "woody" vanilla aromatic

- *Ketone Phenyls*—several of these phenyls accentuate the vanilla odor

- *Phenols*—the main aromatic phenol (eugenol) emits a clove-like aroma; like the ketones, they are amplified when the wood is toasted

There are other compounds that diffuse into the wine but their role remains minor or unknown. The hemicellulose part of wood does have an aromatic effect, but not directly. When the wood is toasted it serves as a base for other odorous compounds.

But the most profound aromatic impact originates with the aldehydes after they are oxidized. Different oaks impart their own unique signature. Note the variations:

❈ ❈ ❈

Total Aromatic Aldehydes (milligrams per gram of wood)
French Oaks

Troncais	4.89 mg/g
Limousin	10.47 mg/g
Gascon	8.12 mg/g
American White Oak	9.59 mg/g
Russian Oak	7.60 mg/g

You will notice some interesting interactions in Figure 16. The amount of phenolic extraction depends on the kind of oak, its size, and length of time ageing in barrel.

Figure 16: Phenolic extraction depends on grapes, wood and ageing

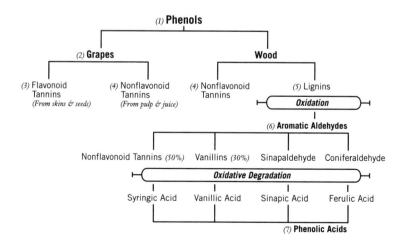

1. **Phenols:** the family of phenolics originating in the grapes and extracted from the wood

2. **Grapes:** from the skins, seeds, and stalks come both flavonoid and non-flavonoid tannins

3. **Flavonoid tannins:** that youthful astringent feeling—with age will condense and precipitate as sediment

4. **Non-flavonoid tannins:** from both grape pulp and wood—remain with the wine, but have no taste or smell—the largest part of the total phenols extracted from the wood

5. **Lignins:** major wood components; are soluble in alcoholic/acid media so are naturals for extraction in wine—with oxygen degradation they basically form four aromatic **aldehydes** (6)—further oxidation leads to the formation of their **phenolic acids** (7).

※ ※ ※

The Dead Zone

"The awkward stage," "the flat spot," "middle-age stagnation," "transformation," "the dumb phase," "it's closed"—whatever your term of choice, it's all referring to a curious phenomenon experienced by most serious winelovers.

It starts with a wine that may show an exuberant, fragrant, drinkable fruitiness shortly after it's bottled, even for a few years. A great future is promised. Then, as if a door had slammed shut the wine becomes essentially mute. Little if anything about it seems to say it's the same wine. In fact, at times it's even worse than mute; the tannins are like a chainsaw on your tongue. But after an indeterminate period of time, it's like the engine's kicked in and the wine is back, better than ever.

This strange event has been observed for a long time. Though disconcerting to winelovers who happen upon the wine while lost in this "valley," it has perplexed producers and retailers even more. Experience has taught them to be patient; they suspect, almost know the resurrection is coming. But how do you explain it to your customers?

A plausible explanation has come to light. Even wine amateurs are aware that as a wine matures the primary grape aromas decline, slowly being replaced with the blossoming, more complex bouquet. But at times, there is a "dead zone." Not with all wines, but enough to be disconcerting.

Plotted on a graph it might appear as in Figure 17. The intensity line on the left shows how dominant the youthful fruit component is

Figure 17: The Dead Zone

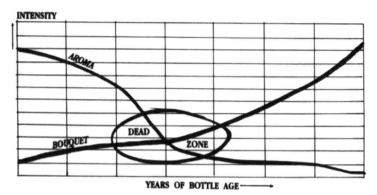

early in the wine's life. As it fades the growing complexity intersects at a particular point. It is here that the "dead spot," "dumb phase," or "closed-in" period could exist in reality, or as the theory goes. If the fruit either fades too quickly or the bouquet is slow in developing, a gap or a valley in the intensity could develop. And that loss of fruit intensity may even reveal the tannins at an awkward, unpleasant stage of their evolution.

When does the "dead zone" appear? How long does it last? Obvious questions, indeed. It should be just as obvious there are no answers to these questions. The intricate interplay of grape variety, terroir, vintage, winemaker, and a dozen other variables creates a profile that no one could predict, nor its start or how long it will persist.

Bottled-Up—The Reductive Effect

From the cask to the bottle may be a short trip, but for the wine a whole new, "reductive" world is experienced. A new set of rules and enacted. In bottle

- the intensity of the oak character softens as the wine becomes less "edgy"

- new aromatic hydrocarbons are formed

- two aromatic chemicals called TDN and vitispirane have been identified in bottle-aged wines, missing in wines still in cask

- with a low pH wine, the reductive ageing is slower, generating more complexity.

The truth is, science doesn't know a whole lot about what takes place in the secretive, reductive atmosphere of the bottle.

But winetasters know! At least from what they can sense in this marvelous transformation from youth to maturity. The "dusty," youthful tannins have become soft and yielding. Words like toasty, honeyed, caramel, nutty, rich, leathery, truffles, licorice, chocolate, and coffee roll off the tongues of winetasters in attempts to describe the wealth of sensory impressions a fully aged wine can convey. With a little patience we can all enjoy such an experience.

Chapter 12

Special Effects

SOME wine components have a very special impact on wine. We need to look at some of them more closely.

✳ ✳ ✳

The Alcohol Equation

Aside from water, alcohol accounts for more of the wine's volume than the long list of other components combined. But is alcohol really necessary in wine?

In light of modern health concerns and the abuse of alcohol, this is a question being asked by a great many consumers these days. Other than the alcoholic effect, doesn't de-alcoholized wine provide us the same tasting pleasures?

Of course, the answer is no! Removing the alcohol from wine might seem like a good thing to some of our social engineers, but not to anyone who has enjoyed a glass of wine at least once in their life. Not even the most modern reverse osmosis techniques leaves a wine that is remotely like the real thing.

Other methods of de-alcoholizing wine, such as distillation, leaves a cooked and stewed cocktail that is simply unacceptable to anyone who still has functioning human sensory organs. So, what does alcohol do for wine?

Aside from its role as a preservative, alcohol has a multi-faceted impact on wine. It is an indispensible natural component. Without alcohol wine often needs additional preservatives just to keep it healthy.

The alcohol we are accustomed to in wine—ethanol—is but one of more than a dozen alcohols, all created quite naturally as by-products of fermentation:

Some Natural Wine Alcohols

Ethanol	Isoamyl alcohol	Tryptophol
Glycol	Act. amyl alcohol	Tyrosol
Propanol	Hexanol	Isopropanol
Heptanol	Phenethyl alcohol	Butanol
Isobutanol	Sec. butanol	Tert. butanol

Ethanol (ethyl alcohol), while in wine, steps back and forth across the line of human perception. Ranging from seven to fourteen percent by volume in table wine it drops below our normal perceptive range (10 percent alcohol), rising to natural levels (non-fortified) of around 13 percent to 14 percent. At this dosage we begin to feel the "heat" of the alcohol as it acts on our tactile, pain receptors, and we begin to appreciate its slightly sweetish impression, as it interacts with other wine components. Even the "higher alcohols," though well below our perception threshold in wine, can still be sensed as they play a hidden role in altering our sense of taste, smell, and feel.

Alcohol can both attenuate and accentuate other wine components. It balances the structure and flavor of wine. It supports a great many wine components without dominating them. Without it, or with low levels of it, wine becomes thin, of poor quality, with a rather retarded future. Alcohol is truly a vital medium for the magical, aromatic components of wine. In a solution of water only, these components just wouldn't make it.

Alcohol is a product of nature and can occur without human involvement. For wine, all of the necessary ingredients are in the grape. Water and sugar in the pulp, flavor and aromatic compounds in the skin, and yeast collected on the outer, waxy surface of the grape. That's all that's needed. By crushing the grapes you introduce the sugar to the yeasts, and the rest comes naturally. Before long you have a complex elixir with hundreds of components. And it's good to drink, too.

Raspberries, strawberries, and bananas have at least seven natural alcohols, oranges fifteen. Even humans produce their own alcohol as a natural product of digestion. Yes, you can register on a sensitive breathalyzer without having taken even one drink. But we as humans prefer alcohol at decent levels. When consumers are given samples of wine to taste blind they invariably choose wines at 12.5 percent alc./vol. over wines of 11.5 percent alc./vol. And our body comes equipped with an enzyme whose sole function is to digest or metabolize alcohol.

We are reminded time and again of the "downside" of alcohol. But in reality it doesn't have one! Abuse it, and it certainly does, but not when kept at moderate consumption levels. If used and enjoyed wisely our health can benefit immeasurably. Individually, the lower risk of heart attack, stroke, and cancer makes it a modern miracle drug. The simple fact is undeniable—moderate wine drinkers live longer and healthier lives than those who abuse alcohol or abstain from it.

But of course, people do abuse it, and the problems and tragedies that that creates are enormous. Weighed in the balance though, we are better off with it than without. If we attack the problem areas (not those who simply use and enjoy it) with wisdom and good sense, that risk will diminish even further.

Not only is alcohol indispensible to wine, without it it is not wine. Treat it well and it will reward you with pleasure and good health.

🀣 🀣 🀣

Carbonic Maceration

This is indeed a special means of treating wine, which in turn makes some wines a special treat. They are unique in the wine world, offering flavors and aromatics to be found nowhere else.

The best known, and certainly the forerunner of the type is Beaujolais Nouveau. The nouveau character has spread from this unique French wine region (the southernmost part of Burgundy) to other regions of France, to Italy, Spain, North America, Australia, and South Africa. So popular is this process it is no longer just an autumnal special event but the whole harvest of some varieties is now subjected to the traditional, or some variation of carbonic maceration.

For many marginal varietals, with rather neutral, uninteresting characters, carbonic maceration has added a new dimension. They become more aromatic with deeper, fresher colors and flavors. They are ready sooner and can be drunk slightly chilled. Their attractiveness quotient takes a major step forward.

Carbonic maceration is not without its detractors. Even in

Beaujolais there are those who charge that no serious wine is ever subjected to this process. That is very probably true. But hardly any nouveau I know of ever makes such a claim. The annual hype over November nouveau doesn't help, either. Some of the more easily jaded palates, and often they're the ones who write about wine, tend to "pooh-pooh" this style of wine.

But precisely what is carbonic maceration and what does it do to the wine? In essence it is anaerobic, whole berry fermentation. Entire bunches of uncrushed grapes, go into special tanks. The tanks are sealed and a different kind of fermentation takes place in a CO_2 atmosphere (sometimes added).

Actually three zones are created within the tank. At the bottom, as you can imagine, the weight of the grapes has crushed most of the berries, which begin to ferment in two or three days, after a heavier than usual dose of yeast is added. This quickly creates a CO_2 atmosphere. The second, or mid-zone, still has whole berries but is submerged in the must. A special alcoholic fermentation, without yeast, is taking place inside the berries (intracellular fermentation). Then finally, there is the top zone which has remained whole, but is surrounded by the CO_2 gas.

The grapes are left in this condition for about 30 days. Something quite special has taken place. More than the usual amount of malic acid has changed to softer forms. More color pigments are drawn from the skins, and very different volatile aromatics have been created, which impart a unique fragrance to the wine (the carbonic maceration nose), quite different to the wine's normal aromatics. A cherry, raspberry aroma is often evident.

The bottom layer of juice is then drained off and the remaining grapes crushed and fermented in a normal fashion. But carbonic maceration has done its job. The normal fermentation can take place at a lower temperature extracting even more fragrant esters and volatiles. It usually happens fairly quickly, in two to four days.

What we now have is a wine with greatly increased aromatics, little of the tannins normal to such a young wine, less and softer acids, somewhat less depth of color, a little less alcohol, and fresher, fruitier flavors. The wine can go to market earlier, sometimes in a matter of weeks to be best served, lightly chilled.

For those who can appreciate these wines for what they are, they are joyous wines. Obviously not long-lasting wines, but they're a genuine pleasure in their vernal freshness and their quaffable, easy nature.

Several glasses of nouveau and a little pâté and bread in a Paris bistro is one of my more memorable late evening recollections.

✹ ✹ ✹

Botrytis Cinerea

It's not a pleasant-sounding name and when grapes are infected with it, it's even uglier in appearance. Ah! but what it does for the wine. It has been called "a great gift from God." It is indeed that to anyone who truly appreciates wine. That doesn't mean everyone will like it. For its devotees though, it is very near the pinnacle a white wine can hope to achieve.

The flavors and aromatics of a botrytis-affected wine are genuinely unique. Attempts to make comparisons are feeble and incomplete. Some of the descriptors include honey, spice, apricot, nutty, toffee, caramel. Put them together in varying proportions and you can imagine why they excite winelovers everywhere.

What is botrytis? It is the Latin name (*Botrytis Cinerea*) for "noble rot." The French call it *pourriture noble*, the Germans *Edelfaule*, the Italians *Mufa Nobile*, and the Hungarians *Aszu*. Regardless of the tongue, it is the name for a very exclusive microscopic fungus related to mushrooms and truffles.

However, in its noble state it is not an easy thing to find. It attacks the grape, shriveling it like a raisin, but transforming the wine to sheer ambrosia.

Ancient stories of its origin have many similarities. It's always a case of an aristocratic vineyard owner off on a long journey—of noble purpose, of course—who returns to find his precious vineyard overrun by this devastating parasite. In sheer desperation he crushes and ferments the grapes, only to discover this unbelievably wonderful wine.

The only problem with these stories is they are supposed to have taken place in several countries, over a period varying by a mere thousand years. Get the picture? Anyway, it seems that the Greeks were aware of botrytis over 2,000 years ago. Regardless, whether or not the botrytis "wheel" had to be re-invented several times, is unimportant. Its most famous home is now in the Bordeaux region of France where some truly incredible Sauternes such as Château d'Yquem are created.

When the conditions are just so, it is responsible for Germany's Trockenbeerenauslesen and Hungary's ancient and luscious Tokaji Aszu. In very limited zones it can also be found in Italy, Austria, Australia, and parts of North America.

The fickle appearance of this pathogenic but at times enriching fungus is very dependent on a narrow band of weather conditions. It is highly unpredictable. Botrytis needs a roller coaster variation in humidities: good humidity to kick it off; dry weather to keep it alive. This humidity yo-yo continues until it is well established. This usually means an alternating of cooler, misty evenings with dry, slightly warmer days. After two to three days the fungus has taken hold.

It's also a little fussy about the kind of grapes it chooses to "kick the stuffings out of." It prefers thinner-skinned grapes (easier to puncture); most reds are not the noble rot's cup of tea (their skins have some resistant element); and it likes more tightly packed bunches of grapes (the moisture hangs around awhile longer in the crevices).

If the ideal weather conditions don't follow its initial beach head, a number of nasties can happen. If the humidity remains, the beneficial noble rot can proceed to its alter ego, gray rot, the advanced stage of noble rot. Gray mold or bunch rot can render the harvest null and void. Additional dangers exist: Other, not so welcomed guests may also arrive—unwanted bacteria, yeasts, and micro-organisms. They, too, attack the compromised grapes and could ruin a whole harvest. It's not difficult to understand why a winemaker isn't instantaneously delirious when the noble fungus makes its first appearance. At harvest, good pickers will smell each bunch to make certain it has not become infected with vinegar bacteria.

When a tiny botrytis fungus spore (wind-carried) lights on the moist surface of the grape, an intriguing process begins (see Figure 18). First, it draws up some of the water, increases in size, and sends out a germinal thread that punctures the grape skin. After "gluing" itself to the grape surface and further attaching suction cups, this spore is here to stay. Home! Then dinner!

With all the nutritional material it needs right there inside the grape it grows quickly, at epidemic rates, first as a transparent spot on the skin then spreading threads in a dense web of fuzzy, gray fungus tissue. With billions of punctures the skin tissue breaks down and the water inside the grape begins to evaporate. The constitution of the berry begins to alter and concentrate; it shrivels like a raisin; aromatic extracts concentrate as do acids and sugars.

But the fungus attack does more than concentrate the grape's constituents. The juice itself is altered in a complex transformation of some of its elements—a tremendous increase in glycerine, for one. Pigments in the skin fall prey, too. For whites, who cares? But for

Figure 18: Botrytis needs high humidity to start and low humidity to finish

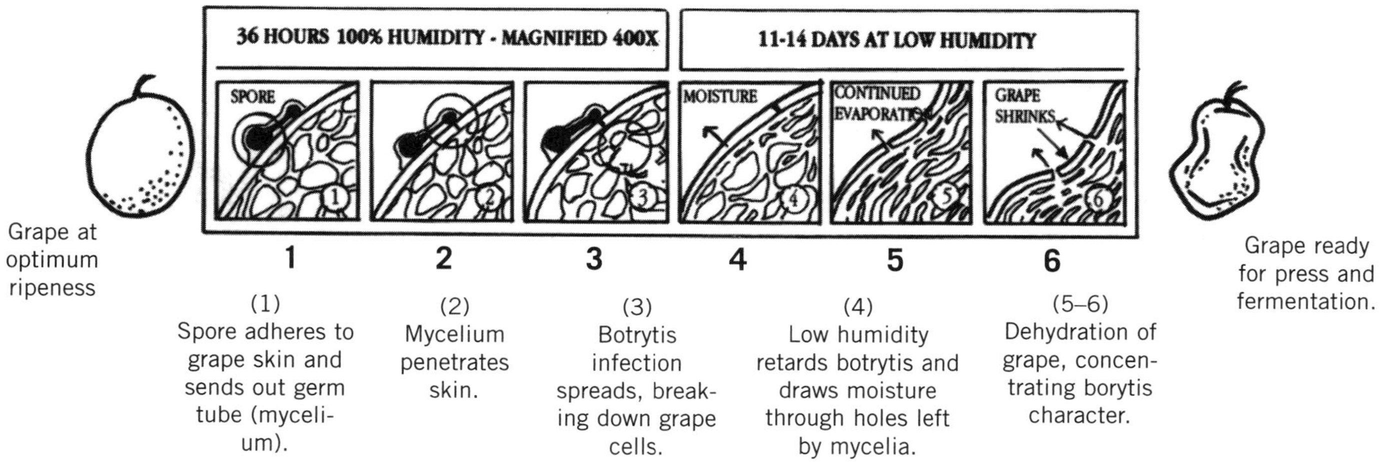

Grape at optimum ripeness

36 HOURS 100% HUMIDITY - MAGNIFIED 400X

11-14 DAYS AT LOW HUMIDITY

SPORE

MOISTURE

CONTINUED EVAPORATE

GRAPE SHRINKS

1   2   3   4   5   6

(1) Spore adheres to grape skin and sends out germ tube (mycelium).

(2) Mycelium penetrates skin.

(3) Botrytis infection spreads, breaking down grape cells.

(4) Low humidity retards botrytis and draws moisture through holes left by mycelia.

(5–6) Dehydration of grape, concentrating borytis character.

Grape ready for press and fermentation.

reds, they are ruined. Not a good thing for a red wine, to have all its red pigments destroyed. This is, of course, a simplification of these incredibly complex events. In the end the grapes appear rotten, unfit for human consumption.

Yet, in the hands of a skilled winemaker, the delights that can be created with this rather ignoble-looking mess are utterly surprising, to say the least. The wine is not only viscous (glycerine), like liquid velvet, but achieves such a marvelous balance of sweetness and acidity it defies appropriate description.

For decades researchers have been trying to understand and analyze the complex makeup of a botrytis-affected (B.A.) wine. In recent years we have begun to shed some light on the mysterious and intriguing aromatics that seem to be unique to B.A. wines. We've discovered it's even more complicated than we thought. The following chart identifies just some of the volatile aromatic compounds found in normal table wines, compared to those of a B.A. wine. The number following each compound represents the typical number of times greater this compound appears in a B.A. wine than in ordinary table wines.

3-Octanol	5
Ethyl acetate	4
Ethyl 9-hydroxynonanoate	5
Ethyl phenylacetate	5
Diethyl succinate	3
Diethyl glutarate	4
4-Nonanolide	12
Furfural	10
Benzaldehyde	3
N-(3 -Methylbutyl) acetamide	2

Further research has identified an acidic substance that plays a huge part in the "botrytis nose" of these wines. It is an aromatic flavor compound found also in sugar, molasses, sake, and flor sherry called *sotolon*. In normal wine you find it at about one ppb. A B.A. wine could have 520 ppb.

Sotolon has a sugar-like, caramel aroma. The aromatic signature of a B.A. wine includes a kind of spicy, apricot, truffles, and honeyed bouquet. It is obviously a very complicated, complex smell. Yet, when sotolon was removed in a lab sample, the wine still had a complex bouquet, but was much like ordinary wines. When sotolon was re-introduced to the sample, the complex, botrytis character returned.

Winemakers who choose to make a B.A. wine are seriously challenged from the start. Components such as volatile acidity (VA) can get out of hand. But when the classic botrytis enacts its impressive transformation, whether it's a Sauternes from France, a Tokaji Aszu from Hungary, a Trockenbeerenauslese from Germany, or one of a growing number of New World B.A. wines, warn your taste buds ahead of time—one of the wine world's greatest treasures is in store.

CHAPTER 13

Some Very Special Tastes

Burnt Wine—Brandy

It is not the objective of this section of *Winetaster's Secrets* to trace the history of brandy, give brand guidance, or even attempt to explain its origins. Other publications have devoted themselves to these delightful tasks. Here are some I recommend:

Handbook of Fine Brandies by Gordon Brown;

Pocket Guide to Cognac and Other Brandies by Nicolas Faith.

My goal is to help you better understand the glorious flavors and aromas of brandy, and how to assess its quality using your own battery of sensory instruments.

An Introduction

The origin of distillation is vague at best. Various historians suggest it began in Egypt, China, the Middle East, with the Moors, and others. Whichever, what we do know is the practice of distilling wine was flourishing by the 16th century. The Dutch stimulated the trade and gave it an odd name: *Brandywijn* or "burnt wine."

In modern terms, true brandies, including those with appellation status (i.e., Cognac, Armagnac, Jerez), are grape spirits (distilled wine) which are acknowledged to improve in quality with proper cask ageing. Since there are few "vintaged" brandies most are products of the blender's art. By skillfully blending brandies of various ages and origin, a fairly consistent product is brought to market year after year—a house style, if you will.

Nevertheless, it is largely the age of the various components of the blend that account for the different levels of brandy quality. Youthful harshness mellows with time in wood. Once bottled all ageing ceases. Simple, inexpensive brandies are usually the youngest. Top quality, expensive brandies almost always use similar base spirits to start with. Age is essentially the only difference.

Brandies develop various aromatic signatures as they age. In youth a grapey, more fruity quality is apparent in the aromatics and on the palate (varies by grape variety). With age comes a more flowery characteristic, including added structure or texture. Further ageing develops a spice and over-ripe fruit quality. Venerable, old brandies often display a more complex spice and dried fruit quality, with a floweriness reminiscent of violets, roses, or iris. With age the wood characteristic often moves from a vanilla oakiness, to cedar, then to sandalwood.

So, it is obvious the effect of proper cask ageing is a crucial factor in brandy quality and in our assessing the quality.

Stylistic variations in brandies are considerable. The choice of pot-stills (alembic) versus continuous stills, double distillations, blends of the two rectification methods, the type of wood, ageing in used sherry barrels, and a number of other techniques, have a strong impact on the finished product and its unique style and character.

Tasting brandy or wine has the same goal—to reveal its character and quality. It's the steps that vary. Pour a glass of wine for a seasoned winelover and invariably he'll start swirling the wine in the glass to release the aromatics. *Do not* do that if it's a brandy, at least not to start with.

Basically, as with wine, we follow the same pattern our human senses dictate: visual—smell—touch—taste. Applied skillfully, these senses will reveal the nature and quality of any brandy.

With an ounce or two of brandy in your glass (egg-shaped crystal winetasting glasses are best), first look for clarity and color. A good brandy will have a clean, bright appearance. Brandy colors range from pee-yellow, through gold and amber, all the way to mahogany. Unless the brandy is quite old it should have no reddish tinges. Young brandies with a reddish hue will probably have had a little too much caramel coloring added.

Unlike wine, brandy tasters go through a series of four nosings. The first three come before you ever swirl the glass. It starts about two inches above the glass. In this smelling zone you sense the woody vanillas more easily. Then, with your nose at the edge of the glass you will experience more intensely those flowery tones. The third smelling zone requires that you stick your proboscis well into the glass. Here you'll smell more of the fruity quality of the brandy. Finally, you can swirl the glass and smell that wonderful blend of aromatics, with dried fruit, herbal, flowers, nuts, and exotic woods. The combinations and accents will depend on the age of the spirits, the kind of wood used, even the original grape variety.

With a drop or two in your mouth you can now appraise the flavors and texture of the brandy. As brandy ages in barrel it concentrates in flavor and body. The more body and structure you experience the more likely there will be older brandies as part of its blend.

A second, larger sip helps you to better get the "in-mouth" odors and feel, including any excessive dryness (from tannins). Brandies can range from quite dry to an easily noticeable sweetness. Though alcohol itself has a sweetish touch to it, sugar syrups are often added to cheap, ordinary brandies to round out their rough edges. At the top of the brandy pyramid, adding sugar is regarded as a definite *faux pas*.

Putting these steps, and many more, together helps you get a profile of the brandy in your glass. Is it worth the price? Does it deserve the name and the fancy bottle? With experience you'll then begin to appreciate the nuances that often define quality, and the many unique styles that are a part of the brandy world today.

The Qualities

As with wine, the quality of brandy varies enormously. The vast majority of brandies, like wine, are ordinary. Only a rare few deserve to be savored, sniffed attentively, and sipped appreciatively.

From grape juice to finished spirit, some brandies reach the bottle in a matter of months, not decades, not even years. Artificial adjuncts are used to mask the raw alcohol and bring to market a spirit that is, at least, drinkable. Wood chips (boise) or "liquid oak," sugar syrup, and caramel coloring, like an alchemist's brew, are the tools of this trade.

Quality brandy, however, requires good wine, careful distillation, fine woods, skilled blenders, and time. The time is needed for the evolution and extraction of aromatic and flavor compounds from the barrel. Age is the major element distinguishing brandy quality classifications.

The Grapes

Tradition and expedience have been the means by which certain grape varieties have been selected for use in modern brandies. Some distillers claim that the coarser the wine the better the brandy.

Many of the base wines used in today's brandies are strict adherents to that philosophy. By far, the grapes of choice yield wines that are thin, acidic and to be quite frank "mean." The most popular is the Ugni Blanc (Trebbiano), used almost exclusively in Cognac and Armagnac. Once widely used, the more flavorful and aromatic Folle Blanche has all but disappeared in these classic regions, due largely to the difficulties this variety presents to the growers in the vineyard. High-yielding, trouble-free varieties are the order of the day.

Strangely enough, brandymakers in other parts of the world often imitate this practice. If not using the same Ugni Blanc grape they will use some local variety, known for its high yields and vinous short-comings. One might assume that having to compete with icons like Cognac and Armagnac there would be some temptation to select more aromatic and interesting varieties as a quality signature, or at least an interesting alternative. Largely, not.

But in America some of the "pot-still" producers have chosen some fascinating varieties to distill. They are using varieties like Chardonnay, Muscat, Pinot Noir, Gamay, and Sauvignon Blanc. Fresh, fragrant and exciting new aromatics are establishing unique monographs for these distillers. With more time and older stocks of spirits to blend, some exciting new brandies of quality will no doubt join the ranks of the traditional.

The Still—Transforming the Wine

With a coarse, unpolished, and low-alcohol wine before him the distiller begins a vigil that will result in a clear white, raw, rather unpleasant-smelling spirit. He may choose to provide a greater concentration ratio of the wine, or to distill it on the lees to achieve greater aromatics, or double distill it for extra smoothness.

Basically, two types of stills (with variations, of course) are in modern use:

Alembic Pot-Still	• single-batch still
	• yields more flavor and aromatics
	• used for double distillations
Continuous still	• continuously distills wines
(the Coffey still)	• yields a more neutral, softer spirit

The size and shape of the stills, and innumerable physical factors, will stamp distinctly different impressions on the raw, young spirit.

The temptation may be to view brandy as a rather simple, uncomplicated alcoholic liquid, in comparison with wine, with its 700-plus known constituents. Brandy complexity is accounted for by over 300 known compounds, taking it far beyond the "simple" category. In Cognac, some 21 different terpene alcohols have been isolated and 37 ketones have been found.

Blending

One of the most crucial components of the magic of brandy is blending. For simple, inexpensive brandies the blending formula may only involve a mix of younger and older spirits. Adjustments of color and sweetness may be all that is needed to achieve their consistent "house style."

Superior brandies may require the interplay of literally hundreds of brandies to achieve even a basic house style. Age, region, grape variety, type of cask, and the distiller are some of the additional components that further complicate the task.

The skilled blender is among the royalty of the brandy world, especially in Cognac. The position is often handed down from generation to generation. I wouldn't even begin to try to explain the complexities of his deliberations. Blending brandies can create a synergism of aromatics, a suppression, or even a cancellation, varying in intensity by a simple change of percentage.

But achieving one blend is just the beginning. Many houses produce several brandies, varying in quality from the simple to the elite. Torres, a fine producer of wine and brandies in the Penedes region of Spain, gives us a very basic example of some of the complexities involved with bringing to market a range of quality brandies (see Figure 19).

Wood—The Secret Ingredient

Without oak our favorite fine brandies would cease to exist; their heart and soul would be missing.

Virtually all of the color, most of the taste, and almost all of the aroma of brandy depend upon oak. As the new spirit slumbers quietly in cask it is continuously extracting a wealth of components. Components that not only bring color, aroma, and taste to the brandy, but with time and oxygen these elements will be transformed even further into new and fascinating sensory experiences.

Since wood and good brandy are inseparable, it's probably not coincidental that they are often found to be geographical neighbors.

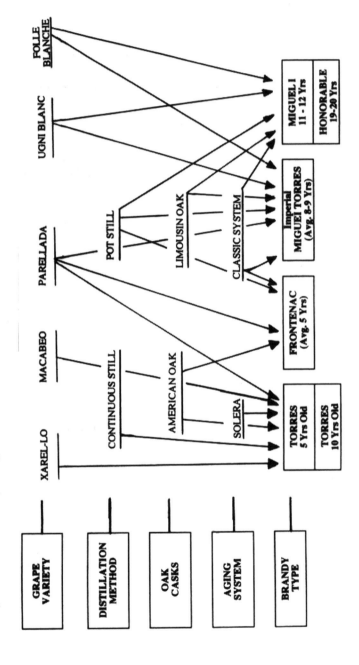

Figure 19: A variety of factors are involved in producing the dirrent Torres brandies

The great Limousin and Troncais forests near Cognac, and the disappearing black Gascon oaks near Armagnac are hardly accidents of nature. The same could probably be said for America's Bourbon whiskies, centered in the southern states near its great forests of American white oak.

Each type of oak has its own story to tell and imparts to the brandy a unique signature of flavors and aromatics. Humans play a minor role in this exchange. By the way they harvest, season, and craft the woods, they can alter the very nature of this contribution. The oaks of France (Limousin, Troncais, Alliers, Vosges, Nevers) are the woods of choice internationally, not only for their intrinsic characteristics, but for the craftsmanship of the French-trained coopers. Both wood and coopers are being exported.

Oak trees are harvested usually in winter when the sap is down. They are split, never sawn. Only the *fut* is used, the part just above the roots, up to the lower branches. The staves are stacked with sufficient air space between them. In sun, rain, wind, even snow, they are allowed to season for periods of four to seven years.

The now silver-gray wood, having lost some of its more aggressive tannins and aromatics, is ready for the cooper's craft. The cooper is viewed in some brandy regions as part of the aristocracy of the trade. Well paid and highly skilled, he plies his art much as it was carried out over a hundred years ago.

In regions such as Cognac the cooper's job is a solitary one—he fashions each barrel from start to finish, without a nail or a drop of glue. If he's skilled he can turn out seven or eight casks a day, casks that sell for about 500 U.S. dollars each.

From the wood itself comes a variety of components that interact with the brandy. Sugars from the wood are liberated and a number of aromatic acids unveil new, complex smells. From these even more esters and lactones are created as the spirit ages and oxidation plays its role. With great age in cask a unique, complex smell develops—rancio.

This is not the rancid smell of stale oils, but the complex buttery, nutty, woody, and vanilla bouquet generated by aldehydes. It's truly unique, a heady experience. Brandy lovers can be found, noses sunken deeply into snifters, inhaling and savoring these marvelous vapors for so long you might suspect they'll never get around to actually tasting it.

Even when the glass has been emptied the experience is not over. Clinging to the side of the glass are dried layers of the least volatile fractions of esters and oak essence. With the more volatile components drained away with the last of the liquid, these forgotten, hidden aromatics remain to entrance the taster.

The Art of Tasting Brandy

Although the principles of tasting wine and brandy have similarities, there are sufficient differences to cause you to make a few adjustments.

The range of brandy aromas and flavors are somewhat narrower than for wine, nevertheless they are just as revealing. As with wine, you start your sensory, qualitative analysis with a **visual** inspection.

Clarity in a good brandy is almost a given; however, rare problems in this area do exist. Some of the more important sources of haze in brandy are listed here:

Calcium—a crystalline deposit; usually caused by contamination with tap water; when the brandy is diluted, poor quality water can be used in some cheap brandies.

Wood extractions—brownish, fluffy deposits can occur when the brandy is diluted; the decrease in alcohol levels can cause some components to precipitate; normally, stabilization processes like those used with top brandies eliminate these deposits (i.e., low temperature stabilization).

Plastics—some plastics (from pipes and connectors) can cause a haze; again, if care is taken the right plastics have no such effect.

Alcohols—higher alcohols (fusel oils) can at times produce a cloudiness if shaken; carefully controlled distillation usually prevents this from happening.

Another reality we must face in judging brandies is that **color** is a poor way to judge their character. It is too easy to manipulate color with the addition of caramel. Almost every producer uses it to ensure that a consistent depth of color is presented, bottle to bottle, year to year. Marketers have some kind of fear that if the color alters somewhat, even from year to year, consumers will flee to their competitors.

The new spirit starts out as clear as water. With time in wood, it travels through a range of colors, some of which are certainly not very appealing. It travels through a light pee-yellow/green, to a yellowish hue; begins to adopt more golden, amber, and brownish tones; and with advanced age, a reddish-mahogany tint begins to show through.

This assumes of course that this is all natural and no caramel coloring has been added. Properly administered, caramel adds only a hint of depth. In excessive amounts it has a sweetening effect and introduces those reddish tinges usually reserved for the true old-timers. It can also add a kind of "bittiness" or grainy effect to the appearance.

Commercial brandy tasters will often taste in blue-colored glasses to eliminate any of the influence a color may have. This is not the real world, so in competitive judgings the blue glasses should be set aside. Color is part of the quality assessment.

Next comes our nose and what we can appreciate from the aromatics of the brandy. Commercial brandy tasters are looking primarily for potential faults. They want a clean nose. They are less interested in the nuances and shadings in the aromatics than winetasters. Opposite is a list of positive and negative aromatics. But wait! *Do not swirl* your glass at this point. Remember, there are four nosings:

1. 2 inches above the glass
—more of the wood and alcohols

2. at the rim of the glass
—more of the fruit and fragrance of flowers

3. nose in the glass
—fruit, spice, and cedar

4. swirl the glass—nose well inside
—dried fruit, nutty, exotic woods

☀ ☀ ☀

Negative Brandy Descriptors

acrolein (acrid odor) milky	sulfury	
leafy	burnt wood	rotten egg
putrid	moldy wood	garlic
cooked	resinous	petroleum
flat	casky	rubbery
heads	wine barrel	dusty
tails	oxidized	

※ ※ ※

Positive Brandy Descriptors

Fruit	Flower	Woody	Herbal/Misc.
apricot	iris	vanilla	tobacco
almond	hyacinth	cigar box	coffee
quince	jasmine	spicy	cacao
fig	lavender	piney	honey
peach	narcissus	cedar	tea
pear	carnation	coconut	nutty
apple	rose	sandalwood	cinnamon
dried fruit	saffron	—	port
muscat	violet	—	walnut
lychee	honeysuckle	—	nutmeg
pineapple	—	—	ginger
prunes	—	—	smokey

※ ※ ※

Some Aromatic Signatures for Broad Age Indication

12–15 years	18–22 years
• Port/Madeira	• jasmine, honeysuckle
• intense oak, vanilla	• walnut, saffron
• nutty, spicy	• gingerbread
30–40 years	**45–55 years**
• cigar box	• violet, rose
• cedar-like	• iris, lychee
• old muscat	• coconut
• nutmeg	• sandalwood
• rancio	• rancio

Some Brandy Terms

adjuncts:	an addition or accompaniment
Aguardenta:	Portuguese for brandy
alembic armagnacais:	specially designed continuous still used for Armagnac
Aguardiente:	Spanish for high-proof spirit
alembic:	pot-still, from Arabic "alembic"
Alquitara:	Spanish term for brandy distilled in pot-stills
Bagaceira:	Portuguese for *marc* (see)
bonbonne:	a glass jar that holds 25 liters, used for old spirits
Brandvin, Brandywijn:	Dutch for brandy meaning "burnt wine"
chai:	ageing warehouse for brandy (cellar or above ground)
Coffey still:	continuous still invented by Edmund Coffey
congeners:	residual chemical components that provide brandy with its flavor, and its drinkers with their hangovers
Grappa:	Italian *marc* (see)
heads:	first spirit from a still. Generally redistilled because it is too strong or impure to use.
heart:	the middle cut—the main spirit used for brandy
lees:	solids left over after fermentation
Limousin:	most popular oak used to mature French and other brandies
marc:	spirit distilled either from the lees left after fermentation or from the pips, skins and stalks after grapes have been pressed
paradis:	cellar for storing very old, rare cognacs
Pomace Brandy:	another term for *marc*
rancio:	the buttery/nutty or woody/vanillin smell of certain fortified wines and very old brandies
tails:	unpleasant end run of spirit from the still—returned for redistillation—too much water
troncais:	type of oak used to mature brandy

For those who have an orientation or an interest in chemistry, some of the aromatic sources are:

coconut	— lactones
general fruitness	— ethyl acetate
pineapple	— ethyl caprylate
floral	— 2-phenyl ethanol
grapey	— ethyl caprate
	— ethyl perargonate
	— ethyl heptanoate
rose	— 9-decen-1-ol

We have not taken into account, of course, the impact that special flavoring agents have on some brandies. Some Spanish brandies are aged in used sherry barrels, as are some single malt scotches; some even have a touch of sherry added. In Greece some brandies have a bit of Muscat wine blended into it. Spices, herbs, and rose petals have all found their way into brandy. A new brand of ice wine with brandy is generating some devoted followers in Canada. The taste and aroma of these additions will have to be assessed on a personal pleasure basis.

Brandy certainly has a sense of feel, a **tactile** property. Fusel oils (higher alcohols) account for much of the "mouth-feel" of brandy. Acids, tannins, sugars, and naturally the main alcohol, ethanol, play a composite role in the "smoothness" of brandy. But keep in mind, an alcohol level of 40 percent by volume is heady stuff. It is very hot, peppery, sometimes even painful in the mouth. When it doesn't react this way, either the brandy is very old, with the alcohol diminished and mellowed by time, or there are a number of adjuncts in your brandy. Components like sugar, glucose, caramel, sherry, and so on, can certainly have a softening influence on the spirit. So, smoothness, though an appreciated quality and evident to a degree in rare, old brandies, is a poor indicator of general quality.

This bridges us nicely into an interesting procedure for enjoying brandy even more—conditioning.

Conditioning

There's little that can be done to soften the impact of a spirit with that much alcohol—that is, without mixing it with something that is going to detract from the pure essence of an unadulterated, well-aged brandy. Some people add water, ice cubes, and other mixers to brandy, and that's okay. You may enjoy the drink. Brandy and fresh orange juice is a favorite personal drink. What you are not enjoying, though, is the pure pleasures of a pure brandy.

And here's where conditioning plays a role. By taking a very small sip or two of the brandy and rolling it around in your mouth you "condition" it to the inevitable aggressive assault of the alcohol. What also occurs is our old friend adaption. With the physical, tactile strength of alcohol your senses don't take long to adapt or close it out. What this does is allow you to better perceive the more subtle, less aggressive aromatics and flavors in the brandy. Then, with a few drops at a time, you can more easily do your taste evaluations.

As you sip a brandy over a period of time you may already have noticed how much less painful the experience becomes. In fact, it's painless after this conditioning and adaption kicks in.

Service and Cellaring

Serving fine brandy in the proper glass adds a civilized and practical note to its enjoyment. Glasses need not be as large as winetasters use. The best shape is what looks like a smaller version of the ISO glass (see page 155). It's the preferred glass in Cognac. It looks a little like the classic sherry "copita" glass, with a little less in-turn at the top.

Snifters have a certain tradition about them, but they are not the best vessels for enjoying the treasures of a fine brandy. Their shape has a tendency to accentuate the alcohol and dampen the aromatics. You can overcome that, of course, by ramming your nose far enough into the glass until it actually touches the liquid. And by all means, avoid those large "balloon-sized" aberrations some restaurants use to impress their clientele. Flower arrangements or goldfish are better suited to these vessels than are brandies, which only get lost in their bucket-size proportions.

Heat is often used to extract additional intensity from brandy. Avoid it—like the plague. Especially offensive and destructive are those burner and cradle contraptions. The flame warms the brandy and with it annihilates virtually every blessing that brandy possessed. The next time one is delivered to your table ask for a stick and marshmallows. Or you could suggest that a third distillation of this grand, pot-still brandy is not really necessary.

Even warming the brandy glass in your hand is too much for the real thing. Our normal body temperature of 98.6°F (or 37°C) is above the optimum temperature for any brandy. What you are really doing is generating an unbalanced evaporation of the brandy's more volatile components. A far more comfortable temperature range for brandy—and your personal pleasure factor—is 70 to 75°F (20–23°C).

Storing good brandy demands a little attention, too. Bottles should be stored upright in the same temperature range you do your red wines. Once opened, brandy is not impervious to deterioration. Younger spirits may remain much the same as when they were first opened for almost a year. Older, more fragile brandies should be kept no longer than six to eight months after opening. The best thing to do with a half bottle of fine brandy? Find another occasion to finish the bottle. How about a sunset?

🐝 🐝 🐝

Ice Wine—A Chilling Experience

"Nectar of the Gods," "liquid gold," "ambrosia," "elixir extraordinaire" are all flights of verbal fantasy that are used by winelovers from time to time. Few wines can legitimately lay claim to these terms. Yet, one wine almost always fits this description—ice wine (*Eiswein*).

This rare specialty of the wine world has entranced winetasters for nearly two centuries. The first successful attempt to press juice from these frozen grapes was recorded in Franconia, Germany, in 1794. They discovered, no doubt to their surprise, here was another way to accomplish a concentration of the sugar, flavors, and aromatics of the grapes.

For 150 years the experience of ice wine depended totally upon nature's surprise. When an early freezing spell caught the harvesters with grapes still on the vine, ice wine became a possibility. The frozen grapes were like so many bunches of hanging marbles.

By the early 1950's a handful of German estates were willing to take a gamble with a small portion of their vineyard. They purposely left some vines unpicked hoping upon hope a cold snap would catch them before they rotted and fell off the vine.

And gamble is the right word. Makers of ice wine risk losing an entire portion of their harvest. If the birds don't get them, perhaps the noble rot will. Birds like grapes. Birds really like sweet grapes. As the grapes super ripen on the vine, well past normal harvest time, it's like a candy store throwing open its doors to a group of sugar-deprived children. More than one ice wine harvest has fallen prey to attack by our fine feathered friends.

Another friend, in its noble state—botrytis—can also turn on these super-sweetened grapes. Should the noble rot continue on too far, before cold temperatures arrest their dehydration process, the grapes may well be ruined. A touch of botrytis can certainly add one more complex note to the symphony of ice wine flavors, but it can be a terminator as well. That's part of the ice wine gamble.

The Grapes

Germany has settled upon the classic Riesling as the ice wine varietal of choice, although they often blend in some Sylvaner to add a bit of flesh, and Scheurebe to bring a little more depth to the aroma.

The grapes used for successful ice wine production should meet specific criteria:

1. tough skins

2. stems that hold on well to the vine

3. late-ripeners

4. an aromatic, fruity variety.

Though Germany is the traditional homeland of ice wine, parts of eastern North America and British Columbia, Canada, may well become the world's major suppliers. This does not mean to suggest they are a "bulk" supplier, with an "ordinaire" quality. In fact, the ice wines of North America have already surpassed Germany in quantity and may have done so in quality, too. North Americans can look to an ice wine harvest nine out of ten years, compared with only one or two per decade in Germany.

The varieties used in North America are much the same as in Germany. Eastern Canadian producers now have a decade of experience with ice wine and have settled on two principal varieties— Riesling and Vidal. They are also using Gewürztraminer, Bacchus, Kerner, Lemberger (a red varietal), and Chancellor (a red hybrid). In theory the Pinot Noir grape should fit most of the ice wine criteria, but I'm not aware of any in production.

Perhaps the biggest surprise to winemakers on both sides of the Atlantic is the Vidal variety. It has turned out to be a major player in this field, at times yielding more fragrant and better structured ice wines than Riesling. Much depends, though, on the skill of the winemaker.

233

From Vine to Wine

To make great ice wine requires more than frozen grapes. Harvesting ice wine can begin anywhere from November to January (of the following year). Ideally, the fall season should be dry and sunny so that the grapes are ripe and healthy. The more ripe the grapes, the better they will withstand the cool temperatures that normally precede the "big freeze."

A temperature of –6 to –8°C (14 to 18°F) has to be achieved to complete the process well. The grapes also need a high sugar content to make the transformation in good shape. Depending upon the vintage, of course, the sugar content of ice wine grapes will vary widely. If too low they could introduce a bitter note to the taste.

In Germany the measurement of sugar in the juice is expressed as *Oechsle*, in North America it's "Brix." To translate, you can divide the Oechsle number by 3.9 to get an approximation of the Brix level. At least 110 Oechsle (28 Brix) is required in Germany for an ice wine—in Canada a minimum of 32 Brix (125 Oechsle) is needed before you can declare an ice wine. In reality the sugar levels normally climb well beyond that. Over 40 Brix is common in Canada. One ice wine in Germany registered nearly 60 Brix at harvest. This is, of course, taking into account the concentration effect of freezing.

Contributing to the $30 to $50 price tag per half bottle of ice wine are the miserly yields. For table wines a yield of 4,000 to 8,000 liters per hectare (2.47 acres) is average. Ice wines may only provide you with 300 to 500 liters. To express it another way, it usually takes about a kilogram of grapes to make a standard 750 ml bottle of finished table wine. With a kilo of shrivelled and frozen ice wine grapes, you will get about 35 to 75 ml of wine.

Pressing the frozen ice wine grapes can be a nippy affair. A nice, warm winery is not the best place to do it. Often the grapes are pressed in small basket presses outside. Some are of the opinion that the colder the pressing temperature the better will be the wine, factoring in the general state of the vintage, of course. The water crystals can be separated from the remaining juice because water freezes at a higher temperature than other juice components, so can be extracted and disposed of. This concentrating process can double the sugar levels, as well as the acids, flavor, and aromatic compounds.

Even getting juice of this nature to ferment can be a challenge. It's ice cold, with great weight and structure, a very heavy juice. In years past it was necessary to warm up a small portion of the juice (about five percent), start it fermenting, then put it back into the chilled must. More recently, strains of very specialized yeasts have been developed that can work at these lower temperatures and in such heavy musts (osmotic pressure). Still, it may take a year or more to develop 10 or 11 percent alcohol by volume.

Tasting the Wine—The Elixir

One of the most attractive aspects of ice wine is that you don't have to wait until the wine reaches a venerable age before you can enjoy its many treasures. No, not for decades, not even for years. Ice wine in its youthful exuberance can be savored when it's just a few years of age. However, with time—five to ten years—a wealth of new aromatics and flavor components begin to emerge; more time, even more complexities. You can choose the style you want and be immensely satisfied with either.

Please don't expect what is often called a "delicate," or "restrained" character from ice wine. It comes out of the glass swinging. Its immediate intensity can be so aggressive there is a tendency to look past a wealth of subtle nuances in every glass. This intensity can challenge a panel of wine judges when a flight or two of ice wines appears in front of them. However, once adaption has taken place for those up-front aromatics, the more complex components emerge.

Ice wine can be a delight to the eye as well as the palate. Even visually you begin to appreciate the enormous structure of an ice wine. The "tears" are shed very slowly, indicating its body and texture. The colors range from a light yellow-golden tone to a deeper, old-gold, and amber tones with age. In youth you may even notice a faint touch of green. However, should you note the deeper golds or amber at a youthful age it may be a warning sign. Perhaps oxidation before bottling has tainted the wine. It is unlikely that it has a long future.

Be prepared for an explosive nasal assault, an enormously pleasant one. An incredibly intense and complex nose is one of ice wine's personality markers. Some who are more used to a restrained, less intense nose are often not quite sure of how to react. They tend to fall back on previous experiences with intense varietals such as Muscat and Labrusca wines. They were never noted for their quality.

Fortunately, this approach does not apply to ice wine. Intensity is a marker of greatness for ice wine. The nuances, finesse, and elegance are there, too. They just happen to come in a rather "loud" package.

It may be difficult to identify a varietal character in ice wine. Many times their unique varietal signature is lost in the deep, complex array of ice wine aromatics. Even personalities as forceful as Gewürztraminer take a back seat to the composite ice wine aroma. Look for these marvelous smells:

Vidal	Riesling
honey	honey
tropical fruit	apricot
mango	pear
pineapple	lemon/lime

With proper ageing the aromas evolve towards dried fruits, brown sugar, raisins, and a creamy caramel. Several decades can be easily handled by a well-made ice wine.

In the mouth further explosions are in store. Not only is the rich sweetness so obvious, but you become aware of an enormous lacing of acid. At times it can be double that of normal table wines (10–15 g/l). Yet, with those enormous residual sugar levels (around 200 g/l, or 20 percent) and the tremendous amounts of extract, what would normally be a mouth-puckering, teeth-rattling level of acidity merely balances the overall impression.

The lush, viscous structure of an ice wine brings great pleasure, as well. The opulence of this style of wine can initially be over-powering, but all the added complexities and nuances are there for the tasting. Delicacy is not a feature of good ice wine. When you do encounter a less intense ice wine you will no doubt enjoy it immensely. Yet, when you recall the explosive power, the layer upon layer of aromatics and flavors contained in a truly great ice wine, it will pale in comparison.

Chapter 14

Wine and Food: A Personal Viewpoint

THE following opinion was expressed in the first edition of *Winetaster's Secrets*. After many years of added experience and great pleasure with wine and food, I will let it stand. I have not changed my view. In fact, the neverending books, articles, and theories of mating wine with food seem to have exploded like a pen full of rabbits—every time you turn around there seems to be a few more.

I would add one comment because of disturbing discussions I've increasingly heard over this past decade. Too many times I've been privy to expressions that suggest these outstanding marriages of wine and food—the events, public or private, in which they are offered for tasting—should be reserved only for those with sufficient experience to appreciate them. It's an easy trap to fall into. But it's wrong.

Whether it's outstanding food/wine or great wines by themselves, share them! Yes, with appreciative, kindred spirits, but add the uninitiated. If they are ever to learn about such pleasures they need to share in such experiences. Both of you will gain.

This may seem slightly out of context for a book such as this. Yet we have spent many pages investigating how to taste and evaluate wines, the goal of which was to increase your appreciation of wine. But there remains one vital thought I feel compelled to add:

Wine is quite capable of standing on its own merits!

I feel the need to make this point strongly because there seems to be a growing trend towards the idea that there is an absolute necessity to marry every wine with an appropriate food, to the extent a wine is often described in terms of what food it should be consumed with. Nonsense! Wine does not need food to be appreciated or improved upon. In fact, many of these unfortunate unions serve only to dilute the appreciation of both.

This mandatory wine/food connection is becoming so widespread today that some wine journalists, educators and connoisseurs, when evaluating a wine, seem to feel their job is incomplete until they have matched that wine with some food or recipe. As a consequence there exists this attitude among some consumers that wine is not much more than a complement to food. It is more. Indeed, it is more.

But please don't misinterpret these comments. I would not for a moment challenge the delightful inclusion of wine with meals, or with food at any time for that matter. They're natural partners. Some of these marriages produce veritable ambrosia. However, to appreciate the genuine pleasures of wine, food is not necessary and can be a considerable distraction at times.

Including a truly fine or great wine with a meal in my view is like driving a Ferrari through rush hour traffic. Granted, if I must suffer the trauma of rush hour city traffic, sitting in a Ferrari is as desirable a way as there is to do it. But that's not the most exhilarating use to which this regal carriage can be put. And so it is for fine and great wines. They have so much more to offer than playing second fiddle to some chef's concoction, as delightful as that concoction might be. More simple, ordinary wines, pleasant wines that can be consumed with only passing interest in their heritage, are the ideal meal mates.

To some this view may be somewhat unsettling, for the inclusion of food with the consumption of all alcoholic beverages is promoted these days in an attempt to counteract some of the images associated with alcohol abuse. To satisfy any concern that this view of mine, if proliferated, would somehow turn the clock back in this respect I must add that the most significant deterrent to abuse is knowledge. When someone takes an interest in wine, pursuing it to greater depths of appreciation and understanding, there is created an increased respect for this beverage and a decreased desire to abuse it—much more so than by simply ingesting some food with your wine. After all, most problem drinkers eat. Education and appreciation are truly the roads to moderation!

The individual personality of a truly fine or great wine, its depth and complexity, all its intriguing attributes of smell, taste and feel—

that's something that should be explored by your senses in an unadulterated fashion. Wine, its appreciation and inclusion as part of life, is an *art*, every bit as interesting, complex and rewarding as other art forms. It's not coincidence that throughout history the love of fine music, art, and literature have been synonymous with the love of fine wines. And, as in the case for those other arts, the art of wine has its roots with the common people. It is not meant to be an elitist pursuit.

For those who may have grown up with wine, and who perhaps now take it almost for granted, giving it no more attention than their morning coffee or tea, as well as for those who are just now making friends with the "product of the vine," there is ever so much to explore, so much to enjoy, so much to gain from wine—the most significant of which is the appreciation for the role wine can play in a moderate life.

Taste on!

Some Tasting Tips

MUCH of what we know, or think we know, about tasting wine comes from the real life experience of winetasters, glass and notebook firmly in hand. This especially applies to tasting events with many samples.

In *Winetaster's Secrets* we certainly haven't been able to cover them all. Some of these omissions are detailed in the following list. There's no master order or logical sequence here, just some tips from tasters who may have had to learn it the hard way.

- To gain anything from a tasting you really do need to *concentrate*—if you don't, much will escape your notice; take it step by step.

- Try to keep each sip of wine at the same volume; this will keep your assessments of different wines on an even playing field.

- Don't rinse too often—rinse (don't gargle) after several wines, swallow the water, then take a break.

- Literally sitting down to taste wines allows for greater concentration—but take a few walking breaks between flights.

- Make allowance for style differences—stronger and bigger is not always better.

- Mouthwashes and toothpastes can affect your tasting for as long as an hour after use; they contain detergents that can seriously affect our taste receptors, causing the wine to taste more acidic, bitter, and less sweet.

- In a flight of wines the first wine is frequently judged rather harshly. The moral: condition your mouth first, with a wine not to be assessed.

- Tasting sequence: driest to sweetest—lowest to highest alcohol—lightest to strongest flavors.

- Regulate your swirling so it's the same for each sample.

- A great nose does not always mean great flavors; don't be prejudiced by one "great" aspect of wine.

- Learn from other tasters (after tasting a sample); tastings are great opportunities to discuss and learn from each other.

- When several wines begin to taste suspiciously alike, be aware that general fatigue and lack of concentration may be occurring—time for a break.

- In serious winetastings make sure the room has proper ventilation; the air should be renewed several times an hour.

- It seems we taste better when we're hungry; that doesn't necessarily indicate a time of day—it tells us to eat lightly before any tasting.

- No matter what system of scoring we use, decisions are not always easy to make. The tendency may be to avoid tough choices and pick the center scale, but don't. Make the choices, or else every wine will tend to be in the same range.

Some Sample Scoring Systems

Numerical Evaluation System

Date _____

		Great	Fine	Ordinary	Poor	Unacceptable
Visual	Surface	4	3	2	1	0
	Clarity/Limpidity	4	3	2	1	0
	Depth/Luminance	4	3	2	1	0
	Tint/Hue	4	3	2	1	0
Olfactory (Nose)	Intensity/Purity	4	3	2	1	0
	Aroma	4	3	2	1	0
	Bouquet	8	6	4	2	0
	Harmony/Balance	8	6	4	2	0
Tactile (Touch)	Body	8	6	4	2	0
	Astringency	4	3	2	1	0
Taste (Gustatory)	Intensity/Purity	4	3	2	1	0
	Sweetness	4	3	2	1	0
	Acidity	8	6	4	2	0
	Bitterness	4	3	2	1	0
	Harmony/Balance	8	6	4	2	0
Flavor (Nose + Taste)	Aftertaste	4	3	2	1	0
	Persistence	8	6	4	2	0
Overall Quality		8	6	4	2	0
						0

Column Total

In my view this wine...

❏ *is declining in quality* ❏ *will improve slightly*

❏ *is at its best now* ❏ *will improve significantly*

Taster _____ No. _____

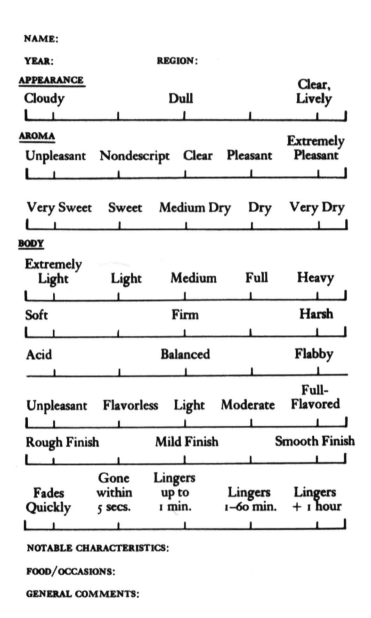

NAME:

YEAR: REGION:

APPEARANCE

| Cloudy | | Dull | | Clear, Lively |

AROMA

| Unpleasant | Nondescript | Clear | Pleasant | Extremely Pleasant |

| Very Sweet | Sweet | Medium Dry | Dry | Very Dry |

BODY

| Extremely Light | Light | Medium | Full | Heavy |

| Soft | | Firm | | Harsh |

| Acid | | Balanced | | Flabby |

| Unpleasant | Flavorless | Light | Moderate | Full-Flavored |

| Rough Finish | | Mild Finish | | Smooth Finish |

| Fades Quickly | Gone within 5 secs. | Lingers up to 1 min. | Lingers 1–60 min. | Lingers + 1 hour |

NOTABLE CHARACTERISTICS:

FOOD/OCCASIONS:

GENERAL COMMENTS:

Handy Wine Measurements

OUR growing sensitivity and evaluation of wine often brings us into contact with measurements that have specific application to wine. Understanding them helps us better understand wine.

The following references are not intended to be precise, scientific formulas, but are approximations that certainly help you to relate one measurement to another. This ease of reference can be of help.

Bottle Sizes

Pony = 187–200 ml

Demi = 375 ml (¹/2 bottle)

Standard = 750 ml (1 bottle)

Magnum = 1.5 liters (2 bottles)

Double Magnum (Marie-Jeanne) = 3.0 liters (4 bottles)

Jeroboam (or Rheoboam for Champagne) = 4.5–5 liters (6 bottles)

Imperial (or Methusalem in Champagne) = 6.0 liters (8 bottles)

Salmanazar = 9.0 liters (12 bottles)

Balthasar = 12.0 liters (15 bottles)

Nebuchadnezzar = 15.0 liters (20 bottles)

Liquid Measurements

1 U.S. gallon = 3.785 liters

1 Imperial gallon = 4.546 liters

1 U.S. quart = 0.946 liters

1 Imperial quart = 1.136 liters

1 U.S. fluid oz. = 29.573 ml

1 Imperial fluid oz. = 28.413 ml

1 U.S. gallon = 5 standard bottles

1 Imperial gallon = 6 standard bottles.

milligrams (mg.) per liter (mg/l) = parts per million

u grams/liter (ug/l) = parts per billion

n grams/liter (ng/l) = parts per trillion

Tiny fractions of wine components are at times measured in parts per million (ppm) and parts per billion (ppb). We can certainly read these numbers, but at times we don't completely grasp how small they really are. For example:

1 ppm (1 mg/l) is like 1 inch to 16 miles

1 ppb (1 ug/l) is like 1 inch to 16,000 miles

1 ppt (trillion) (1 ng/l) is like 1 inch to 16,000,000 miles

Putting it in another way: One part per million (1 mg/L) is about equivalent to taking an Aspirin, dividing it into 300 equal parts, then dissolving one piece in a quart of water.

Translating some of the European numbers (metric) to North American numbers can present a challenge at times. And I mean more than just converting metric to Imperial or the U.S. system of measurement. Sizes and the way some measurements are made can be quite different.

Measurements of sugar, for example, are expressed as *Oechsle* in Germany, *Baume* in France, and *Brix* in North America. Here are some approximate conversions:

Oechsle divided by 3.9 = Brix

Baume x 1.95 = Brix

Some other measurement conversions worth noting are:

1 hectoliter (hl) = 100 liters

1 hectare (ha) = 2.47 acres

grams per liter (g/l) divided by 10 = percentage

hectoliters (hl) x 22 = U.S. gallons

hl x 26 = Imperial gallons

hl/ha divided by 15 = tons per acre

1 case of standard bottles of wine holds 12 bottles = 9 liters.

Total acids in wine are generally expressed as grams per liter (g/l) tartaric. In France and other parts of Europe they express total acids as g/l sulfuric acid. To convert:

g/l sulfuric x 1.531 = g/l tartaric

% Alcohol by volume x 2 = U.S. Proof

% Alcohol by volume x 1.75 = British Proof

For example: 40% alc./vol. = 80 proof U.S.

40% alc./vol. = 70 proof British

Glossary

An Introduction

One of the most difficult and frustrating facets of wine education is finding ideas and words to communicate sensory experiences to others. The reality is that that may not always be possible. For example, there are so many odors, foul and friendly, we can never hope to identify them all, let alone describe them to others.

Some fascinating research has been done to help us appreciate how difficult it is for us to even understand our personal terms of reference. Volunteers were asked to taste a series of wines and write down a description of each sample. A month later, with notes in hand, they were allowed to taste the same wines and try to identify them from their own written descriptions. They all did very badly.

At times we simply run into a brick wall—the inexpressible. Sometimes there are no words in our vocabulary that allow us to extract some of the perceptions we have in our mind. It is frustrating indeed. We can empathize with Orizet's plea: "I need to invent the words!"

So, it's obvious we will stumble and at times wonder whether our senses of smell and taste have taken a vacation. But keep at it. The ability to convey sensations means we have come to understand them ourselves. Perhaps the best we can do for now is to approximate our perceptions. Our continued efforts will be instructive and rewarding.

Yet, we've come a very long way. Our vinous vocabulary today consists of about one thousand, reasonably understood words. A few hundred years ago it was fewer than a hundred.

The concepts of how to describe wine are varied, too. There is the "technical-chemical" vocabulary, the "fruits-and-vegetable" comparison group, even the "cute and colorful similes" approach. Sometimes you wonder if the chalkboard of your face is not the best of all communication devices. Of course, a few salient but demonstrative hand and arm gestures can add a clarifying note. Even a small "grunt" has effectively transmitted an idea to crowds of people.

While the language of the chemist has a certain precision to it, for most winelovers it is a foreign tongue. Would describing a Cabernet Sauvignon be better understood if we included the technical descriptor "n-octonal and 2-methoxy-3-isobutylpyrazine"? Hardly!

Comparisons such as blackcurrant, cigar box, and cedar may be more approachable. However, how many who understand the words can honestly say they know what a real blackcurrant, a cigar box, or cedar truly smell like? Some do, of course; some think they do; a great many haven't the vaguest idea of what we're talking about.

Those fond of colorful, imaginative similes revel in their use. But suggesting a wine has a smell reminiscent of "cellar dust" or a character like "a bespectacled bank clerk"—really, are we entertaining or communicating? Both, you say! There *is* communication, no doubt. But is it accurate, is it going to help others understand more about the wine, or more about you and your marvelous ability to grab their attention?

Admittedly, the winetaster's lexicon leaves a good deal to be desired. Everyone seems to have his own personal wine vocabulary, including yours truly. It's not that winetasters cannot communicate efficiently; it's just that too many of us are wont to forget that words should be a means to accurately transmit thoughts to others, not solely to oneself.

So, what has developed over the past few decades is this generation's wine jargon. It sounds elegant, sophisticated, and highly colorful, but in truth confuses almost everyone but the user, and at times even him. At most wine-related affairs these flamboyant, ambiguous wine terms fill the air like raindrops in a monsoon.

But I'm happy to see that, perhaps from sheer necessity alone, a number of wine words are becoming more universally understood in wine circles. Even the wine scientist and the connoisseur are more frequently talking about the same things these days when they use certain words. Mind you, I don't mean to create any false hopes for a final linguistic fusion. The gap between the usage of accurate and obscure wine words remains distinctly chasmic.

And, once more I must explain that I have not taken it upon myself to try to resolve the differences in the following Glossary.

Hopefully these few pages will shed a bit of light on the matter. If it accomplishes that I'll consider it a worthwhile exercise. If it further confuses the issue—my apologies.

But in all fairness, there is a decided tendency in virtually every field of endeavor to condense what is most accurately described by several words down to a single, hopefully succinct term. As is so often the case that selected word falls short in some respects, or leaves itself open for rather liberal interpretations. Much of the current wine jargon merely echoes this pattern.

For all winetasters—scientists, professionals, connoisseurs, buffs and yes, most important, everyday wine consumers—there is need to simplify and universalize wine language. This is not an attempt to start a crusade or movement but simply to raise somewhat the conscious need to be more specific in the way we describe the grandest beverage of all.

❉ ❉ ❉

ACETALDEHYDE—sherry-like aroma—formed by oxidized alcohol

ACETIC—the taste and odor of vinegar—caused by acetic acid (taste) and ethyl acetate (smell)—a negative factor—from several causes—excessive air contact a major culprit.

ACETONE—wrongly identified nail polish odor associated with Pinotage—correctly amylacetate

ACID—referring to desirable pleasant acids originating from the fruit and the fermentation process creating the tart, crispness of a wine—an essential component in sound wines—contributor to a wine's bouquet development—preservative

ACUITY—a keen sense of perception

AFTERTASTE—the lingering FLAVOR experienced after swallowing some wine—quality wines have a balanced, pleasant length of flavor, while ordinary wines are often characterized by a short finish—if too long it can also be a fault, or if it is an unpleasant bitter tone

AGGRESSIVE—a taste or smell sensation that is strongly forward and immediately sensed

AGUSTIA—inability to taste

ALCOHOL—a basic wine component ranging from 7–20 percent to 30–45 percent in brandies—several types are found in wine, the major one being ethyl alcohol—perceptible on the nose, in a tactile sense (see HOT) and by taste (sweetish)—accounts for much of a wine's body—a factor that should be balanced for the type of wine—a.k.a. ethanol

ALDEHYDE—odorous element produced by oxidation of primary alcohols

ALEMBIC—a pot still

AMPELOGRAPHY—science of identifying and describing grape varieties

ANOSMIA—inability to smell

ANTHOCYANINS—color matter, pigments located just under the skin of the grape

APPLES—malic acid smell—immature grapes or wine

AROMA—a wine odor originating with the fruit, the grape itself— varies in nature according to grape variety—declines with age

AROMATIC—a richness of PRIMARY AROMA

AROMATICS—substances capable of stimulating a smell

ASTRINGENCY—a tactile (touch) stimulation originating with the wine's tannins—described as harsh, rough, coarse—often leaves a gritty feeling on the teeth and lips—as the wine ages the tannins should decrease leaving a smooth wine some refer to as soft and velvety —effect increased by excessive acid

ASZU—Hungarian word meaning shrivelled, referring to NOBLE ROT

AUSTERE—a bit severe, but may develop with age

※ ※ ※

BACKWARD—underdeveloped, slow ageing

BAKED—caramel-like odor from wines that may literally have been heated—Madeira, Marsala, and some sherry-like dessert wines possess this character—more loosely applied to table wines from hotter climates with a dried, raisiny character—overheated grapes from a hot climate or season

BALANCE—the pleasing harmony of a wine's taste, olfactory, and tactile elements—no excesses or deficiencies

BANANA—an odor fault caused by isoamyl acetate, frostbitten grapes, or old wine in poor shape

BARRIQUE—barrel of usually 225 liters

BEERY—an odor fault originating in benzoquinone or a secondary bottle fermentation

BEETROOT—supposed descriptor for Pinot Noir aroma

BIG—a rather ambiguous term used to describe wines with a healthy complement of various wine constituents such as extract, alcohol, tannins, acids, and so on.

BITE—suggests a strong measure of acidity—more common to youthful wines and wines with solid tannins—softens with age

BITTERNESS—one of the four true taste stimulations—best detected on the rear surface of the tongue—can have more than one source—youthful bitterness should disappear with age—a degree of bitterness may characterize some wines for their lifespan—some tasters accustomed to it defend wines with a touch of bitterness—most significant question to ask: is the bitterness offensive?

BITTERS—substances added to wine to add an appetite-stimulating bitterness—from plant extracts and oils—quinine has a similar effect

BLAND—mild, with little character—not a positive assessment

BODEGA—a Spanish shipper or producer of wine; wine cellar; ware house

BODY—a tactile sensation—texture, viscosity, and consistency are close synonyms—created primarily by the alcohol content—glycerine, residual sugars, extract and tannins also play a role—opposite of full-bodied is thin

BOTRYTIS—*Botrytis Cinera*—see NOBLE ROT

BOTTLE-AGE—reductive (without air) ageing of wine—develops most of its complex bouquet—softens acids and tannins

BOTTLE SICKNESS—temporary wine ailment after bottling—adjustment to oxygen and/or carbon dioxide, SO_2, and H_2S—usually disappears by itself or soon after opening

BOUQUET—odors created from the fermentation process and from subsequent wood and bottle ageing—technically, the slow oxidation of the wine's fruit acids, esters and alcohols—a complex odor structure that should grow with proper ageing—includes "bouquet of fermentation" and "bouquet of age"

BREED—a vague term supposedly referring to the factors such as superior grape variety, ideal soil, and climate conditions, etc., which account for a quality wine—we could do well without the word or having it better defined

BRETTANOMYCES—a yeast that can create acetic and butyric acids in wine causing off-odors of vinegar, sweat, ammonia

BRIGHT (Brilliant)—total lack of observable suspended material affecting the clarity of a wine—limpid, a synonym

BRIX—a measurement of sugar content (weight of sugar per volume of sugar solution) in grapes, must, or wine

BUNCH ROT—see NOBLE ROT

BUTTERY—smell from DIACETYL, a by-product of MALO-LACTIC FERMENTATION—positive at low to moderate levels—in excess, it is unpleasant and a wine fault

※ ※ ※

CARAMEL(IZED)—toffee-like odor of wines that have been heated or have had cooked musts added to them—found in wines like Madeira, Marsala, some types of sherries, and some sherry-like dessert wines

CARBON DIOXIDE (CO_2)—odorless gas—causes effervescence in liquids—by-product of fermentation—can be invisible, to light (petillant), to foamy, and sparkling

CARBONIC MACERATION—method of whole-berry fermentation using uncrushed grapes in a CO_2 atmosphere (intracellular fermentation)—produces fresh, very fruity wines for early consumption—started in Beaujolais and has spread to many other vineyard regions

CATS PEE—unusual, but graphic smell of some wines on occasion (e.g., Riesling and Sauvignon Blanc)

CAUDALIE—measurement of P.A.I. (persistent aromatic intensity)—1 caudalie = 1 second of aromatic intensity

CHARACTER—ambiguous reference to quality either of specific components or to the wine in general terms—like the word personality, what is meaningful is what type not how much—generally used as a positive term

CHARACTERISTIC—a good substitute word when you're not certain of the appropriate specific term—broadly meant to identify a certain nature related to such things as grape variety, region, district, or vintage

CHAPTALIZATION—adding sugar to grape must to create more alcohol during fermentation—when done judiciously it improves the wine and its health

CHROMATOGRAPHY—liquid or gas chromatography (GC)—instruments used to analyze chemical composition of a substance's components

CLARITY—opposite of cloudy or turbid—a clear wine devoid of visible particles in suspension

CLEAN—freedom from off odors and tastes—a basic starting point for wine quality—both ordinary and great wines should be clean

CLEAR—not crystal clarity—an unacceptable level, with perhaps some discernable suspended particles

CLONE—a vine propagated from a single source asexually to create a desired difference in the vineyard or winery

CLOSED—a wine said to be going through a "dumb" stage where its aromatics are hidden—often temporary

CLOUDY—abundant suspended particles (colloidal) sufficient to seriously impair the clarity of the wine

CLOYING—an excessive, lingering, flabby, sweetness—sometimes accompanied by low acidity

COARSE—primarily a reference to the harshness caused by the combination of too much acidity and bitterness—not the roughness of a fine young wine, rather that of a poorly made one with little hope of improvement

COMMON—ordinary, but clean and drinkable

COMPLEXITY—the existence of numerous components evident in the nose and taste of a wine—supposedly indicates quality grapes, proper processing, and perceptible wood ageing

COOKED—heavy, sweetish, plummy aroma—often from grapes subjected to excessive heat

COOPERAGE—wine storage units (barrels, casks, vats) usually made of wood

CORKED (Corky)—musty odor from a cork that has been affected by bacteria or chemicals used in processing the corks—the musty, moldy odor eventually infects the wine—easily identified—TCA (trichloroanisole)

CRISP—firm, but not mouth-puckering acidy—adds a note of "drinkability" and refreshment to the wine

CROSS—a variety of grape created by crossbreeding members of the same grape species (i.e., Vinifera x Vinifera)

🐜 🐜 🐜

DELICATE—misused term—often a polite way of expressing a deficiency—some use it to define something less than distinguished

DEPTH—a rich, multi-faceted wine with all its components in harmony—layers of aromatics and flavors

DEVELOPED—a wine with its bouquet of age (tertiary) evident, having reached or is close to its personal peak of quality and maturity, without going past it

DIACETYL—a buttery aromatic compound found in many Californian Chardonnays

DISTINGUISHED—loose term used to describe a wine of exceptional character and quality

DRY—the absence of perceptible sweetness—usually below 0.7 percent residual sugar (7 g/l)

DULL—(a) see CLOUDY (b) low acidity

DUMB—a "flat spot" in a wine's development—an educated guess that defines a young, undeveloped wine that will blossom forth with quality when it matures—also descriptive of some users of this word when such predictions are unfounded

DUSTY—reference to overly tannic wines

🐜 🐜 🐜

EARTHY—in-mouth odor supposedly indicative of certain soils—as many descriptions for this word as there are tasters—can come from a chemical called "giosmin"

EGGS, ROTTEN—an odor fault from hydrogen sulfide (H_2S)

ELEGANT—more suited to the fashion trade than to wine

ESTERS—organic aromatic compounds formed by a reaction between an organic acid and alcohol—responsible for a significant portion of wine odors

ETHANOL—ethyl alcohol—product of yeast/sugar fermentation

ETHYL ACETATE—chemical formed when acetic acid reacts with ethanol producing potent aromatic odor of nail polish remover

EUCALYPTUS—descriptive of this "mint-like" odor in some wines—often eucalyptus trees grow nearby

EXTRACT—soluble wine solids (minus sugar)—contributor to the body and character of a wine

☙ ☙ ☙

FAT—full-bodied—good glycerine, extract, alcohol

FIERY—loaded with alcohol

FINE—(1) overused commercial wine term—properly applied it indicates a quality level above "vin ordinaire," less than "great" (2) wine clarification process

FINESSE—non-specific term for wine—despite attempts to define it, they all seem to differ

FINISH—see AFTERTASTE—a long, pleasant and balanced end to the wine, after swallowing

FIRM—well structured in the mouth—good acid/tannin balance

FLABBY—lack of structure—low acid—short finish

FLAT—(a) low acidity and flavor; (b) sparkling wine that has lost its bubbles

FLAVONOID—group of aromatic pigments (yellow, red, blue) found in flowers and fruits—anthocyanin is one of four types

FLAVOR—stimulation perceived by combined sensitivity of nose and taste receptors—"in-mouth odors"—degrees of flavor are often determined by the length of that flavor, expressed as FINISH or AFTERTASTE—flavor = *nose + tactile + taste + common chemical sense*

FLINTY—find another word for what you think this means—said to be of gun-flint—haven't fired a musket in years

FLOR—specific yeast that grows on the surface of fino and amontillado sherries in barrel—shields it from oxidative effects and adds a unique odor and flavor component

FLOWERY—a floral-like fragrance similar to that of certain flowers—detected in the nose of the wine

FORWARD—advanced maturity in respect to the age of the wine

FOXY—a wet-fur, musky-like odor and taste exhibited by some native North American species of grapes, primarily Vitis Labrusca—largely, created by methyl and ethyl anthranilate—these chemical substances are not generally found in Vitis Vinifera (European grapes)—a non qualitative factor unless it is too persistent and exaggerated

FRAGRANT—it sounds like too nice a wine-word to give up, but I don't know what it means specifically—a type of pleasant odor?

FRESH—broad terminology for wines exhibiting a youthful nature

FRUITY—pleasant, aromatic taste and smell of fresh grapes—usually associated with good levels of fruit acids and sugars

FULL-BODIED—see BODY—most appropriate to dessert wines with higher sugar, glycerine, extract, and alcohol content

※ ※ ※

GAMEY—overripe note—not pleasant unless you have learned to enjoy it

GARLIC—hydrogen sulfide off-odor

GERANIUM—off-odor of geranium when sorbic acid attacked by lactic-acid bacteria

GOUT DE TERROIR—see EARTHY

GRAPEY—heavy grape aroma originating with varieties like the Muscat family, Labrusca's, and some German crosses

GREAT—care needed in where this word is applied—reserved for the quality-elite of wines—they must prove it in the glass, a reputation is not enough

GREEN—the odor and taste from unripe grapes when made into wine—high malic acid a major factor—acidulous

GRIP—when good acids meet firm tannins, surrounded by good levels of alcohol you have grip—great Ports have grip

GRITTY—coarse, rough texture that can be felt in the mouth

※ ※ ※

HARD (harsh)—used to describe youthful tannic state of a wine, with additional excesses in acid, occasionally accompanied by low alcohol—time may cure the condition

HARMONY—see BALANCE

HAZY—not as serious as CLOUDY but sufficient suspended material to detract from the wine's appearance

HEAVY—FULL-BODIED taken to excess

HECTARE—a metric land measurement equal to 2.471 acres

HECTOLITRE—a metric measurement of capacity equal to 100 liters

HEDONISTIC—expression of pure, individual, unimpeded pleasure

HERBACEOUS—natural wine odors reminiscent of herbs—not from the addition of botanicals such as done with Vermouths, and so on.

HIGH-TONED—excess of volatile acids—evident on the nose and in taste

HOLLOW—a wine with a good initial impression (attack) and perhaps even a wonderful finish, but the center, the middle is missing

HONEYED—as close as you can get to describing an odor given off by some well-aged, sweet wines like Sauternes, Beerenauslese, Trockenbeerenauslese and Tokaji—even some fully matured dry wines will have this aromatic

HOT—mild pain sensation from high alcohol content—also described as fiery

HYBRID—a cross between two species of grapes (e.g., Labrusca x Vinifera)

HYDROGEN SULFIDE (H_2S)—a rotten-egg smell

✱ ✱ ✱

INKY—(1) unpleasant metallic, iron taste; (2) heavy dark color—too deep to see through

INSIPID—without character or spine (ACID)—flavors are almost non-existent, too

✱ ✱ ✱

LEES—(1) a residue that settles out of wine—when wine is kept in contact with it a more complex bouquet develops; (2) collection of blue jeans

LEGS—rivulets that slide down the sides of the glass—called "arches" or "tears"

LENGTH—the pleasantly long finish and aftertaste of the wine—if too long it can wear out its welcome in some wines (e.g., some Labruscas, and Muscats)

LIGHT—deficiency of elements that create body—not unpleasant—can contribute to balance in a wine with low alcohol

LIMPID—see CLARITY

❋ ❋ ❋

MACERATION—extraction of aromatic and flavor compounds from skin contact during and after fermenting grapes

MADIERIZED—usually refers to white wines that, due to improper storage, show the heavy signs of oxidation in taste and color—see BAKED—will exhibit gold, amber, and brown tinges of color

MALIC ACID—the major organic acid of unripe grapes—resembles the acidic taste in green apples—as grapes ripen malic acid decreases —see MALO-LACTIC FERMENTATION

MALO-LACTIC FERMENTATION (MLF)—a bacterial fermentation that converts malic acid to lactic acid—softens acid perception and adds DIACETYL, but can also reduce fruitiness, add odor faults, and cause sedimentation

MATURITY—pinnacle of quality for each grape or wine—the time to each this stage is quite individual—bouquet and color are the major indicators for this stage of development in wine

MELLOW—another equivocal wine term—has traditionally meant a softness in the wine—a term used to describe red wine with a touch of residual sugar—could also indicate the approach to maturity

MERCAPTANS—a sour, skunky, rubbery odor due to the breakdown of sulfur in a reductive (no air) atmosphere—natural gas smell and garlic are two more descriptors

METALLIC—rarely related to actual metals in wine, but extreme rarities of iron and copper excesses can create this sensation—more often it refers to a metallic-like sensation of low alcohol, high acid dry whites—some highly astringent, acidic reds can also create this sensation

METHODE CHAMPENOISE—champagne-method—a second fermentation in bottle to create sparkling wines—includes traditional grape varieties, TERROIR and complete process

MOLDY—an odor of mold infecting the wine—can originate from poorly maintained containers that have had mold growing in them—also from grapes that have been affected by the non-beneficial mold called *pourriture gris* (bunch rot)—can also originate with unclean barrels

MOUSY—an acetic acid–like odor and taste caused by yeast bacteria—most often occurs in late-harvested grapes that were low in organic acids

MUSHROOM—odor developed in rare, old, well-cellared wines (e.g., Barolo)

MUSKY—peculiar, characteristic odor exhibited in wines from the Muscat family retaining some sugar—can be found in some Labrusca grapes or their hybrids

MUST—unfermented grape juice and/or mash

MUSTY—dubious wine term—probably a mild example of something else

✳ ✳ ✳

NERVOUS—French expression for acidity that is "racy" and lively

NEUTRAL—a wine exhibiting low intensity in olfactory, tactile, and taste sensations—little to cause offense, little to make it memorable

NOBLE—aristocratic but foggy term—supposedly used to distinguish wines that are truly superior

NOBLE ROT—a potentially beneficial fungus that can attack red and white grapes—most often negative for reds—under specific conditions it can create uniquely honey-rich, sweet wines of great power and longevity (e.g., Sauternes, Trockenbeerenauslese)—called *pourriture noble* in France, *Edelfaule* in Germany, and *muffa nobile* in Italy, *aszu* in Hungary—technically, *Botrytis Cinerea*

NOSE—broad term describing the collective oenological elements assessed by the olfactory organ of your proboscis (English translation)—general wine odors, including aroma and bouquet

NOUVEAU—wines made to be drunk young—often uses CARBONIC MACERATION whole berry fermentation

NUTTY—pungent, nut-like odor and taste—often found in Amontillado type sherries and Tawny Ports—probably from wood and acetaldehydes

✳ ✳ ✳

OAK—superior wood for wine barrel construction—imparts a variety of substances to ageing wine, including a number of aromatics, the most important of which is "vanillin" often identified as the "oaky" odor

ODOR(S)—broad term used to discuss all wine smells, aroma, bouquet, even off-odors

OFF—seriously negative odor or taste—opposite of clean

OLFACTORY—the sense of smell

OPALESCENCE—a type of milkiness, often associated with iridescence

ORDINARY—a wine with few if any outstanding characteristics, but without faults—can be drinkable, enjoyable

ORGANOLEPTIC—in this case, a sensory evaluation of wine—more than a casual inspection is intimated, analytical, systematic

OXIDIZED—probably better expressed as "over oxidized"—exposure to too much air—may result from advanced age or from poor handling, processing or storage—basically you are smelling a substance called acetaldehyde—stale, off-odor

✳ ✳ ✳

PASTEURIZATION—heat treatment (at 70°C/158°F or higher) that destroys any biological elements

PEPPERY—type of harsh, stimulating aromatic component—can be a positive note of complexity—can also be a fault if too raw

PERFUME—a refined, quality odor—a diffusive and attractive scent

PETILLANT—light bubbliness (French)—2 atmospheres or less pressure

PETROL—oily, gasoline smell—I think it's usually misapplied—more like the pungency of white truffles—an indicator of maturity in wines such as Riesling

pH—measure of the strength or activity of wine acids

PHENOLS—color pigments and tannins

PHYLLOXERA—see NOBLE ROT

PIGMENTS—anthocyanin, phenols—coloring matter

PIQUANT—fresh acidity—when mixed with some sweetness and body gives a refreshing quality

PLUMMY—(1) a purplish tint (2) over-ripe fruit quality

POLYPHENOLS—family of organic chemicals which include tannins

POOR—as a general quality level for wine this word identifies wines with little merit or distinction, but are certainly drinkable—a stage below "vin ordinaires"

PRICKED—an awkward expression that is supposed to define a wine with excessive volatile acidity (vinegar), but may still be in the drinkable stage

PRICKLY—tactile sensation of (1) effervescence, (2) high acidity, (3) burnt-match smell of sulfur

PRIMARY AROMA—aroma of the grapes, their fruit

PUNGENT—vague term to be used at your own risk—can indicate an excess of several aromatics

✺ ✺ ✺

QUAFFABLE—a wine style that invites hearty consumption—easy to swallow (e.g., Beaujolais—Vinho Verde)

✺ ✺ ✺

RACY—usually refers to a liveliness based on high acids

RAISINY—a wine odor created by using grapes that are partially or completely dried (pasito)—also evident to a lesser degree in some wines produced from grapes grown in hot climates—concentrated character in some ice wines

RANCIO—not to be confused with the generally understood English word, rancid—it is not this word—it is the buttery/nutty, ALDEHYDE associated smell of certain fortified wines (e.g., Oloroso sherries) deliberately aged in limited contact with air—the more woody/vanillin smell of very old brandies that have spent a long time in oak

REDUCTIVE—ageing odors generated without air (in bottle)—can be excessive creating faults—opposite of oxidative

RICH—in-depth quality of several wine components (flavor, sweetness, fruit, extracts)—or a deep, complex mixture of all of these

RIPE—(1) the personal peak for an individual wine—a fully mature wine before its decline—it remains in this state for various lengths of time, unique to each wine; (2) fully matured grapes

ROBUST—good structure and alcohol balance, but mature and rounded

ROUGH—another term to describe the astringent tactile stimulation when it is excessive

ROUND—balanced maturity—soft in-mouth texture

RUBBERY—a negative, self-descriptive odor of complex chemical origin—usually mercaptans

※ ※ ※

SALTY—true taste stimulation—the normal concentrations of sodium in wines are below human sensory thresholds—occasionally some tasters claim to sense a salty tang in some Manzanilla and old, dry flor sherries—perceptible to some tasters when ion exchange resins are poorly applied—influences other stimulations, even below thresholds

SAPID—any substance that stimulates our taste receptors

SAVOR—to smell wine by exhaling odors from the mouth through the nose—I say smelling is smelling

SAUERKRAUT—an excess of Lactic acid—most often from too strong a malo-lactic fermentation

SCENTED—see PERFUME

SECONDARY AROMA—new aromatics developed as a result of the fermentation process (fermentation bouquet)

SHARP—well-known wine educator and author (I couldn't let it go by) see TART (no, not referring to me)

SHORT—quick collapse of flavors in-mouth—poor length

SILKY—soft structure—a smooth texture or weave of components

SMOKEY—uncertain significance—easier to sense than describe

SMOOTH—opposite to ASTRINGENT, HARSH, ROUGH—a soft, slick texture—tactile, not taste

SOFT—used to describe too many characteristics—mellow?

SOLID—ample amount of various wine components (e.g., tannins)

SORBIC ACID—acid added to wine as a preservative—limited applications—can sometimes be detected by a geranium-like odor when attacked by bacteria

SOUND—a wine basic—no faults in visual—nose—tactile—taste

SOUR—(1) laboratory language for the true acid (not acetic acid) taste—see TART and ACID; (2) commonly used to describe an overly acidic condition

SPARKLING—full °2C effervescence of a secondary fermentation

SPICY—the spice-like odor and taste of some grape varieties—an out standing example is the Gewürztraminer

SPRITZIG—see PETILLANT

STABILIZATION—processes involving the removal of protein, tar trates, coloring matter, and so on. from the wine to attain clarity, as well as chemical and biological stability

STEELY—a firm level of acid in a well-structured wine

STEMMY (stalky)—a green, wet, wood-like odor and taste usually caused by improper removal of grape stems from the must

STIMULUS—anything that generates a sensory perception

STIMULUS ERROR—incorrect judgment resulting from the influence of factors irrelevant to the wine under evaluation

SUBTLE—if you need a definition for this word, please start over at page 1

SUGAR—a group of carbohydrates with a sweet taste sensation—a vital component in wine—no sugar, no wine

SULFUR—almost a necessity in the wine industry—small amounts are naturally produced in wine—added in various forms at different stages of processing—acts as a sterilizing agent, killing bacteria and germs without destroying yeast cells—an anti-browning agent—separates into free and chemically-bound (inactivated) sulfur—free is what can be detected on the nose, when above 50 parts per million—burnt-match smell

SUPPLE—flexible, vibrant—not harsh, but yielding on the taste—attractive texture

SWEET—a true taste stimulation originating from several wine sources, primarily natural sugars (fructose, sucrose, and glucose)—

also capable of demonstrating a mild sweetness are glycerine, alcohol and some strains of yeast—sweetness is neither an absolute positive or negative factor—needs to be balanced with other elements like acid and alcohol—natural grape sugars can "dry-out" with age while added sweetness usually remains

🐞 🐞 🐞

TACTILE—anything that elicits a physical feeling—a stimulation of touch-related sensors

TANNIN—an organic element found in the skins, stalks and pips of grapes—it can also be extracted from wooden barrels during ageing—creates ASTRINGENT feeling—tactile sense not a taste— necessary for beneficial ageing of wine—most prominent in young red wines, as white wines are generally fermented off their skins— precipitates out as part of a deposit during the ageing process—a major wine preservative—a polyphenolic

TART—too much acid without sufficient sugar or other components to balance it out—may decrease with some ageing—malic and tartaric acids are usually the cause

TARTARIC ACID—a major, organic wine acid—largely responsible for the crisp, acidic tastes in wine with sufficient quantities—can also create TARTRATES

TARTRATES—tartaric acid salts (potassium bitartrate in wine)—can form crystals in wine and adhere to the cork or precipitate as a grainy or flake-like sediment

TEINTURIER—red or black grapes with deeply colored juice—can be varieties in which the grape pulp has a reddish tint even before crushing (e.g., Alicante Bouschet, Rubired)

TERROIR—vineyard environment (soil, climate, etc.)

TERTIARY AROMA—bouquet of age—comes with reductive ageing and the formation of new compounds, and the increase in intensity of others

THIN—opposite of FULL-BODIED—often described in terms of being watery

THRESHOLD—a point beyond which you lose the ability to sense stimulations—with exercise improvements can be made—thresholds naturally vary between individuals and source of stimulation

TOAST –Y, –ED—(1) odor reminiscent of toasted bread; (2) heat applied to the inside of oak barrels

TOTAL PERCEPTION—combination of all wine perceptions—wine should be assessed as a single entity—taster comes to recognize the whole, not the individual parts

❀ ❀ ❀

ULLAGE—space between the bottom of the inserted cork and the surface of the wine in bottle—causes of increased ullage are various—effects: possible oxidation, spoilage

❀ ❀ ❀

VANILLA—a degradation of lignins extracted from oak casks—enriches wine with a vanilla odor—highly appreciated for wines and brandies —in excess it can be a negative, masking other wine aromatics and tastes

VARIETAL—a single grape variety—a wine with a distinctive varietal aroma and taste

VELVET(Y)—texture, a tactile description—use carefully as it can change definition according to the user

VINEGAR—acetic acid (odor and taste) and ethyl acetate (smell)—see ACETIC

VINICULTURE—the art of making wine

VIN ORDINAIRE—French term for ORDINARY wine

VINUOUS—a simple, detectable winey nature minus distinction or varietal qualities—see NEUTRAL

VISCOUS—heavily structured—round, oily in the mouth—visually appreciated as "tears" slide slowly down the sides of the glass

VITICULTURE—the science of growing grapes

VOLATILE—chemicals that become gaseous from a liquid at various temperatures

VOLATILE ACIDITY—(VA) see ACETIC

❀ ❀ ❀

WATERY—see THIN

WEAK—the reasoning behind using this word in a glossary

WEIGHT—light compared to heavy wines—should not be used as a synonym for "texture"—cream vs. water is a good illustration of the differences—cream has more texture than water, but is lighter and will float on water

WISHY-WASHY—see WEAK

WOODY—odor and taste of wood extracted from barrel ageing (usually oak)—if excessive it can be a fault

※ ※ ※

YEAST—a monocellular, microscopic fungus that acts as a catalyst in fermentation

YEASTY—odor of fermenting or fermented yeasts—should disappear within months following a wine's primary fermentation—dead or spent yeasts have a different aromatic signature (autolysis)

※ ※ ※

ZEST/ZING—crisp, aggressive acids—these were questionable words to use in our glossary, however, I didn't want to end at "Y."

The International Language of Wine

IT is difficult enough trying to achieve precision in your own tongue, let alone other languages. However, at the risk of offending five other ethnic groups, I have included a brief listing of wine terms and their corresponding translations. Quite reasonably the list could have been lengthier, but this is as far as I feel competent to travel this road at this time.

English	French	Italian	German	Spanish	Portuguese
acidity	acidité	acidita	saeure	acidez	acidez
acidulous	aigrelet	acidulo	sauer	acidulo	acre
aftertaste	arriere-gout	retrogusto	Nachge-schmack	retrogusto	resaibo
agreeable	aimable	amabile	lieblich	agradable	agradavel
aroma	arome	aroma	Aroma	aroma	roma
astringent	astringent	allappante	adstringierend	astringente	adstringente
austere	austere	austero	rauh	acerbo	austero
authentic	authentique	genuino	sortenrein	autentico	genuino
balanced	equilibre	equilibrato	ausgeglichen	equilibrado	equilibrado
bitter	amer	amaro	bitter	amargo	amango
blending	coupage	taglio	Verschneiden	mezella	mescia
body	corps	corpo	Korper	cuerpo	corpo
bottle	bouteille	bottiglia	Flasche	botella	garrafa
bottling	mis en bouteille	imbottiglia-mento	Flaschen-fullung	embotellando	engaraffa mento

English	French	Italian	German	Spanish	Portuguese
bouquet	bouquet	uquet	Bukett	aroma	bouqua
bright	brilliant	brillante	glanzhell	brillante	brilhante
brut	brut	brut	brut	bruto	bruto
chaptalizaton	chaptalisation	zuccheraggio	Zuckerung	azucarado	chaptal-izacao
characterless	fade	vuoto	charakterlos	insipido	insipido
clean	net	netto	sauber	limpo	boa prova
clear	clair	spogliato	geklart	claro	limpo
closed	ferme	muto	stummge-machter	apagado	amuado
cork	bouchon	tappo	Korken	tapon	rolha
delicate	delicat	delicato	fein	delicado	delicado
dry	sec	secco	trocken	seco	seco
easy to drink	goulqant	passante	sufllg	ligero	chelo
elegant	elegant	elegante	elegant	elegante	elegante
extract, dry	extrait-sec total	estratto	Gesamt-extrackt	extracto seco	extracto seco
fermentation	fermentation	fermentazione	Garung	fermentacion	fermentacao
flat	plat	insipido	fad	insipido	chato
flavor	saveur, gout	sapore	Geschmack	sabor, gusto	sabor, gusto
flavorful	savoureux	sapido	Gesmackrell	sabroso	saboroso
foam	mousse	spuma	Sektschaum	espuma	espuma
fresh	frais	fresco	frisch	frescor	fresco
full	plein	pieno	voll	lieno	encorpado
generous	genereux	generoso	edel	generoso	generoso
hard	dur	duro	hart	duro, verde	duro, rijo
harmonious	harmonieux	armonico	ausgeglichen	equilibrado	equilibrado
lively	vivace	vivace	lebendig	vivaz	vivaco
madierized	maderise	maderizzato	rauhgeschmack	maderizado	madeirizado
mature	mur	maturo	reif	maduro	maduro
mouth-filling	plein	pastoso	wuchtig	pastoso	pastoso
must	mout	mosto	Most	mosto	mosto
neuual	neuue	neuuo	neutral	neuuo	neuuo
perlage	perlage	perlage	perlen	aguaja	eferve-scencia
perfumed	bouquet	profumato	bukaueich	aromatico	perfumado
raisined	passerille	passito	trockenbeerwein—	—	—
rich, full-bodied	etoffe	stoffa	koperreich	concuerpo	robusto
robust	corse	robusto	kraftig	robusto	forte

English	French	Italian	German	Spanish	Portuguese
rough, coarse	rude	ruvido	herb	basto-aspero	travoso
round	rond	rotondo	rund	redondo	redondo
salty	sale	salato	salzig	salado	salgado
sediment	depots	deposito	Depot	deposito	deposito
semi-sweet	doux	abboccato	suss	abocado	doce
smooth, velvety	veloute	vellutaio	rund und samtig	suave	—
spoiled	bacterien	malato	bakterienkrank	pasado	—
sugar	sucre	zucchero	Zucker a	zucares	acucares
supple	souple	morbido	geschmeidig	suave	—
sweet	doux	dolce	sehr suss	dulce	doce
tart	acerbe	acerbo	grun	acido	acerbo
tastevin	tastevin	"tastevin"	Probetasse	taza de catar	tambu-ladeira
thin	decharne	debole	Korperarm-(mager)	aguardo	descarnado
turbid	trouble	torbido	trub	turbio	turvo
unctuous	onctueux	grasso	geschmeidig	untuoso	untuoso
vine	vigne	vite	Weinreb	vina	videira
vine variety	cepage	vitigno	Rebsorte	cepas-	casta
vinous	vineux	vinoso	weinig	vinoso	vinoso
vintage	millesime	annata	jahrgang	anada	colheita
viscous	filant	filante	lind, zah,	viscoso	oleoso,
	olig	filante	filante		
warm	chaud	caldo	feurig	caliente	quente
wine	vin	vino	Wein	vino	vinho
young	jeune	pronto (pronto beva)	jung	joven	vinho feito

Bibliography

Ackerman, Diane. *A Natural History of the Senses.* New York: Vintage Books, 1991.

Amerine, Maynard A. and Edward B. Roessler. *Wines: Their Sensory Evaluation.* San Francisco: W.H. Freeman & Co., 1976.

———. and Vernon L. Singleton. *Wine: An Introduction.* Berkeley: University of California Press, 1978.

Baldy, Marian W. *The University Wine Course: A Wine Appreciation Text and Self Tutorial.* Wine Appreciation Guild, 1993.

Bespaloff, Alexis. *Wine: A Complete Introduction.* New York: New American Library, 1980.

Boies, Lawrence R. *Fundamentals of Otolaryngology.* Toronto: W.B. Saunders, 1989.

Brillat-Savarin, A. *Physiologie du gout* (1839).

Broadbent, Michael. *Complete Guide to Winetasting and Wine Cellars.* New York: Simon and Schuster, 1984.

Brown, Gordon. *A Handbook of Fine Brandies: The Definitive Taster's Guide to the World's Brandies.* London: Garamond, 1990.

Cadiau, Paul. *Lexiwine.* London: I B D Ltd., 1987.

Chaptal, J.A. *L'Art de faire le vin* (1807).

Chauchard, P. *Les messages de nos sens.* Paris: Presses universitaire de France, 1944.

Faith, Nicolas. *The Simon and Schuster Pocket Guide to Cognac and Other Brandies.* New York: Simon and Schuster, 1987.

———. *Cognac.* Boston: David Godine Publishers, 1987.

Fincher, Jack. *The Brain: Mystery of Matter and Mind.* Toronto: Torstar Books, 1981.

Galet, Pierre. *Practical Ampelography: Grapevine Identification.* New York: Cornell Press, 1979.

———. *Cepages et vignobles de France, Vol. II and III.* Montpellier: Imprimerie du Paysan du midi, 1958, 1962.

Got, Norbert. *La Degustation des vins.* Beziers: SODIEP, 1953.

Gunyon, R.E.H. *The Wines of Central and South-East Europe.* London: Duckworth, 1971.

Hunt, Morton. *The Universe Within: A New Science Explores the Human Mind.* New York: Simon and Schuster, 1982.

Leglise, Max. *Une initiation à la degustation des grands vins.* Lausanne: DIVO, 1976.

Levine, W. Michael and Jeremy M. Shefner. *Fundamentals of Sensation and Perception.* Pacific Grove, CA: Brooks-Cole, 1990.

Mey, Wim. *Sherry.* Rhoon, Netherlands: Asjoburo, 1988.

Nykanen, L. and P. Lehtonen, eds. *Flavour Research of Alcoholic Beverages, Vol. 3.* Helsinki: Foundation for Biotechnical and Industrial Fermentation Research, 1984.

Papo, Luigi. *Italian Brandy.* Florence, Italy: Alinari, 1987.

Peppercorn, David. *Drinking Wine: A Complete Guide.* New York: Harbor House, 1979.

Peynaud, Emile, and Michael Broadbent. *The Taste of Wine: The Art and Science of Wine Appreciation.* New York: John Wiley and Sons, 1996.

Poupon, P. *Nouvelles pensées d'un degustateur.* Paris: Bibliothèque de la Confrérie des Chevaliers du Tastevin, 1974.

———. *Plaisirs de la degustation.* Paris: Presses universitaires de France, 1973.

Pusais, et al. *Precis d'initiation a la degustation.* Institut technique de vin, 1969.

Quimme, Peter. *Signet Book of American Wine.* 3rd ed. New York: Signet, 1980.

Ratti, Renato. *Come degustare i vini.* Brescia: AEB, 1971.

Restak, Richard M. *The Brain: The Last Frontier.* New York: Doubleday, 1979.

Ribereau-Gayon, Jean et al. *Sciences et techniques du vin.* Paris: Dunod, 1972.

Robinson, Jancis. *Vines, Grapes, and Wines: A First Complete Guide to Grapes.* New York: Knopf, 1986.

Samalens, Jean and Georges. *Armagnac.* London: Christie's Wine Publications, 1980.

Snow, James. *Introduction to Otolaryngology.* Chicago: Year Book Medical Publishers, 1979.

Spurrier, Michael, and Steven Dovaz. *Academie du Vin Complete Wine Course: A Comprehensive Course in Wine Appreciation, Tasting and Study.* New York: Putnam, 1983.

Thompson, Richard. *The Brain: A Neuroscience Primer.* San Francisco: W.H. Freeman and Co., 2000.

Vedel, Andre, et al. *Essai sur la degustation des vins.* Macon, France: Societé d'edition et l'informations viti-vinicoles, 1972.

Young, Alan. *Making Sense of Wine Tasting.* London: Lennard Publishing, 1987.

Young, J. Z. *Programs of the Brain.* Oxford, U.K.: Oxford University Press, 1981.

Index